THEY CAME AS FRIENDS

ATLANTIC OCEAN
OKNEY ISLANDS
SHETLAND ISLANDS
No. Ireland
BELFAST
Scotland
EDINBURGH
rish
ree State
DUBLIN
IRISH SEA
NORTH SEA
England
LONDON
ENGLISH CHANNEL
'S GRAVENHAGE
Netherlands
Belgium
France

TO THOSE WHO FELL

THE GERMANS have never been able to understand the strength that lies in the democratic way of life. They have seen the weaknesses in the system. And they have scoffed at them. But because they themselves possess no democratic instincts or traditions, because dictatorship in some form or other has always prevailed in Germany, the Germans are blind to the forces that sustain democracy.

This has always been a weak point in Germany's relations with other nations. And because Adolf Hitler is the very prototype of everything German, his eyes also are closed.

The fact that the Germans chose "more peaceful" methods when they started to introduce the New Order in Norway was therefore not due to any sudden and inexplicable understanding of the ideals of democracy. Quite the opposite. Hitler, racial fanatic that he is, has always suffered from a frustrated love for the Scandinavian peoples, and it is on this belittled love that the National Socialist theories of the Nordic race are based. That is why Hitler expected his ideas to be met with understanding in Norway. And even though he did take into account that democratic prejudices and conceptions would have to be overcome, he nevertheless hoped and believed that the Norwegians, as "blood-related Germanics," would—after due consideration—adjust themselves to a "greater Germanic international fellowship under Germany's leadership." For this reason Norway was not to be terrorized into the New Order, as Poland was.

To Hitler, Norway was the great experimental field for the transplantation of National Socialist ideas in foreign soil. And he gambled everything on the success of the experiment.

He had reckoned without democracy. He did not realize that what he took to be signs of weakness were in reality signs of strength. He did not understand that the victories which he apparently won at the start in reality constituted the prerequisites for his defeat. He believed that democracy was nothing but a system and that merely by obliterating the institutions created by democracy he would stand as victor over the system. He did not understand that fundamentally democracy is a way of living which will die only when the last democrat lies six feet under the sod

Adolf Hitler had not only come to a foreign land. He had also ventured into a world that was entirely foreign to him.

Developments of the past year reveal with brutal frankness that the two theories could not be exchanged, one taking the place of the other. The "peaceful" methods have, therefore, today given way to open terror. Today conditions in Norway are exactly the same as in other occupied countries.

This has been Adolf Hitler's great defeat.

And it is the story of this defeat that this book tries to tell. It is also an attempt to show, by portraying that which happened in Norway, what must inevitably be the development in any democracy put to the same test.

It is the story of democracy's strength. It is well worth noting that the Norwegian home front to an overwhelming degree has fought an open fight with genuinely democratic weapons. One after the other, institutions and individuals have stood up to the occupying power—ready and willing to take the consequences of their action. They have not been crawling around under cover, for they have nothing to hide.

Conditions have made it necessary to carry out the preparations for the home front's various actions in a way that might be described as "underground." But the fight itself has been fought in the clear light of day.

Mistakes were made in Norway, and much could and should probably have been done otherwise. But the Norwegian home front, which has itself supplied the material for this book, and which today slaves under the yoke of nazism, has a message for the world at large. Let it be heard.

CONTENTS

I. "WE COME AS FRIENDS"

1. SHIPS MEET IN THE NIGHT

THERE WAS A HEAVY SWELL RUNNING, and the lonely little patrol boat rose and settled rather cumbersomely as it made its way along the Norwegian coast. It wasn't much as warships go.

The April night was inky black, but the first gusts of warm air had swept in from the south, signifying the approach of spring and conjuring up a faint mist from the sea.

Slightly to the port the lookout could discern a darker streak amidst all the black—the coast. There was not a single light. From Lindesnes to North Cape the coast was blacked out. Even the lighthouses were dark—the lighthouses which are the only salvation for strange ships that venture in among the 150,000 islands that shield Norway from the fury of the sea.

It was also dark and quiet aboard the patrol boat, which bore the name *Pol III*. The men had little to talk about that had not already been said a hundred times. Silently they stood at their stations and peered into the blackness. The night had only two sounds—the rhythmical throbbing of engines and the slapping of the sea against the boat's sides.

The many unspoken words were an extra burden upon the little craft as it plowed on through the night. They whispered admonishingly from the rigging, sighed despairingly with the breeze, and sang out reassuringly from the hum of the engines. They were words of fear and hope and faith and doubt. The crew sensed them. They came from days and nights of endless waiting, from accounts of the war and of the misfortune abroad in the world. The result was a sense of unsafe safety, with nerves drawn as tight as the strings on a violin, instantly susceptible to every influence.

The patrol boat was only a small part of Norway, but figuratively it was all of Norway in that early spring of 1940. And its fate, oddly enough, foreshadowed Norway's fate.

The skipper of the *Pol III* stood on the bridge, his eyes fixed on the wavering compass card. Below, the chief engineer checked his engines. With smarting eyes the lookout strove to penetrate the night. In their bunks the men off duty were sleeping a sound and dreamless sleep—the well-earned possession of every honest workingman.

A warning cry from the watch in the bow ripped through the night:

"Ship ahead!"

The words were repeated on the bridge, passed along, and quickly multiplied to a profusion of words shouted by sleepy voices, bewildered voices, disbelieving voices.

A strong, steady voice pierced the confusion:

"All men to their stations! Clear the decks for action! We are opening fire!"

From the cannon on the foredeck a red tongue of fire shot defiantly out into the dark.

For the first time in 126 years Norwegians had fired a shot against a foreign power. The time was a few minutes before midnight of April 8, 1940.

The fleet of warships heading up Oslo Fiord was imposing enough—battleships and heavy cruisers, destroyers and lightning-fast motor torpedo boats. Behind these waddled the bulging troop transports and cargo ships. It was difficult to estimate the number. Darkness hid the greater part, and the ships were only faintly discernible silhouettes moving through the night.

From the start it was a hopeless situation for the *Pol III,* with a single, small cannon against a whole navy. But there was no doubt or hesitation in the mind of Captain Welding Olsen or among his men, for a grim determination to act had swept overboard all previous uncertainties and apprehensions. The *Pol III* cannon barked. And guns on the warships roared in reply.

The action was brief. The foreign warships had not slackened their speed. Virtually undisturbed, they sailed on while a couple of guns were assigned the task of eliminating the patrol boat. Soon the *Pol III* ceased to bark, and the stillness returned. Only the white streaks on the water showed the direction the ships had taken.

The *Pol III,* its rudder gone, drifted helplessly on the sea. The boat was battered and sprayed with blood. On the bridge no skipper remained. With both his legs shot away, Captain Olsen slid himself over the rail and vanished. "I'm no use any more," he said. "But they'll never get me alive!"

The *Pol III* did not go down. With its dead and dying it tossed about at the mercy of wind and weather. Those of the crew who had come through alive were dazed by the shock of their experience. But gradually the survivors began to show signs of life, and little by little they began to restore order. For the *Pol III* was still afloat, and a ship that floats is a ship that can be turned to good use—providing you have a crew and the determination to survive.

Ships had met in the night, and all this had happened. They might easily have gone by each other, if fate had wanted it that way. And this would have been avoided.

This thought haunted many of the *Pol III* survivors during those first hours. Some blamed the skipper for not having followed another course, but that did not make better seamen out of the critics. The others, those who could look ahead, began readying the ship for resumed voyage, and they were the ones who eventually saved the craft. They were also the first to notice that a new day was breaking.

2. THE SINGLE PURPOSE

THE GERMAN ATTACK on Norway was launched simultaneously all along the coast the night before April 9, 1940, and it came as a complete surprise to the Norwegian people and to their Government.

There had been signs of stormy weather during the seven months since Germany, with her brutal assault on Poland, had started the Second World War. There had been voices of warning, too, voices that spoke of the looming danger. And of course most Norwegians were conscious of a lurking fear that this time it would not be possible for their country to keep out of it, as it had during the war of 1914–18. But the course had been laid out, once and for all. As early as the first days of September 1939, the Norwegian Government had officially declared that Norway intended to remain neutral. A united popular will supported this declaration.

These seven months, however, had been full of difficulties for the governmental authorities. With the Norwegian coast as exposed as it is, it was inevitable that intricate crises should arise almost daily between Norway and one or the other of the warring powers. This was not because Norway was pursuing a policy that could be called unneutral. Quite the opposite: Norway was being scolded and criticized by both the Germans and the Allies for observing all too rigidly the international laws pertaining to neutrality. Thanks to its clear and firm position, the Government succeeded in riding out each of these storms. The apparent successes thus scored by Norwegian foreign policy had undoubtedly contributed towards creating in both the people and the Government a false sense of security.

At the moment when the Germans attacked, diplomatic relations between Norway and Germany were better than at any time since the outbreak of the war. The knotty *"Altmark affair"* was, seemingly, shelved and forgotten. And Norway had been entirely spared the war-of-nerves treatment which up to then was the established introductory chapter to all of Hitler's conquests.

That the attack also came as a surprise to the Allies seemed beyond doubt when the British fleet proved unable to interfere effectively with the German operations.

A sea-borne invasion supplemented by air power, such as the one that occurred in Norway, had never been treated in any military textbooks. Until it actually came, the idea was generally dismissed as a reckless stunt, lacking every practical possibility of success. The modest Norwegian defense force was by no means ready for such an attack. The naval and coastal defense forces had been mobilized, but most of them were still inadequately equipped. The only Norwegian land forces of any significance were stationed along the Norwegian-Finnish border, which had been under constant guard ever since the Russo-Finnish war began.

Hitler's surprise tactics produced complete success. Yet a single effective counterstroke by the Allies during the first hours of the attack might well have saved Norway. If the Norwegian

Navy and coastal defenses had received aid from the outside
at that moment the result would probably have been entirely
different. Alone, however, they could do little to prevent the
landing of troops. And alone they could not stop the landed
enemy troops from receiving supplies.

Neutral observers have estimated that Hitler lost from one
fourth to one third of his then existing Navy in invading
Norway. These were severe losses. But for each ship that went
down, several slipped by, and German soldiers by the tens of
thousands poured into the country at countless points along
the 3,000-mile coast.

When the Allies came to their senses after the attack it was
too late. By then the greater part of the Norwegian Navy had
been sunk; by then the Germans had succeeded in capturing
all the airfields in southern Norway. With additional planes
on the Danish coast, they had gained full control of the easterly
part of the North Sea as well as the Kattegat and Skagerrak.
Allied surface ships could not reasonably run the risk of operating so near the German air bases, and thus the German supply
lines were secure. Norway's chance of obtaining aid from the
outside was cut off, and the small Norwegian fighting forces
were left to handle the situation alone.

Most of these developments occurred in the course of the
first day. But simultaneously something else was happening,
something that was to prove of decisive importance to Norway's continued fight and also to the future war effort of the
Allies. A few hours after the German attack had commenced
—more exactly, about five o'clock in the morning of April 9
—the German Minister to Norway, Dr. Bräuer, called at the
Norwegian Foreign Office to present Adolf Hitler's ultimatum.

He was not unexpected.

The Norwegian Prime Minister and his cabinet had convened at the close of the Storting (Parliament) meeting late in
the evening of April 8. The group was still in session when first

reports of the German assault arrived. From then on, minute by minute, the Government was kept posted on the course of events. No ultimatum from the German Minister was needed to tell that Norway was at war.

Oslo's air-raid sirens had sounded at twenty minutes past midnight, and simultaneously electric current had been cut off in all sections of the city. Save for dim lights in a couple of offices, the Foreign Department was completely blacked out when Dr. Bräuer arrived. He was admitted to an ante-room, and there the Norwegian Foreign Minister, carrying a flickering candle in his hand, came to meet him. No explanations were necessary. Dr. Bräuer handed over the ultimatum and was left in the anteroom while the Foreign Minister returned to his waiting colleagues with the document.

The situation was hopeless, and the Norwegian Government realized it. It would have been only natural to accept the German ultimatum, and that was exactly what the Germans expected. But it didn't happen. In the inner room sat a group of men face to face with the greatest responsibility of their careers. In the unreal glow of the candles Norway's neutrality policy received its deathblow. In the midst of despair and confusion the Norwegian Government reached a decision which determined the entire future policy of the country. Unanimously, and after only a few minutes of consultation, the German ultimatum was rejected.

Norway had elected to take up the fight.

The decision was unanimously approved by the Storting, which convened at Hamar later that same morning. What was probably even more significant, the Storting at this same meeting, and by another unanimous vote, ordered the King and Government to continue the fight against the invader from outside Norway's boundaries, if this should eventually prove necessary.

And with that a clear and certain line of action had been

laid down—a single purpose which was to run like a red thread through the history of Norway's struggle for freedom both at home and abroad. Thereby, also, Norway's merchant fleet of more than a thousand ships—the fourth largest in the world—was saved for the cause of the United Nations, and history alone will be able to tell what this has meant in the world-wide war between civilization and barbarism.

The Storting's action at Hamar that day laid the foundation for an active Norwegian home front, assuring continued participation in the fight by a united civilian population. Its decision staved off the domestic political division and dissension which the Germans had counted on.

The line of action was drawn. Since then Norway has followed it.

3. ANYTHING BUT QUISLING

CONFUSION WAS RAMPANT in all quarters those first hours and days after the German attack, and because of this the country's military achievements were not what they might have been. The same thing happened later in other countries where the people's desire for peace was just as firmly rooted as in Norway.

One of the chief causes of the confusion was, of course, the surprise attack. Event followed unexpected event at a terrific pace. In a flash, the old familiar concepts crumbled into dust. The confusion spread to the man in the street; no one knew what or where; the world was out of kilter.

But an even more important cause was the strong undercurrent of pacifism permeating all modern Norwegian culture. One hundred and twenty-six years of peace had produced a rather general contempt for and disbelief in military might, a contempt and disbelief which could not be completely erased in the course of a few days or hours. Not even the Norwegians' ingrained hatred for everything smacking of nazism—a fixation which had found clear and unmistakable expression during the war in Spain as well as during later developments in Middle Europe, and which made Norway a haven for fugitives from nazism—could alter the situation. Unconditionally, the average Norwegian's sympathies were with the Allies, but he had not yet built up any clear and full understanding of the extent and significance of the war that was being fought. Even though he inwardly realized that only a firm and united action by the democratic countries could stop Hitler, he withdrew instinctively from the self-evident conclusion.

What happened in the course of that spring night in 1940 called for a complete re-evaluation of an entire people's living, and practically every Norwegian had to go through the process. It was a battle each man had to fight out with himself before he could take up the fight against the invader.

These first days were a critical period both for the nation and for the individual citizen, and it is not improbable that the Germans, by clever maneuvering, could have used the situation in such a way as to have made all further resistance impossible.

What really was the deciding factor is difficult to say, because there were so many involved. There was the instinctive urge of self-defense. There were the so-called "Vienna children" —the German youngsters who were brought to Norway after the First World War to enjoy the many benefits which war-torn Germany could not provide. Now they returned with weapons in their hands. There was the fact that many of the "refugees" from nazism turned out to be spies after having benefited from Norwegian hospitality for years. There was the common man's natural indignation over the intrusion of strangers who seemed bent on destroying the fruits of his labor. And there was Quisling—yes, maybe first and foremost there was Vidkun Quisling!

All through the land people sat in front of their radios trying to learn what was taking place. Then suddenly a hoarse

and guttural voice reached them over the air waves—Quisling's. At six-thirty o'clock in the evening of April 9 he spoke
over the Oslo radio urging Norwegians to desist from further
resistance while he simultaneously "deposed" the country's
legal Government and presented himself as Prime Minister.

In that instant thousands of Norwegian pacifists found the
answer they had been seeking: anything else, perhaps—but
not Quisling. Not a broken-down politician who for ten years
had been the laughingstock of the people. Not a traitor. "If
the choice is between war and Quisling, we'll take war."

That same evening the greatest migration in modern
Norwegian history got under way. Oslo and most other major
cities along the coast were already in the hands of the Germans,
but no German could halt the thousands of young and old
men and women who shouldered their rucksacks, slipped
through the streets, and disappeared into the surrounding
forests. They walked in silence, following many routes. But
all had the same goal, no matter whether they came from
Oslo, Bergen, Kristiansund, or Trondheim—to reach the interior and there join up with the forces which, under the
leadership of King and Government, were already at grips
with the enemy.

This was the beginning of a bloody fight destined to last
sixty-two days and nights—the heroic but hopeless war which
the Norwegian forces waged against a vastly superior enemy.

Those sixty-two days became a true epic of individual
heroism and sacrifice and, simultaneously, a tragic admission
that you cannot stop armored tanks with bare fists. Despite the
aid of British, French, and Polish relief troops—none of them
sizable—it was finally necessary to discontinue the opposition
on June 11, 1940. Norwegian troops, aided by Allied forces,
had by that time reconquered Narvik, thus handing Hitler
his first defeat on land, but at the same time events on the

Western Front were approaching a crisis, and it was necessary to recall all Allied troops from Norway.

Four days before the surrender—on June 7, 1940—the King and Government had acted on the orders given them by the last free session of the Norwegian Storting: they had departed for London, there to continue the war against the invader.

Quisling's initial Government was short-lived. Just as the people had refused to approve the traitor and had taken up arms instead, so had the Oslo authorities refused to have anything to do with him. In the governmental departments and in all other public offices he was simply ignored; police officials refused to obey orders coming from him; Oslo's municipal government served notice that it did not intend to co-operate with him.

The Germans could see that governmental administration was threatened with chaos, and they backed down under the pressure. At noon on April 15, 1940, the Quisling Government was forced to resign; during its six-day career Quisling had not even been able to get his cabinet together for a meeting!

On the initiative of the Supreme Court there was then established a so-called Administrative Council whose duty it was to look after the civil administration of the sections of the country already under occupation. At that moment this meant Oslo and the surrounding countryside. This Council enjoyed the support of the large national labor and business organizations, of the press, and of the ordinary citizen. A sigh of relief rose from the entire country when Quisling resigned.

No one can yet say whether the establishment of the Administrative Council was a wise move. Probably results would have been better if Norwegians from the very start had left all civil administration to the Germans and consciously and exclusively devoted themselves to sabotage and resistance. But the fact was they had not yet completely recovered from the shock. They still had a long way to go before reaching that clear understanding which is prerequisite to united opposition.

The Administrative Council was a temporary agency, created to cope with the emergency, and not a revolutionary unit at odds with the legal Government in London, such as Quisling's Government had been. The Council was composed of respected Norwegian citizens, most of whose names had never been mentioned in connection with politics, and its single task was to see to the welfare of the civilian population in the sections already occupied. The chairman of the Council was Paal Berg, a justice in the Supreme Court, and by way of Stockholm he got in touch with the King and Government and secured approval of what had been done. The Council had no departments for foreign affairs and military organization.

This peaceful solution to a difficult situation was unconditionally a blessing to the civilian population, but at the same time it represented a danger which hardly anyone clearly understood. The Germans, however, saw the possibilities created by the development and systematically set to work to exploit them.

During the battle in Oslo Fiord on the night of invasion, Norwegian forces had succeeded in sinking several German ships, including the cruiser *Blücher,* which was Germany's newest warship. The German occupation plans suffered a severe setback when the *Blücher* went down in flames. It was carrying hundreds of German "Norway experts" who had long been in training for the administration of the country. This is probably the explanation for the German authorities' willingness to pass the reins to the Administrative Council.

On April 24 one of Hitler's most trusted men, Josef Terboven, arrived in Norway, and on the same day through a *Führerverordnung* he was made "Reichskommissar für die

besetzen norwegischen Gebiete." Terboven immediately established himself in the Storting building with his staff, which
quickly grew to more than a thousand "experts." Originally it
was said that the Reichskommissariat was to serve as an aid to
the German fighting forces, but it soon appeared that its real
duty was to wipe out every trace of independent Norwegian
government and to re-create the country into a Nazi *Führer*
state. But it took time for the truth to dawn upon those whom
Terboven had been assigned to bring into line.

Terboven systematically took advantage of the Administrative Council's strong position among the people in order to
smoke-screen his own activities, and in difficult situations he
used the Council as a buffer between himself and the people.

4. POLITICAL INTERLUDE

FROM THE BEGINNING the German slogan had been: "We come as friends." The German authorities said so, the German soldiers repeated it. The Norwegian press and radio, both of which had been promptly brought under German control, were compelled to emphasize it: "The Germans are here as our friends."

Germany, it was proclaimed, had come to "protect" Norway, to protect the country against war and misery. It was the sin of the Norwegian governmental authorities that this offer had been misunderstood. That, said the Germans, was why this ridiculous war had started. The blood of the innocent dead was on the hands of the King and his Government. The British warships were actually on their way to Norway when Hitler decided to act. It had been a matter of hours—of ten hours, to be exact. The Germans like to be exact. By exactly ten hours had the Germans beaten the British in the race to the Norwegian coast!

The conduct of the German soldiers towards the civilian population was correct in the extreme. They were modest, they assisted old women across the streets, they smiled at the children. Their bands played rollicking American dance tunes and the troops sang as they marched through the streets.

And they went mad trying to understand the icy disdain in which the Norwegians held them. This is not intended as irony. They actually were driven to distraction in trying to understand it. Did not the Norwegians, like the Germans, belong to the loudly acclaimed "Nordic race"? Were not their interests therefore linked with Germany's? Why, then, this frigid attitude? Why was it German soldiers were vanishing without trace in Oslo's blacked-out streets?

The German soldiers were confused, and they read anew those "rules of conduct" which had been given them by their Government's propagandists. Had a mistake been made somewhere?

An "unsuspecting" Norwegian editor who had come into possession of a copy of these rules published them in his newspaper. Here they are:

GUIDES ON HOW ONE SHOULD CONDUCT ONESELF IN PERSONAL CONTACT WITH THE NORWEGIAN POPULATION

All soldiers should be aware they have not entered enemy country, but that the troops have arrived to protect the country and its people.

Therefore, take note of the following:

1. The Norwegian is deeply patriotic. He feels intimate kinship with other "Nordic" races. Therefore you must avoid hurting his national honor.

2. The Norwegian has a great love of liberty and independence. He rejects coercion of any kind. He does not believe in military discipline. Therefore, few orders, no commands, for they fill him with repugnance and have no effect whatever. Explain to him and convince him objectively. Humorous conversation is the most effective. Unnecessary sharpness and patronizing treatment will offend his self-esteem.

3. The Norwegian is irresponsible, just like the French peasant: taciturn and reserved in character, slow of thought and action. Avoid outbursts of temper. Take it easy.

4. According to the ancient Germanic conception, the Norwegian's home is sacred. He is hospitable but has a strong sense of property. Frequently the houses are kept unlocked. Robbery is all but unknown and is considered a shameful act. Avoid unlawful interference. Pilfering is considered robbery and is forbidden in all circumstances.

5. The Norwegian understands nothing about war. This seafaring and trading people sympathizes with England; they are suspicious of Russia. Furthermore, Norwegians have little understanding of the aims of National Socialism. Avoid political discussions.

6. The Norwegian loves his home, and he takes pleasure in a comfortable existence. He can be won with friendly gestures, with small courtesies and a little flattery. No importunities, which are particularly to be avoided in the case of women.

7. The German language is understood almost everywhere, but be careful to speak slowly and distinctly.

But at the same time German placards on every wall were screaming their warnings:

"DEATH BY SHOOTING will be the punishment for those who . . ."

And at the same time Norwegian newspapers were forced to publish articles that were written in the German propaganda department and which explained to the Norwegians in detail what an uninformed and uncultured people they were, how helpless they had been when it came to running their own country, and how hopelessly incompetent they were in every other respect.

At the same time the Germans raised the swastika over the Storting building and placed a bust of Hitler in the main entrance. At the same time they were quartering their soldiers in schools and government buildings and even in the National Theater, the nation's pride and the home of Ibsen's dramas.

At the same time they set to work ransacking stores and warehouses for everything of value. German soldiers and civilians, who arrived in constantly increasing numbers, invaded the shops and restaurants. They spent thousands upon thousands of Norwegian kroner. In the beginning they paid with a special type of currency, called *Reichskreditkassenschein,* issued in connection with the invasion and which by German dictum was a valid medium of exchange. But it did not take long before they discovered that the Norwegians would rather give their goods away than hand out Norwegian bills and coins as change. After that the Germans found it more practical to print Norwegian notes. Norwegian humor, so highly lauded in the Germans' rules, was not slow in producing fitting comment. The only free press in the country, it was said, was the printing press of the German-controlled Bank of Norway.

Relations between the occupation forces and the population were not good. An amazing number of Norwegians proved unable to understand German, despite the fact that German as well as English was a required subject in Norwegian schools. People no longer left their homes unlocked. Norwegians still did not like military discipline and authority. Understanding of the goals of National Socialism was still completely lacking.

The German officers and soldiers were treated with formal courtesy, and altercations of importance seldom arose. But under the surface things were seething. That hatred of Germans which during the first days of the invasion existed only in the imagination of the attackers now derived nourishment from great and small humiliations and grew from day to day.

But confusion was still rife. The occupied sections were left without leaders, and the number of occupied sections increased steadily as the Norwegian forces had to withdraw farther and farther northwards. Many of the responsible authorities, quite reasonably, remained with the King and his Government during the fighting. This included the leaders of the National Labor Federation, the country's largest and most important organization. It also included departmental chiefs, the director of the public health service, and other administrators.

Those who had remained behind tried to make the best of a difficult situation, but it was inevitable that some friction should arise between the authorities in unoccupied Norway and those men who in the absence of the leaders had been forced to take the reins in the occupied areas. All communications were cut off, and one group knew little or nothing about the other's plans or difficulties. The Germans tried in every way to fan the embers into flames, and gradually the situation developed exactly as they wanted it to. They made it a policy to sow suspicion of the nation's old leaders and to stir up ill will against them. It was easier to control a disunited people.

As the Norwegian retreat continued northwards considerable dissatisfaction with the Royal Government arose. General recognition of the inadequate Norwegian defense system demanded that someone be the goat. Disappointment over the weak assistance provided by the Allies made conditions worse. The Germans kept fanning the embers. They forced the newspapers to publish "eye-witness accounts" of the low morale of British troops, of how the British regularly kept the Norwegian troops in front of them as a shield, of how the relief troops from abroad had been raising mischief in the towns and hamlets to which they came. It was not only a matter of getting the Royal Government into disrepute: the Germans were determined that all sympathy for England should be completely uprooted.

People in and around the capital had experienced comparatively little of the war. Aside from the few bombs that had been dropped in various parts of Oslo on April 9, no war damage of consequence had been suffered there. And they received no reports on the Germans' ruthless action at Kristiansund, Elverum, and Bodö until long afterwards. Newspapers were prohibited from mentioning destruction by the Germans. Only subjects "of a positive, rather than negative nature" should be publicized. Only reports that "the difficulties had been overcome and life was going on as usual" could get into print.

At the same time the Germans turned a new man loose in the political arena—a minor Norwegian politician named Victor Mogens. For many years Mogens had been a vigorous opponent of the Nygaardsvold Government, which was composed of members of the Labor party, Norway's largest political group. He had his own party, the Fedrelandslaget (i.e., the Fatherland League), and his pet issue had always been national defense. It was known that he was pro-German, but he had never revealed any wholehearted sympathy for nazism.

Unlike Quisling, Mogens was a clever man. Therefore he was dangerous. During those days a small group of pro-German and compromise-minded Norwegians, under the leadership of Mogens, received wide freedom of action, and they made use of the opportunity to the utmost. Victor Mogens made several speeches over the Oslo radio, and his speeches were "must" material for all newspapers. He took his stand on constitutional ground. He attacked Vidkun Quisling, ridiculed him, and condemned him. He declared that Norwegian armed resistance had been both natural and right, but he scored the Nygaardsvold Government for having permitted the country to be so poorly prepared to fight and for not having given up the fight when southern Norway had to be surrendered and it was clear that the war was lost. His policy was that Norway should try to make the best of a bad situation, that Germany had already all but won the war, and that there was nothing to be gained by quarreling with the inevitable.

Mogens received some support from conservative quarters where the Nygaardsvold Government, because it was a Labor Government, had never been popular. And to a certain extent he also received support from people within the Labor party itself. In the midst of this period of confusion Mogens was busy building up a position for himself.

The Germans maintained they had come as friends. But they also said that the occupation was only one phase in the war against England, and that it was their intention to abandon the country as soon as the war was over.

This *might* be true. To all appearances the Germans in those early days did not meddle with Norway's domestic politics. The Administrative Council appeared to have a completely free hand in dealing with matters that had no direct bearing on the German war program. Actually this was not the case, but only a few "insiders" knew it.

Developments proceeded exactly as the Germans wished. With press and radio under their control and with untrained people in positions of leadership, the Germans ran things to suit their own pleasure.

The nation had entered upon a new and dangerous period, but scarcely anyone realized it. It all looked as if the worst were over. True, it was unpleasant to live under German occupation, but it would have been far more unpleasant to engage in war. This was a comment occasionally heard.

Many of the followers whom Mogens enlisted from the Labor party reasoned precisely this way. They also felt that in a coalition of the Fedrelandslaget and the Labor party the latter would in the long run become the stronger part. Besides, those rights and benefits which the working classes had gained for themselves after years of struggle were far too valuable to surrender without a murmur.

Some representatives of the business world supported Mogens for exactly opposite reasons. They saw in him and in co-operation with the Germans a chance to destroy the labor organizations and trade-unions, once and for all.

But among Mogens' followers were also some who supported him not because of any secret or selfish motives, but solely for patriotic reasons.

The situation on the war fronts was far from bright. Holland and Belgium had given up; France's vast Army fell apart like a house of cards. The British Expeditionary Forces evacuated Dunkirk. The Western Front disintegrated. It was doubtful whether England could continue the war after France had fallen. And one thing was certain: America would never get into the war. The Norwegian newspapers were compelled to print column upon column of reports of American isolationist meetings. Statements by Charles Lindbergh and other prominent America-Firsters were presented as official American foreign policy.

Germany was going to win. The war would probably be over before fall. What use was there in little Norway's continuing the resistance? Wouldn't it be wiser to recognize the situation and try to make the best of it? Defeatism had the upper hand in all influential circles, and the epidemic had begun to spread to the masses. Only along the coast and in the war-torn areas did the people wait for the hour of revenge.

5. THE LIGHT BEFORE DAWN

SOUTHERN NORWAY was abandoned by the Norwegian forces on April 28, and for this part of the country the war was over. Bloody battles were still being fought in northern Norway, where the German troops at Narvik were under constant attack by the Norwegians, but northern Norway was far away—almost in another world for those who lived in the southern part. The war had moved on into the distance, and people gradually began to adjust themselves to conditions as they were.

They were not pleased with these conditions, but it did not appear that much could be done to improve the situation. People confined themselves to maintaining a sharp line between themselves and the occupation troops, and the few who ventured to mingle with the strangers were subjected to an ostracism approaching deliberate persecution. Girls who, dazzled by the splendid uniforms, consented to engagements with German soldiers were given a special treatment by their erstwhile friends: their hair was cut off. Storekeepers who failed to understand that their first duty was to take care of their

Norwegian patrons soon discovered the power of the boycott. Norwegian Nazis were nowhere to be seen, and Vidkun Quisling had vanished completely.

Quisling's disappearance caused much comment. It seemed to strengthen the Germans' declaration that the occupation was only temporary and that they had no intention of meddling with Norwegian government. Gradually the belief gained currency that Quisling—who had always been known as a political adventurer—had merely made use of an opportunity to try a *coup d'état*, but that the Germans had eliminated him when they realized that his presence would hinder their own war program against England.

Slowly life returned to a somewhat calm and accustomed pace. People tried to forget the occupation and its discomforts. Those returning from the fighting in the north, filled with bitterness and hate for the invader, met with disillusioning scenes. They found the theaters open and café life in full swing. In the newspapers they found long reports of peaceful sports contests—contests in which no Germans participated, to be sure, but nevertheless . . .

The people in southern Norway had experienced little of the horrors of war. They had not seen the bombed towns and burning hospitals which the German "protection forces" had left in their wake. They had not seen people, grimy with gunpowder and tears, standing in the midst of the ruins of their homes, helplessly shaking their fists at the planes. They lived in a world completely isolated from its surroundings.

The Germans, confident of victory, could afford to display some generosity in their treatment of the civilian population. And as long as the fighting continued in the north it was to the Germans' interest to see to it that the latent ill will against them in the south did not flare up anew. They wanted no sabotaging of industry. They wanted no riots or revolts that would necessitate a revelation of their true selves and purposes.

They saw to it that everyone returning from the north was isolated and denied permission to function in any public capacity. They wanted no monkey wrenches thrown into the machinery, which was once again running smoothly.

The Norwegian people were to be put to work for the German war machine, and whether this was accomplished through the aid of Victor Mogens or through other more un-suspecting souls was of minor importance. What mattered was to lure people to the belief that they themselves had set up the New Order. If this plan were to succeed the Germans would need the help of the leading, "realistic-minded" circles, whose representatives could dispel any suspicions arising among the people. It should be remembered that defeatism was prev-alent chiefly among the higher, more "intellectual" classes. The common man never gave up hope, not even during the critical period when the Western Front collapsed. His thinking did not follow the lines of reason or of military science. He simply believed stubbornly and steadfastly in justice and in a just retribution.

It was at this time that the Royal Government, now situated in London, succeeded in establishing connections with the people at home. This was accomplished through regular broad-casts via British Broadcasting Company facilities three times a day.

The antidote for defeatism had been found.

Partly because of this, partly because their successes on the Western Front betokened an early victory, the Germans decided to nazify Norway at one fell stroke. This happened in the middle of June.

The battles in northern Norway ceased on June 11, but it had long been plain to most leading Norwegians that the Administrative Council arrangement was not satisfactory. Originally the Council had been formed to look after the administration of the capital and its immediate surroundings, but the course of the war had constantly placed additional occupied areas under its leadership. Something had to be done to improve conditions.

It was approximately at the time of the surrender in northern Norway that this question was taken up for discussion at a meeting of representatives of the country's four leading political parties. The meeting was held in Oslo, and it was agreed to seek a solution whereby the Administrative Council could continue its work after being reorganized and strengthened. The representatives understood quite clearly the Germans' political intrigue, and they regarded the Council as an effective brake on those nazification attempts which were being made through willing Norwegian tools such as Victor Mogens. The meeting also gave the Council a unanimous vote of confidence, but this was never made public, for on June 13 the Germans launched their attack.

It was the presidium of the Storting, along with representatives of the four major political parties, the National Labor Federation, and the Administrative Council, that had to absorb the force of the first blow. On June 13 these men were presented with a number of demands by the Germans, the most important being that King Haakon and his Government be deposed and that the authority given them by the Storting on April 9 be revoked. Further, the Germans demanded the establishment of a "National Council" which until further notice should take over the functions of the King and Government. The Storting should be summoned to enact these measures, the Germans insisted—although they did not want the Storting to convene until there was assurance that its decisions would be as they wanted them!

The Germans requested an answer to their demands by June 17.

The Storting presidium's protest against the basis of the

negotiations was met with unmistakable German replies: If the Norwegians themselves could find no solution, then the Germans would take over the civil administration of the country. If no agreement were reached, the Germans would be "forced" to regard it as an expression of "hostile sentiment," and this would lead to "unpleasant consequences." The threats of reprisal also hinted that all Norwegians fit for military duty would be interned and sent to labor camps in Germany.

There was no reason to doubt that the Germans meant what they said. Further, prospects on the war fronts seemed to offer nothing but catastrophe. The Western Front had collapsed; the very day after the Germans in Norway had made their demands, other Germans were marching into Paris. If the war were not already lost, the best one could hope for was a long and weary struggle. It was a matter of so adjusting oneself as to make the occupation as tolerable as possible as long as it lasted.

Finally, the Norwegian negotiators were trained in democracy, and their ingrained democratic habits of thinking certainly played a part. There were still many uncertainties with regard to the Germans' plans, and to these Norwegians the term "negotiations" sounded like good, old-fashioned democracy.

The nature of the German demands soon became known in the better-informed Norwegian circles, and there were two points of view: one, that all negotiations should be dropped forthwith; the other, that the situation was such that no possibilities should go unexplored. The latter view won out, and, despite the humiliations that followed, the solution was in certain respects the right one. Public opinion in June 1940 was still not ripe for a showdown. And the decision to try the path of negotiation had its definite effect on later opposition to German encroachments. A democratic people such as the Norwegians needed proof that all decent means had been tried before they, as a united opposition, were willing to stand the suffering which a war to the death would bring with it.

At this time only the negotiators themselves and a small group close to them knew what was going on. The Germans had entered into the negotiations on the condition that the public should not be kept informed. That, too, was why they had allowed the Norwegians only four days in which to formulate their reply. They had no faith in the public, and they did not want to give the negotiators a chance to seek advice from the people.

At the very first meeting between the Norwegian negotiators and the "Regierungspräsident," Dr. Delbrügge, who led the negotiations for the Germans, it became clear that the German demand for the removal of King Haakon and his Government was nothing less than an ultimatum. The negotiations were to be concerned only with the methods to be employed! Threats of reprisal followed in quick and endless succession, and on the evening of June 17 the Storting presidium had to submit its reply. It indicated willingness to request the King to abdicate. The original German demands called for deposition of the King, but to this the Norwegians would not agree. And for that reason the Storting was not summoned. After a few days' consideration the Germans accepted the reply as submitted, and in due course the request for abdication was sent to the King in London by way of Stockholm.

The Norwegian people still knew nothing of what had happened, but it had long been suspected that something was brewing—largely because Norwegian newspapers from one end of the country to the other had for days been carrying identical attacks on the King and his Government. Such unanimity in the democratic Norwegian press could not help but stir up suspicion.

On July 8 King Haakon made his reply over the London radio. A detailed account of the negotiations preceded the King's address, which emphasized that the Storting presidium's request "cannot be regarded as an expression of the free Norwegian attitude, but only as the result of pressure exercised through military occupation." Joy swept like a tidal wave through the country.

The King's reply became a plan and a guide for the home front, which was now slowly beginning to organize itself. The contact between the two fronts—the home front and the external front—had been made. The Government and the people were once more united. The action taken by the Storting at its last free meeting on April 9 now acquired significance which became clear to every Norwegian. The war was not yet lost. Amid all the confusion and despair the single purpose was again discernible.

The Norwegians set to work to compose their own "rules of conduct" to match those carried by the Germans. Nobody knew who first wrote them, but soon they were being typed in shops and offices everywhere and distributed to the people by the thousands:

THE TEN COMMANDMENTS FOR TRUE NORWEGIANS

1. Thou shalt obey King Haakon, whom thou thyself hast elected.

2. Thou shalt detest Hitler and all his works, and never forget that, without a declaration of war, he made his coassassins fall upon peaceable people.

3. Thou shalt remember forever how the German Nazis, without military reason, made their aviators wipe out Norwegian farms, villages, and towns, in order to satisfy their blood lust and spread terror.

4. Thou shalt despise any form of treason and remember that its punishment is death.

5. Thou shalt regard as a traitor every Norwegian who, as a

private individual, keeps company with Germans or Quislings at home, in the streets, or in restaurants.

6. So, too, thou shalt regard every member of the Storting who votes in favor of deposing our gallant King and our legal Government, who are the only ones who are able, in freedom and independence, to work for the liberty of Norway.

7. Thou shalt take note that a Government of German lackeys will be judged by the whole world as a Government of rebels and bring upon us universal contempt.

8. Thou shalt daily impress upon thy children and all thy acquaintances that they are Norwegians and must remain so.

9. Thou shalt remember that only a German defeat can give us our liberty again.

10. God save the King and the Fatherland!

II. THE FACE BEHIND THE MASK

1. THE NORTH SEA BRIDGED

PEOPLE COULD NOT REMEMBER having had such a glorious summer in many years. Day after day there were scintillating skies, and the nights were short and silvery gray and filled with a thousand scents of fertile soil. The black-out which for months had been oppressing minds and gnawing at nerves became a joke without sense or purpose. People tore the black paper away from windows and let the cool, sweet air flow in. They set their radios on the window ledges and tuned in London at full volume. The Norwegian BBC broadcasts in the evening, at midnight, and in the morning had become the fixed points around which all life revolved. The few minutes that each broadcast lasted were sacred. Telephone calls made while the program was on went unanswered. It was no use ringing the doorbell, not even at the homes of one's best friends. Nobody would answer. Nobody wanted to miss a word of the program. If one were invited out for the evening, no questions were asked about what to wear. The only question was: Shall we come before or after London? The German-controlled Oslo radio was no longer of any account. All through the country radios remained tuned to a single station.

The enchantment was complete. Gone was the bed of thorns. To tune in London was like tearing the black-out shades from the windows. Fresh air poured in. It was not necessarily good news that came from London, but, good and bad, it was the words of free men spoken in a free land. They were words that brought hope and faith and assurance of future liberation and of happy days to come.

The information service, which later became so effective that the Germans in their desperation confiscated all radios and imposed the death penalty for all who listened to foreign stations, was still in its infancy. The individual Norwegian's freedom of movement was for the time being not noticeably restricted, and the need for news of Norway by way of London was still not great. It was news from abroad that people wanted: news of developments on the war fronts, news about the Royal Norwegian Government's activities. And pep talks, too. Later, when travel limitations were imposed and when the various sections became more or less isolated from each other, the situation changed.

That summer was an eventful period, but most people knew little of what was going on behind the scenes. Secret newspapers appeared, but only to a limited extent and very irregularly. There were, for instance, very few who knew that the Germans had placed the political parties as well as the National Labor Federation and the Employers' Association under financial guardianship. People were more interested in what the German troops were doing. It was obvious that they were getting ready for something.

As is the custom in Norway, thousands of people spent their vacations that summer at the seashore. They camped in tents and houses and huts. The beaches were packed with sun worshipers. The sun shone on the just and the unjust. It shone also on the German soldiers who in great numbers had been transferred from inland districts to the coast, and who spent hours each day in the ocean. They were rehearsing the invasion of England.

The maneuvers were conducted with typical German thoroughness. Tanks and planes and trains and infantry were active. Innocent and peaceful islands were "invaded" with clash and clatter. German soldiers, seasick and sopping wet, bustled about everywhere along the coast. Weird rumors were in circulation, and some of them were doubtless true. Near Egersund people had seen German soldiers who daily practiced swimming on horseback. At Stavanger, it was said, the German soldiers had mutinied and refused to board any troop transport.

It was a commonly known fact that the British were sinking German ships along the Norwegian coast almost daily. The burial of German soldiers had become matter of course in the coastal villages.

"We are sailing against England," sang the German soldiers.

"But you will never reach that land!" intoned the people, keeping time with the drumbeats that followed the tuneful boast. And behind the marching German troops ran small boys making the motions of swimming.

Everywhere people were deriving pleasure from quoting Churchill's words: "We are waiting for the invasion. So are the fishes!"

But it was only on the surface that this kind of humor prevailed, because there was no doubt that the Germans were going about their preparations with deadly seriousness. The Nazi authorities had requisitioned thousands of Norwegian fishing boats, armed them, and concentrated them at all the strategic points along the coast.

The tension was great, and an almost unhealthy optimism spread among the people. Hitler was on the verge of putting his invasion plans into effect. But Norwegians, who were accustomed to boats and to the sea, drew their own conclusions when they saw how miserably the Germans handled the stolen craft. They knew what the outcome would be. Hitler was staking everything on one card! It was obvious that he would lose. There would be a terrible blood bath. Maybe the war would be over by fall, anyhow—and with the Germans beaten!

Meanwhile the clouds above the horizon drew together, betokening bad weather. Without anyone's knowing where the rumors came from, Quisling's name suddenly reappeared in the gossip. It was said that he was in Germany and that he had by no means given up after his setback of April. People were on the alert again. Quisling—that meant only one thing: strife. The people's attention was torn away from the invasion maneuvers. At this time, too, the first efforts were being made to improve the organized opposition to the Germans. Small groups, or "cells," were formed. They worked independently of each other, and their spheres of action were for the time being limited to their most immediate surroundings. Simultaneously the major political parties were clearing the decks for action. They knew Quisling and how he felt and what he thought about them.

It had been the Germans' intention to summon the Storting after the King gave his reply on July 8, and to have it set up the promised National Council. Even the date for the convening of the Storting had been fixed. This was to take place on July 25. And in this connection there occurred an episode which, even though it is unimportant, revealed how little the Germans understood the people they had set out to govern.

When discussion developed as to where the Storting session should be held, a cynic among the Norwegian negotiators suggested Eidsvold—Norway's "Independence Hall"—the place where the Norwegian Constitution came into being in 1814. To every right-thinking Norwegian, Eidsvold is sacred

ground. The Germans snatched up the cynic's suggestion with
enthusiasm. Of course, Eidsvold should be the meeting place!
It would supply precisely the desired festive touch to the event.
Donnerwetter! To think that no one had hit upon that idea
before!

The Germans announced their decision. The result was a
storm of indignation. The Germans couldn't understand it.
They were annoyed and shaken by it. They had really meant
it well! Least of all had they intended it as an affront.

The enterprising German officer who had first approved
the suggestion was shortly afterwards transferred to Poland.
Later the plans for a National Council drifted into endless
revision, and the meeting of the Storting was never held.

The Reichskommissariat had its hands full with other problems, and the first of these was that of "neutralizing" the
National Labor Federation, which was the country's most influential force. Norway had only this one national labor organization, but it was nation-wide and had long since gained
common acceptance as a natural and necessary part of the
Norwegian social structure.

The initial attack on the organization had occurred in May
when the Germans struck at the workingman's standard of
living by dictating a drastic reduction of wages. As early as
April 23 the German authorities had set up new rules governing disputes over wages and working conditions—rules which
left such matters to the Germans to decide. But for tactical
reasons the occupying power had, by and large, been quite
obliging to the labor organization during those first months.
The Germans had, for instance, yielded to the Norwegian
Seamen's Union's point-blank refusal to have any part in the
shipping of German troops and matériel while the fighting
was still going on.

The situation had changed, however, and the Germans
were slowly but surely beginning to reveal their true character.

But they still moved cautiously. What they wanted to do was to divide the organization from within. They enlisted the aid of some confused souls who allowed themselves to be influenced by National Socialism's terminology about war against capitalism and English plutocracy and imperialism. But the coup did not become anything more than a tempest in a teapot; when the "opposition," as the pro-Nazi group called itself, met in Oslo to set up a new program for labor, only eighty-five persons were present, and most of them refused to sign the appeal. When representatives of the four major political parties got together for their meetings on August 5, they had the support of the National Labor Federation. Everybody realized fully the danger that loomed ahead.

The rumor that Quisling was in Germany was now confirmed. Further, it became known that he had received the Germans' promise that his Nasjonal Samling party would be strongly represented in the proposed National Council. In addition, it was said that Hitler had promised him that he would be allowed to form a government. All this made counterstrokes necessary.

The political parties established a central committee whose duty was to draw up a joint declaration and to formulate a joint program. This work was completed on August 24. The program was brief and to the point: The parties agreed to shelve all former dissension and to unite in a single task—that of re-creating a free Norway.

The declaration was signed by the Labor party, the Right (Conservative) party, the Left (Liberal) party, the Farmers' party, and also by the Christian Peoples' party, which joined the others after the agreement had been worked out. Together, these five parties represented 92 per cent of all the voters of Norway. On the same day that the declaration was signed it received the unanimous endorsement of all of Norway's leading business and professional associations.

On August 26 the Germans prohibited the proposed co-operation. On September 7 they demanded that the negotiations which had been held in June should be resumed. This time they insisted that the Norwegians take action on King Haakon's rejection of the request that he abdicate. The Germans wanted him deposed, then and there. The Storting's presidium immediately decided to summon members of that body to a meeting on September 10.

It may have been purely coincidental that the Germans launched these new negotiations just at the time of the violent air raids on London. But it may also have been planned that way. The June negotiations had taken place when the terrible impression left by the collapsing Western Front was still fresh on the mind, and possibly the Germans thought that the Norwegian negotiators would be more tractable with the echoes of the London bombardment ringing in their ears. If it was planned that way, the Germans were right in timing it so, for the events of the summer had turned the tide of public sentiment. The wave of defeatism that had followed the fall of France was now ebbing fast. The invasion plans were still only plans, and German soldiers still perched along the Norwegian coast looking longingly towards the west. The song "Wir fahren gegen England [We Are Sailing against England]" was no longer quite so popular.

Other factors also played a part. For one thing, it gradually became terrifyingly clear to Norwegians what an enormous drain on the country's supplies was resulting from the presence of the occupation forces. As the queues in front of food shops grew longer, as tobacco disappeared, as the army of German civilians took on the characteristics of a swarm of grasshoppers, the Norwegians ceased to make fun of the German soldiers who ate chocolate bars spread thickly with butter. The number of arrested Norwegians was steadily increasing, and the first death sentences had been pronounced.

The hatred for the invaders became a force which it grew ever more difficult to keep in check. The men who faced the Germans at the conference table were representative of this new feeling. They had come from all parts of Norway, and the angry voices of the people were still echoing in their ears. Yet they had not given up their confidence that the differences with the Nazis could be solved by democratic methods. They still had a lesson to learn. And they still hoped for some way of avoiding that unspeakable humiliation—Quisling.

To Norwegians, Quisling was the worst that could happen. The Germans knew this, and they made no effort to conceal the fact that he was the trump card they were holding in reserve. Just a few days before the negotiations opened he had returned from his sojourn in Germany, and the swastikaed celebrities who turned out to greet him at the Oslo airport supplied abundant proof that Quisling was not to be passed over lightly any longer. His name hovered like a sword of Damocles over the conference table throughout the days that followed.

It soon developed in the negotiations that the Norwegian representatives were definitely opposed to the deposition of the King. They knew that the people of Norway, who ordinarily displayed no great respect for royalty, and who during the years of peace had seldom given their own monarch any serious thought, had now definitely rallied around King Haakon VII as the symbol of the whole country's future.

But they also knew, or thought they knew, that the people were ready to make considerable concessions in order to be spared Quisling. For this reason a small majority of the Storting men appeared willing to consider suspending the Royal House for the duration of the war, but only on certain conditions. These conditions were quite well defined: The Germans should supply written guaranties that the proposed National Council be permitted to govern the country accord-

ing to Norwegian law; the German police should not interfere
with Norwegian civil courts; the German authorities should
not exercise censorship; Norway's finances should not be destroyed; amnesty should be given all persons arrested or sentenced because of the occupation. It was the last act of the
comedy that the Germans had been staging since the middle
of June.

The Germans carried on the negotiations in a spirit of
conscious swindle. Not once was the Storting permitted to
convene for a plenary meeting. Practically no written or clearly
formulated propositions were presented by the Nazis. They
transferred their blitzkrieg tactics from the battlefield to the
conference table. The individual political party groups within
the Storting were directed to hold separate sessions. Again
and again the group leaders were summoned to "consultations"
with the German authorities, and there they were alternately
threatened, enticed, flattered, and threatened anew. Everything
proceeded at breakneck pace. The Germans demanded votes
taken on the shortest possible notice. Proposition followed
proposition, some in Norwegian and some in German. One
group was informed that the other had yielded, and vice versa.
The Storting was never permitted to assemble as a whole.
Plainly the object was to crush the Norwegian centers of
resistance individually so that the front which had been created
by the autumn's events would collapse all along the line.

The Norwegian defenses swayed and shook under the attack. But on September 18 the leaders rallied all forces for
a counterstroke. The Storting's presidium sent the German
authorities a note wherein the Norwegian counterdemands
were clearly and precisely set forth. It concluded with the
statement that if these demands were not granted the negotiations were to be regarded as ended.

Surprisingly, the presidium's note brought no direct reply
from the Germans. Certainly one guaranty, more or less, could

be of no importance in the Germans' records. The explanation came a few days later, when the Germans brutally ripped off their mask and bared their true face.

The following day the Storting members left Oslo to return to their homes.

2. NAZI LESSON IN PERSPICUITY

THE OSLO THEATER was filled to the doors, and laughter billowed through the darkness. A summer of censored newspapers had taught people to read between the lines. With Gestapo agents on all street corners, in restaurants and hotels, they had also learned to seek out the hidden meanings in everyday phrases. Their ears were attuned to words and accents.

Songs followed skits like the spokes in a wheel, and the entire revue was a concealed sneer at the occupying power. The crowd enjoyed itself tremendously and shamelessly. Not even the most thorough and methodical "expert training" for occupation soldiers in Berlin had succeeded in producing an effective weapon against the intimacy and comradeship that here existed between actors and audience.

The show was nearing its end, and the German officers scattered about in the theater moved restlessly in their chairs. They sensed that the laughter was directed at them. Yet they found nothing to criticize in the antics of the performers. The revue had been carefully censored beforehand by the Reichskommissariat's department of "cultural and theatrical activity," and it was unthinkable that mistakes could have been made so high in the ranks.

The laughter on all sides rose to new heights, and if the ears of the *Herrenvolk* had been trained to pick up finer sounds than the rumble of tanks and the explosion of bombs they would have caught the dangerous undertone. Two actors were on the stage. They were whispering to each other. Suddenly one cried out in surprise:

"You don't say! Why, that's impossible!"

More actors appeared and joined the others. The whispering continued, grew louder; the voices became incensed, angry.

"It can't be!"

"That would be an insult!"

"We'll never agree to it!"

"Anything else, maybe, but not that!"

Then one voice, louder than the rest:

"They won't dare—they won't dare to offer us that! Why, remember how people took it the last time!"

The audience had become deathly silent. The German officers looked around. The faces near them had become so grim, so bitter. Such quiet seemed eerie where people should be enjoying themselves, where there should be laughter. Then suddenly the tension on the stage was relieved. A man came running in and gasped:

"Have you heard the latest? They've raised the liquor prices again!"

The German officers sank back in their chairs, once more at ease. They nodded to each other, haughtily.

"Those Norwegians! What childish fools!"

The Germans had not taken warning. They tried it anyhow. Quisling stood on the threshold.

The Germans' efforts to create a National Council—a "government" which would run their errands—met with no success. The Storting members had gone home. The next move was up to the occupying power.

On Monday, September 23, Oslo's chief of police was dismissed—the same man who in April had refused to obey Quisling's orders. Simultaneously there occurred a shake-up of high police officials. A few Quisling followers began to appear publicly in uniform. This added a new touch to the street scene. Political uniforms had been prohibited in Norway for many years. The country's lone pro-Nazi newspaper, *Fritt Folk,* flared up worse than ever before. Its threats were no longer cloaked.

The presence of Nazis was a provocation, and on Tuesday, September 24, the boil not only came to a head but burst open. It began at a little restaurant for students at Oslo University. A small group of Nazi students had been inviting trouble for several days, and now patience with them had reached an end. Two young boys and a girl wearing the brown-shirted uniforms of the Nasjonal Samling party entered the restaurant and raised a commotion. They were promptly thrown out, but only after their brown shirts had been torn to shreds. Embarrassed but enraged, the three left. Ten minutes later they were back again, and with them came a score of others. Led by a German civilian, they marched into University Square.

Two or three hundred Norwegian students stood in the Square watching the proceedings in silence. The Nazis lined up in front of them, took off their shoulder belts, unpocketed their blackjacks, and made ready for battle. University Square was strangely quiet. What was taking place seemed unreal and unbelievable. This was Oslo. This was not Prague or Vienna. Behind the group lay Karl Johan Street with the *Studenterlund* and the National Theater, and before them were the university buildings with the venerable main hall in the center. Above them domed a Norwegian September sky, with clear, cool air.

The German leading the group finally broke the silence. He was a little fellow, with a Tirolean cap and an exact copy of Hitler's mustache. With a snarling voice he ordered his "troops" to attack. The leather straps and blackjacks whistled through the air. It took the students a few seconds to awaken from the strange spell. But when they did they were fighting mad, and they set to work to maul the disturbers of the peace. Quickly they demonstrated that there was also such a thing as Norwegian thoroughness. Within a few minutes seven or eight of the Quislings were lying unconscious in the Square. The others ensconced themselves on the stone steps in front of one of the buildings. The German had vanished completely.

University Square borders on Oslo's main thoroughfare, and the row had begun at four o'clock, just as thousands of people were on their way home from work. Thus the students were given ample reinforcements. Office workers and laborers, errand boys and others, rushed in to lend a hand. And they meant business.

Someone called the police. Was not Norway a land of law and order? It was the duty of the police to look after the rowdies and the unruly. Soon the police arrived—tall, light-haired men with open, honest faces. They were strangely white around the gills. The crowd separated in order to let the police through. Now those Nazi hooligans would get what they had coming to them!

Then it happened. The police lined up against the crowd, driving it back. Other police formed a protective circle around the Quislings, and there was no mistaking the triumphant shouts from the steps. The police continued to force the crowd back. It was obvious they were unhappy.

"It's orders," they explained when people looked at them questioningly, unbelievingly.

"We're acting on orders," they said.

The Quislings who had remained on their feet now marched away. People stared at them in silence.

Suddenly the victors—the Quislings—commenced singing the national anthem. It sounded thin and strange coming from that group, and instantly the jeering began. It rose like a storm from the crowd and spread along Karl Johan Street. Never before in Norway's history had the national anthem been drowned out so completely.

It was some time before street life returned to normal. People drifted about restlessly. They were unsatisfied and unsure. Something had happened—something that they could not quite understand. They also had a feeling that they should have done something about it, that they themselves had not been true to their purpose.

The following day—September 25—all newspapers carried a front-page notice that ordered all people to listen to the Oslo radio at six o'clock that evening. Reichskommissar Terboven was to make an address "of historic significance." The Reichskommissar had not spoken over a Norwegian radio since June 1, and at that time he had concerned himself chiefly with "the cheap and cowardly practice of those young boys who shave the heads of girls who sympathize with the protecting power." It was not likely that this speech was to deal with such trivial matters.

But no matter what people had expected, Terboven's address exceeded their most extravagant imaginings. By the time the Reichskommissar concluded his half-hour utterance, it was clear to Norwegians just what kind of "guests" they had in the country. Gone were all fine phrases and pleasantries. Gone were all assurances of friendship and interdependence, of mutual interests and "protection" from war and misery.

The mask had been cast away. The wolf had emerged.

Terboven had promised a speech of "historic significance." And there is scarcely any doubt that his speech will go down in the history not only of Norway, but of the world. In the course of half an hour the entire Nazi mentality was laid bare. In the course of half an hour the justification for the war against nazism was firmly established. In the course of half an hour all hopes of a negotiated peace were trampled in the dust.

Since June the Norwegian authorities had been conferring with the Germans in an effort to find an honorable and defensible solution to a difficult situation. Maybe they were naïve in believing that it was of any use to negotiate with the Germans. Maybe they should have realized from the beginning that it was futile. But they were upright men, and they believed they were doing right by their country and its cause.

Terboven revealed in his speech that the Germans' purposes had not for one moment been honorable. Openly and unblushingly he told his hundreds of thousands of listeners that the negotiations had been launched with only one purpose in view: to make the Storting, its presidium, and the Administrative Council into the whole country's laughingstock. The Norwegian people were to be shown their responsible leaders as they really were—"as a collection of individuals who are politically corrupt from one end to the other, separately and as a whole."

Terboven's speech was true to the basic rule that Hitler has laid out for all propaganda, that only really great lies are believed. He stated that the Storting had been called together and that it had deposed the King and his Government with more than the legally required two-thirds majority. He insisted the Storting members had offered only one countersuggestion: that they should continue to receive their regular salaries. He heaped lie upon lie before he finally concluded:

The King and his Government had been deposed. They would never again be allowed to enter the country.

The Administrative Council had been dismissed.

All political parties, with the exception of the Nasjonal Samling, were dissolved.

The forming of groups or organizations for political activity was prohibited.

The Reichskommissar then reported that he had appointed thirteen "acting ministers" for the various governmental departments and that these men would henceforth manage the affairs of state. He read the list of thirteen names. Practically all of them were members of the Nasjonal Samling.

When Terboven turned away from the microphone a heavy silence lay over the entire land. Only the clatter of German boots was heard in the otherwise deserted streets. The heels were of iron.

3. VIDKUN QUISLING

"THE TROUBLE with the Norwegian people is that they have been debrutalized!"

The fuming, squeaky voice rose to a shrill falsetto.

Listeners who had gathered around the orator roared with laughter. He was a tiny little man with thick-lensed glasses— almost a dwarf in uniform—and with brown shirt, black tie, blue ski pants, shoulder belt, and blue ski cap set at a ridiculous angle on the busy little head. People laughed, but as they laughed they stared at the little orator with disbelieving eyes. Such things as this simply did not happen!

The voice grew more and more angry:

"Norwegians have grown soft under the democratic system. They have forgotten their racial heritage. They have forgotten from whom they are descended. The viking blood has turned to water!"

That brought a new roar of laughter.

"But there will be changes made. We must revert to our true selves. We are going to be the leaders of the North. Norway is not only going to be free. Norway is also going to be great! Iceland, Greenland, the Faeroes, the Shetland Islands, the Orkney Islands—all these will again be ours. They will be parts of the great new Norwegian empire!"

The words and the scene were comical, and at the same time profoundly unpleasant. It was as if the cool and clear September air had suddenly unloosed a sickening stench.

Listeners turned away and walked on—uncertain, half laughing, half shuddering.

And suddenly the little orator was left standing absolutely alone in University Square. He looked around him, uncertainly.

Then, like a child in a fit of temper, he screamed:

"Just wait! Just wait! You'll find out!"

Running awkwardly, he vanished into the university gardens.

It was said that the Germans had become enraged back in April when they discovered that the Nasjonal Samling was not a political party but just a hodgepodge of spiritually crippled individuals. They had refused to believe it when they were told that the Nasjonal Samling had not managed to elect any of its members to the Storting. They had been dumfounded when they discovered how Vidkun Quisling had stuffed them full of lies.

All this, of course, was only talk. The German diplomatic representation in Norway and the thousands of German spies who had been active for years, partly in the guise of tourists and partly as "refugees," knew how matters stood. It may well be, however, that the German soldiers and the minor occupational authorities were amazed at the discoveries they made.

Here lies the explanation for the dissension that has existed ever since the invasion between the occupation authorities, especially the military men, and the authorities in Berlin over the effectiveness of using Quisling and his party.

Vidkun Abraham Lauritz Quisling was born in Telemark

in southern Norway on July 18, 1887. His parents were ordinary folk of Norwegian *bonde* ancestry.

The boy was very gifted, and he received a good education, such as Norway provides for all. People who knew him during his school years say that he was a "shining light" and that he was ambitious far beyond the ordinary. He was regularly the highest in his class, and if he did not manage to maintain that position by honorable means he did not hesitate to employ others.

He *insisted* upon being first—in the classroom and among his comrades. And if he thought he had been wronged, he never forgot it.

He was graduated from the Norwegian military academy as the highest man in his class. A brilliant military career seemed to be awaiting him. Promotions came to him regularly, and during the First World War he was sent to Petrograd as the Norwegian military attaché. He was an able linguist.

During his stay in Russia, Quisling met Norway's outstanding humanitarian, Fridtjof Nansen, and became his assistant in the great task of alleviating distress in war-torn areas. Nansen needed a man who knew the Russian language, and Quisling, with his education and natural talents, was well qualified for the work at hand. Beyond that, little was heard about him in this connection. Nansen was the soul of the vast relief work. Quisling was only one of his many helpers.

Towards the close of the 1920s Quisling became interested in the National Socialist currents in Germany, as a means of attaining power. But he hesitated to take a definite stand. What he had seen in Russia prevented him from feeling sure that communism was not the best course to adopt in plotting his future career. During a visit to Norway he sent out his first feeler: he offered the Norwegian Labor party his services in organizing a "Red Guard," pointing out that he would bring to the task the fruits of his experience in Russia and as a member of the Norwegian General Staff. The Labor party turned him down.

Political conditions in Norway were at that time unclear, and Quisling continued to feel his way along.

His chance came in 1930. Circumstances had brought it about that the young Farmers' party was to form a government. This development came rather suddenly and unexpectedly, and the party had not yet produced any group of important leaders. Among other things, it proved difficult to find a man for the position of Minister of Defense. Finally the choice fell to Quisling.

The Farmers' party Government never managed to get firmly established, and Quisling's presence by no means eased the situation. An indication of how people—even his best friends—regarded him was provided by a minor incident at the Grand Café in Oslo shortly before his appointment became known.

Quisling was seated in the café with some friends. He had just been informed of his selection, and he could not restrain his pride and joy.

"Gentlemen," he whispered confidentially across the table, "I have just accepted appointment as Minister of Defense!"

For a moment the group around the table was silent. Then one of the men stood up and raised his glass.

"In that case," he said, "I think it is in order to say: 'God save our King and native land!'"

Quisling's career as Minister of Defense was very turbulent, and one public scandal followed the other. The affair which aroused most widespread attention sprang from Quisling's assertion that he had been attacked in the department offices by a group of men who threw pepper in his eyes. That gave the whole country a hearty laugh, and at one stroke Quisling was turned into a public joke. But the people were also disgusted with him. No proof of the attack was ever produced, and Quisling was unable to give even the vaguest description of his attackers. There was no doubt among the people that the "attack" had occurred only in Quisling's lively imagination.

During his brief period as a member of the Government, Quisling also managed to get himself hated by the entire Norwegian working class. On two occasions he called out troops to deal with laborers participating in legal strikes. Therefore he was assured of the intense opposition of Norwegian trade-union organizations when he came to power in September 1940.

His record as Minister of Defense had definitely made Quisling an impossible man in Norwegian politics. That is why, on May 17, 1933, he launched his own political party, giving it the name "Nasjonal Samling," which means national unity. This event caused no special stir, nor did the fact that in his program Quisling had plagiarized the ideology of German National Socialism. In the fall of that year Quisling's party entered candidates in the Storting elections, but the result was disappointing. Only a scant 2 per cent of the votes cast went to the Nasjonal Samling, and even under Norway's rules of proportional representation the party did not succeed in placing a single one of its representatives in the Storting. At the next Storting elections, held in 1936, the party made even a poorer showing, despite a tremendous campaign carried on through the aid of certain wealthy men who were anti-labor. Quisling himself toured the country in an automobile built to resemble a tank and equipped with a loud-speaker. Again and again incensed voters would break up his meetings and send Quisling and his *Hird* on their way. The *Hird,* expanded since the invasion, is Quisling's band of storm-troopers. Back in 1936 it was not much more than a kind of bodyguard.

In the Storting elections of 1936 the Nasjonal Samling votes dropped to 1.83 per cent of the total cast. In local elections the following year (1937), the Nasjonal Samling ob-

tained only the faintest shadow of support: fifteen one-hundredths of 1 per cent of the votes cast in the rural districts,
and six one-hundredths of 1 per cent of those cast in towns.
That was the end. From that time, up to 1940, the Nasjonal
Samling was only a ghost organization. It was never mentioned
any more, except as a joke.

The Nasjonal Samling newspaper, *Fritt Folk,* appeared as
a small four-page weekly, and its circulation dropped steadily.
The followers which the party had had—chiefly businessmen
who were anti-labor plus thrill-seeking boys who were cap-
tivated by the thought of wearing uniforms—also lost all
interest. The rich men dropped out because the enterprise
was producing no returns. The young people quit when the
law prohibiting the wearing of political uniforms went into
effect: no uniforms, no fun. In 1936 a split also occurred
within the party when practically all of its few respected
members took warning of developments in Middle Europe and
thereupon took their leave of the budding Norwegian *Führer.*

During the early spring of 1940 Nasjonal Samling activities
were to some extent revived. Now and then a placard bearing the NS colors—red and yellow—was to be seen along
the streets. They were torn down almost the moment they
appeared. People attached no special importance to this. Storting elections were scheduled for later that year, and perhaps
the Nasjonal Samling was planning to set up candidates again.

Only the most politically alert wondered at this reawaken-
ing. It was obvious that the party had obtained new funds.
But where from? Could it be true that there were still some
Norwegian businessmen who were willing to waste money
on something so sure to fail? The mystery increased when
on April 1, 1940, the newspaper *Fritt Folk,* which had been
struggling along as a third-rate weekly publication, suddenly
blossomed out as a daily. Some guessed that the money had
come from Germany, but few took warning.

It is impossible to say to what extent Quisling was kept informed of the German plans to invade Norway. Careful generals as the Germans are, it seems unbelievable that they would have disclosed their military secrets to such an unreliable person. But there can be no doubt that Quisling knew there was something in the wind. Probably he received his tip-off just before things began to happen. At any rate, on the evening of April 8 he moved from his apartment in the outskirts of Oslo to the centrally situated Hotel Continental, and late in the evening of the same day some of his youthful followers scattered handbills about the streets—handbills demanding that the Government resign.

The practical use that the Germans had for Quisling during the invasion was infinitesimal, aside from the confusion he managed to create when he spoke over the Oslo radio on the evening of April 9 and reported that mobilization had ceased. Even this contribution was of doubtful value to the Germans, because whatever confusion he created was far outweighed by the anger which his appearance on the radio aroused.

The party had no one in a position to influence the course of the war. The Royal Government has not yet succeeded in proving any clear-cut cases of treason among the Norwegian military forces. The case of the Narvik commandant —the notorious Colonel Sundlo—who surrendered the town without a struggle is still unclear. The man later joined forces with Quisling and so far as that is concerned is a traitor, but there are many indications that his conduct during the invasion can be attributed simply to a lack of courage.

However, there is no doubt about Quisling's treason. It was, figuratively, his voice that had sounded in a sob-choked falsetto over University Square that clear September day of 1940: "Just wait! Just wait! You'll find out!"

Quisling had much to avenge, many humiliations that ached

for repayment in kind. And all the querulous malcontents of the country, all those who had felt themselves humiliated and misunderstood, all those who in honest competition had been unable to assert themselves—all these now joined forces with him. They comprise his Nasjonal Samling of today.

4. THE FIRST DEFEAT— AND THE FIRST VICTORIES

THE EVENTS of late summer and early fall of 1940 had to a certain extent stabilized the front lines of resistance. But the Germans wanted no stable front against them. For them it became a matter of forcing the attack, of ripping up the resisters' positions and creating confusion in the ranks. The blitzkrieg tactics employed during the negotiations were resumed. And well informed as the Germans were about the Norwegian social structure, they realized that their aims could best be accomplished by a systematic destruction of the country's strong organizations. To them these organizations were hostile units. They had to be crushed separately before they got a chance to agree on a common plan of action.

The Germans also knew that the strongest and most dangerous of these units was the National Labor Federation (Arbeidernes Faglige Landsorganisasjon). With a membership of more than 350,000, the Federation was the main force within the Norwegian people's army of a scant three million.

The Germans had not waited long after their arrival before directing their first blow at the Federation. Late in April the Reichskommissariat had taken for itself the final say in all disputes arising over wages and working conditions.

The second blow came in May, when, by German orders, wages for Norwegian labor were reduced 7 per cent.

A still more serious blow fell on the Federation after the Norwegian surrender in June. The Federation leaders—and this included the very top men—who had accompanied the King and Government northwards during the campaign and who had returned to Oslo after the cessation of open hostilities, were refused permission to resume their duties. This was to prove catastrophic when the Germans launched their main attack. The first omens of this appeared during the negotiations in September.

When the political parties set up their common front in August, the Federation joined with other major organizations in supporting the move. The Federation had also participated in the abortive negotiations regarding the proposed National Council. But suddenly the Federation leadership sounded a retreat. The secretariat resolved to withdraw from the battle. It was declared that the organization could no longer concern itself with questions of a political nature; that it should not appoint representatives to the National Council if this were formed; that in the future it should concern itself only with social and labor problems.

This was nothing less than an escape from the world of reality, and the resolution no doubt drew its inspiration from German quarters. The leadership saw the storm approaching. It tried to avoid it by seeking shelter. Naturally this scheme failed; it did provide a few days' postponement, but nothing more than that.

The German assault came on the evening of September 25, and it was an attack from ambush. The first indication of it was an apparently innocent announcement made over the Oslo radio, which stated that the National Labor Federation would continue to function as before, but that it had been necessary to make certain changes in the leadership.

The acting president of the organization was out of town on a business trip at the time, so it fell to the vice-president to take up negotiations with the Germans on the following day. These continued quietly for a few days, and then on September 28 the Germans gave the vice-president the choice of resigning together with the president or taking the responsibility for the dissolution of the organization. He was not given an opportunity to consult with other members of the secretariat. His answer had to be made on the spot. The vice-president decided against taking the responsibility for a break, and thus the "push" resulted in a German victory. Men from the organization's "opposition group," used as tools by the Germans earlier in the summer, now moved up into positions of leadership.

The rank-and-file members of the organization reacted violently to what had happened, and the sentiment throughout the country was greatly perturbed. Authorities had their hands full in keeping the resentment from breaking out in riots. At regular intervals during the days that followed a statement was read over the Oslo radio. It strongly emphasized that the National Labor Federation would continue its activity as before, and that in reality nothing had been changed. Workers, however, were not content with this, and those "representatives" whom the new leadership sent out into the country to explain the situation were given a hot reception. And when the various trade-unions were presented with a "declaration of loyalty," to be signed and returned, most of them refused to comply.

The National Labor Federation had been forced to capitulate under the brunt of the Germans' surprise tactics. The same fate would probably have befallen almost any Norwegian organization at that moment. An entirely new situation had arisen suddenly and unexpectedly, and for lack of experience in dealing with such situations no adequate method of defense was immediately available.

The scorched-earth policy was still not recognized as an effective war weapon. As in other countries, it had cost the workers of Norway many years of toil and sacrifice to build up an organization capable of safeguarding their interests. To destroy this organization voluntarily, and before being absolutely certain it was going to be used against its members, was a terrifying decision to make, especially when the responsibility for the decision was placed on a single man's shoulders.

But what happened to the National Labor Federation became a valuable lesson for the other organizations in the country. Proof that the lesson had been taken to heart was provided as early as November, when the Nazis, employing the same tactics, tried to gain control of the National Athletic Association, which had a membership almost as great as that of the Federation, roughly about 300,000.

The leadership of this organization had kept in close contact with all sports clubs and other suborganizations throughout the country, and it had taken appropriate measures. So, when the Nazis struck on November 22, things began to happen. All the Association's leaders refused to co-operate in the "New Ordering"—i.e., nazification. They resigned from their offices. The same thing happened in all the suborganizations —the associations of skiers, skaters, swimmers, football players, track athletes, and so on. And the same thing happened in every single one of the country's more than 3,000 local sports clubs.

Threats were of no use, nor were attempts at bribery. For the first time the Germans were confronted with an absolutely united front. This was possible because all Norwegian athletic groups are united in a central organization. Norway has never had any professional sports worth mentioning. The Norwegian Athletic Association was the country's largest youth organization, and it penetrated all classes of society. Young factory hands as well as rich men's sons were welcome in the Association, providing they went in for sports of any kind.

When the Nazis at length realized that their attack had failed, they resorted to countermeasures bordering on panic. In the first round they flooded the young people of the athletic organizations with promises and assurances. The State would appropriate vast sums for sports activities and facilities. Swimming pools and athletic fields, ski hills and clubhouses were to be built here, there, and everywhere. The sports leaders had only to speak up and say what they wanted. Nothing was out of reach. The men of the New Order had "the fullest understanding of the importance of athletics to society," it was said, and they intended to do all in their power to promote sports in the land.

To all this the sports leaders replied that their only wish was to be left alone. They pointed out that the Athletic Association had been built on purely democratic principles, that it had satisfactorily stood the test of years, and that nobody wanted to see any *Führer* system injected into it. Furthermore, nobody intended to co-operate in any reorganization of any kind whatsoever.

Next came the threats. The first of these were directed at individuals. The leaders were put under pressure, but they did not yield an inch. Then the Nazis turned their attention to various sports stars. They were to be compelled to co-operate with the New Order. Their names were banners which the youngsters would follow. They were told they were under certain obligations to the country's youth, obligations which they must not forget—or else! But the stars replied as the leaders had done. They positively refused.

The most unmistakable of these replies came from Birger

Ruud, Norway's foremost skier and holder of several Olympic championships. "When the day comes that it is my 'duty' to take part in a contest," declared Ruud, "on that day I will burn my skis!"

The Nazis then went after the individual sports clubs, threatening to confiscate their property and funds. Most of the clubs owned a ski hill, an athletic field, a hut or house—either alone or in conjunction with other clubs.

"Help yourself!" was their answer. "You can take what we own, but you can't force us to do something we don't want to do!"

The Nazis did not dare retreat. They had announced their course, and they had to follow it. Norway's Athletic Association was dissolved. All property and all funds were confiscated. A new organization was set up under a new leadership. Large and splendid offices were opened in Oslo. The next step was to find leaders for the various suborganizations, and it was no easy task. Therefore the Nazis requested the directing boards of these groups to appoint *Führers* for their respective branches of athletics.

In the midst of the strife these boards had not lost their sense of humor. They yielded with surprising readiness to the order, and within a few days the new national athletic leadership triumphantly published the names of those men who were to direct Norwegian athletic activity in the future. The Nazis discovered too late that they had been "taken for a ride." The list of names which they published set the whole country laughing. But the directing boards were innocent. How could the Swimming Association's directors, for instance, know that the man they had proposed as *Führer* was at that very moment in jail, serving a sentence after having been convicted as a common thief!

The new athletic association tried to arrange contests. Its intention was to cement "the good relations existing between

Norwegians and the occupying forces" through "peaceful competition on the athletic field." But it proved impossible to obtain Norwegian participants. Norwegians had no desire to compete with representatives of a nation that had laid Norwegian towns in ruins and killed their comrades. They stayed away.

The Nazis warned that they were planning to arrange Norwegian-German boxing and wrestling matches, and that without regard for any individual's sympathies or antipathies they would designate the members of the Norwegian teams. And they did so. Names of those selected were published in the newspapers. The athletes had their defense plans ready. The selected boxers and wrestlers simply piled on weight through overeating until they thus disqualified themselves and blasted all hopes of any international meet.

Then the Nazis made a new and desperate effort. The various athletic teams were to be usurped one by one. Each club was assigned a new chairman—in most cases a complete stranger to the members. With the excuse that the whole athletic program was to be rearranged, all the clubs in certain towns and villages were merged into one. The real reason for this, however, was that the Nazis did not have enough men to fill the chairmanships.

Members of the clubs, predominantly young people, wasted no time in replying to the usurpation scheme. By the thousands and tens of thousands they simply resigned from membership. Almost before they could count to ten the Nazis were left with the empty shells of what had shortly before been thriving sports clubs. To be sure, they had grabbed the clubs and associations and all their worldly possessions. But all this was of secondary importance; it was the youth of Norway that they wanted, and that prize had slipped through their fingers.

For the first time the scorched-earth policy had been tried in occupied Norway, and it had succeeded completely. All the sports-minded young people of Norway went on strike, and it was a unanimous strike. Since November 1940 not a single athletic contest has been staged in Norway, with the exception of a number of small meets wherein the participants have been Germans and members of Quisling's *Hird*. It has not even been possible to hold the annual Holmenkollen ski tournament, traditionally the greatest athletic event in a country renowned for its winter sports.

Norwegian sports fans have followed the athletes. Ever since the strike began the grandstands have remained empty. And if there occasionally turns up a vacillating soul among the sports-minded young people, he is quickly put to rights. His companions see to that. To protect their democratic traditions, the Norwegians at home have frequently found it worth while to exercise a bit of dictatorship within their own ranks. It is quite effective.

In April 1942 the Nazi national sports *Führer,* Egil Reichborn-Kjennerud, resigned from his office. He had grown tired of trying to bring the athletes into line. In acknowledging his failure he revealed that he had enlisted for service with the German forces in Russia. The Nazi newspaper, *Fritt Folk,* thought the occasion worthy of a special interview with the unhappy warrior. In that newspaper Reichborn-Kjennerud said:

Ever since the first day I started traveling around the country, and up to today, I have not heard an indecent word from any athlete. I have sat in numerous meetings with sports people who did not approve of the work I was doing. They have frankly stated their opinions, and many was the time I had to leave with my task still unaccomplished. But even at that, I did not leave with a heavy heart. I had met young people who were cultured and patriotic. That these young people—loyal as they had been to their old leaders—did not immediately make an about-face, simply because a traveling salesman in sports came to town, seems to me to be a credit to these young people.

In the first serious attack upon it, the National Labor Federation had been taken by surprise. The National Athletic Association learned a lesson from the Federation's mistake. In turn, other Norwegian organizations profited by the example set by the Athletic Association. The work which had begun on a small scale in midsummer, and which was given shape and purpose by the joint program of the political parties, was now picking up speed. With all their tactical errors and encroachments, the Germans had hastened it along. The Norwegian home front was in the process of becoming a reality.

5. NO NORWEGIAN FOR SALE

THOUSANDS OF PEOPLE jammed the downtown streets of Bergen. The city had never before seen such crowds, except on the most important national holidays. But the people were in no festive mood on October 17, 1940. The atmosphere was electric.

The main gathering point for the crowds was the square in front of the Hotel Norge and the surrounding streets. In that hotel Vidkun Quisling was staying. He had ventured into the lion's den itself, the old Hanseatic city of Bergen. Probably in no other Norwegian town was patriotism so firmly embedded. Some hundreds of years before Bergen had learned what it means to be under German influence. The yoke had then been thrown off, and now thousands of threads and shipping connections tied the city to countries west of the sea.

A steady murmur rising from the throng sounded almost like distant thunder. As the tension increased, people began to show signs of restlessness. Something had to happen.

Suddenly, from somewhere, a shout was heard:

"We want to see the *Führer!*"

It caught on, and was quickly repeated by other voices. In a twinkling the whole mass was shouting:

"We want to see the *Führer!* We want to see the *Führer!*"

People waved hats and handkerchiefs. The shouts rolled thunderously against the hotel windows.

They were heard. Soon Vidkun Abraham Lauritz Quisling appeared on the hotel balcony. His face beamed with pride and expectation as he slowly approached the balustrade. At last he was to realize a long-cherished dream. He raised his arm in the Nazi salute. He was the *Führer* receiving the plaudits of the multitude. This was indeed news, and the *Fritt Folk* photographer, jittery with excitement, ran around like a chicken with its head cut off.

But all at once the crowd set up a new cry—or rather, a myriad of cries. The air turned blue with epithets hurled at the man on the balcony. Words of abuse and derision echoed and re-echoed through the streets. Gradually the many shouts merged into a single one, rising rhythmically, relentlessly from the thousands of throats:

"Traitor! Traitor! Traitor!"

On and on went this chant. Finally it gave way to booing; and while they booed, people took to bombarding the hotel with stones, rotten eggs, anything. There was the clatter of broken glass.

For a moment Quisling stood there dumbstruck, his face gray. Then he had made a quick about-face and vanished out of sight and out of danger. Later that day he was to speak in one of the city's largest halls. When the time came for his address, the hall was still empty.

Outside, the streets were still jammed with people. Members of the *Hird,* swinging clubs and blackjacks, charged at the crowd. In a moment a general riot developed. It ended only when German soldiers arrived and formed protective circles around the *Hird* youths. All together, fourteen injured persons were taken to hospitals, and in two cases the wounds proved fatal.

When Quisling left Bergen late that evening, a wide area surrounding the railroad station was blocked off to the public by German soldiers with fixed bayonets.

Reichskommissar Josef Terboven's speech over the Oslo radio on September 25 had not granted "governmental power" to Quisling and his Nasjonal Samling party. To be sure, practically all of the thirteen "constituted ministers" were NS members, but Terboven had clearly emphasized that these "ministers" would be merely his personal representatives in the various governmental departments, and that all their decisions were subject to the approval of the Reichskommissar. The "constituted ministers" were never to convene as a government. In no time at all everybody was referring to them as Terboven's "prostituted" ministers.

But the Nasjonal Samling had, since September 25, become Norway's only "legal" political party, and Quisling was the party's leader. No one was in doubt as to what this meant. No one doubted that Quisling had been assigned the task of nazifying Norway.

At Stavanger the newspaper *May First* put the sentiment of the people into words when on September 26 it published the following editorial under the title of "No Norwegian for Sale!"

Reichskommissar Terboven directed the libelous accusation at our Storting members that they were willing to throw overboard everything sacred to them as long as they were able to safeguard their material existence. The Storting members can and will certainly account for their actions, both to their constituents and to their consciences.

But the Storting members are not alone affected.

We—98 per cent of the Norwegian people—have elected them as our highest representatives. In the eyes of the world and in our own eyes, Terboven's accusation is one which strikes at the people.

The libel must be washed away.

We are a law-abiding people with an aversion to everything which can disrupt the public peace, and we will fulfill our social obligations to our work and our families as long as no power prevents us from doing so.

But there is one clear path to follow. If any of us should be confronted with the question of discarding that which we have subscribed to in earnest conviction of what best serves our people in order to go over to something which we have fought and despised—the consideration being that we in this way will preserve our own material advantages—then the rule is that no Norwegian is for sale!

Trond Hegna, the editor who had written the editorial, was immediately arrested by the Gestapo. But he had created a battle cry for the Norwegian home front, and within a few days his editorial in mimeographed form was being read in all parts of the country.

The banning of political parties, with the exception of the Nasjonal Samling, produced immediate results. As early as the afternoon of September 25 the Gestapo had taken over the national headquarters of the parties and had confiscated all their property. Not even Victor Mogens' party, the Fedrelandslaget, was spared, and thereby the occupying power effectively gagged the one man who at a certain stage actually stood a slight chance of appeasing the Norwegians.

The ban also affected the parties' suborganizations, such as the women's auxiliaries and the youth clubs. It extended even further than that. Masonic lodges were shut down, and the same was true for the Student Association in Oslo and the Oxford Group Movement. The latter, because of its English name, was suspected of being affiliated with the British Secret Service.

The Nasjonal Samling, which during preceding years had been barely able to make ends meet if at all, was now suddenly wallowing in wealth. All the confiscated funds and possessions of the prohibited parties were placed at the disposal of Quisling and his followers. This included not only cash sums, bank credits, and moneys of all kinds, but also buildings and other real estate, such as the Labor party's "people's houses" in all parts of the country, the Masonic clubhouse, and the Conservative party's building in Oslo—the most modern structure in the country. The Labor party's official newspaper, *Arbeiderbladet,* had been ordered suspended at the end of August, and thereby Quisling's sheet, *Fritt Folk,* was given a home, one of the largest and most modern printing plants in the country. The sudden wealth went to the Quislings' heads, and within a remarkably short time the party's pets were equipped with modern automobiles, private chauffeurs, new country homes, and all other finery.

More serious was the steady stream of new decrees handed down those first days after September 25. At one stroke they put an end to the foundations of justice upon which Norwegian society had been built.

First the legal protection of public officials was suspended. A decree issued on October 4 declared that "all men in the public service whose political affiliations do not constitute a guaranty that they will co-operate for the new political order can be dismissed from the service." The decree denied public officials the right to have their cases tried in the courts, thus removing one of the pillars of the Norwegian social structure. The Norwegian public service had through the years been built in such a way that its members were completely protected against upheavals and dismissals when government control shifted from one party to another. Men and women in the public service had every reasonable assurance of the permanence of their jobs, no matter what parties were in power.

The decree led immediately to a series of dismissals and transfers. Shortly afterwards Quisling received the Germans' permission to set up the Nasjonal Samling's Personnel Office for Public Service to place Nazis in all governmental positions. All persons seeking a position in the public service were required to designate present and former political party affiliations. This rule applied to charwomen as well as to applicants for top-ranking positions.

By establishing this Personnel Office the Nazis hoped to provide themselves with a weapon by which to force Norwegians into the party, the plan being that none but party members should be considered for employment. It soon became apparent, however, that loyal Norwegians would not permit themselves to be driven into the Nazi ranks, even at the cost of their jobs, and the underground promptly devised a scheme for giving financial support to those who lost positions or were denied them for political reasons.

Another decree which appeared at this time established a "People's Court" which was to try all persons accused of hostility towards "the party in power," which the Nasjonal Samling now considered itself to be. The decree stated that a majority of the Court's members should be NS men, thus setting up a system under which the complainants would also, in fact, serve as the judges.

The Nasjonal Samling ran into no end of difficulties in finding a lawyer who was willing to preside in this People's Court. By the time the period for making applications for the position had expired, not a single man had indicated any interest. The Nasjonal Samling was therefore compelled to draft an obscure lawyer, whose only qualification for the position was his membership in the party.

The first case to be brought before this Court was one affecting the sixteen Labor party representatives who were members of the Oslo municipal governing body. They had drawn up a statement which they planned to submit to the entire governing body for approval, but the Nazis had got wind of the statement before it had been acted upon. It proposed that the Oslo governing body should reject a Nazi order that it work, from then on, "in harmony with the New Order and the Nasjonal Samling's policies." The sixteen Laborites pointed out that members of the body had been elected to office on quite different premises. The People's Court sentenced all sixteen men to long terms in prison.

The third decree appeared on October 14, and with this decree it became still more evident that Quisling, despite his loud boasts of power, was merely doing the bidding of his German masters. The decree was to deal with "control of unemployment." It declared that all persons out of work would have to accept the jobs assigned to them, the conditions to be laid down by the Germans. It was plain that the decree was designed as a "legal" basis for later shipment of Norwegian labor to Germany.

The decree also stipulated that all forest and agricultural workers, as well as fishermen and seamen, were no longer free to change to different lines of work, and that they were prohibited from changing their places of residence. This applied also to the workers' children. In short, it meant slavery.

At the same time the Germans unloosed a terrific propaganda barrage aimed at luring Norwegian workers to go to Germany as volunteers. It was officially stated that Germany could provide work for 50,000 to 100,000 Norwegians, and the Nasjonal Samling entered into an agreement with the Germans for the delivery of 5,000 workers as a starter.

On paper the offer made to the Norwegian workers seemed attractive enough, but the fish didn't go for the bait. The Norwegians knew that wages in Germany were 40 to 60 per cent below those in Norway, and they also had a well-founded apprehension that the imported workers would be placed in plants especially exposed to air attacks. The unemployed—and the number had been mounting steadily—stayed away from the registration offices where the colorful placards proffered pleasant days in the Third Reich. They were afraid that if they registered for work in Norway they would instead be forced to go to Germany.

The result of the tremendous campaign was that a scant 500 persons, including a large number of women of dubious reputation, were sent southwards on January 1, 1941. Thousands of people had gathered at the railroad station to witness the departure. When the train started to move they held their noses and made believe they were pushing the cars to get rid of them as soon as possible.

During the fall of 1940 churches and schools were made well aware that they, too, were inside the danger zone. The Nazi authorities wanted to lay hold of the children, the nation's future. Also, they wanted to control religious activity, which they regarded as an obstacle to the New Order.

The initial attack on the Church was weak, and it was promptly repelled. In Norway all radio broadcasting stations are owned and operated by the Government, and divine services were a regular feature on the programs. The Nazis demanded the right to censor all sermons before they went on the air. The clergy's answer to this was a point-blank refusal to take part in the broadcast. And that was that, for the time being.

The position of the schools was more difficult, and methods employed against them were also more ruthless.

Ever since April the Norwegian schools had been operating under trying conditions. It goes without saying that all schools were closed while open warfare was in progress. Afterwards they gradually resumed, but it was far from easy. A large number of the school buildings had been requisitioned by the occupying forces and were put to use as soldiers' barracks. In Oslo, for instance, only seven of the city's thirty-three public schools were available for their intended purpose, education. It was repeatedly promised that the schools would be vacated by the Germans as soon as they had been given time to build regular barracks, but that promise—like so many others from the same source—was never fulfilled. Barracks were built in large numbers, but most of them still stand empty. The Germans had quickly discovered that the British fliers used the barracks as targets for their bombs, and they found it safer to live as near the civilian population as possible.

Early in October the Nazi authorities decided that the schools should devote a part of their time "to introducing children to the New Order." This decision was met with a storm of protest from teachers and pupils. Speakers sent into the schools by the Nasjonal Samling were booed and jeered by the children. Teacher organizations protested formally against this encroachment on education.

A number of teachers were arrested at that time, and several schools were closed following altercations between pupils and Quisling's *Hird*. Some of these collisions were bloody, especially those at a number of Oslo schools where detachments of full-grown *Hird* men attacked pupils with clubs and blackjacks. Most sensational of all was the row at the Oslo Business College on November 30; afterwards several pupils and three teachers —including the head of the school—had to be removed to hospitals for medical treatment.

The *Hird's* attacks created complete chaos, and throughout southern Norway the school-age youth went on strike by refusing to attend classes. In this they were supported by parents and teachers, and school after school was forced to close.

It was not until the Germans, who at this time wanted no

domestic disturbances, stepped in and placed a restraining hand on the *Hird* that schools got going once again. For the time being the Nasjonal Samling was forbidden by the Germans to proceed with its program of nazifying the schools.

The Quislings were abundantly active in other fields, however. Their feverish attempts to recruit new members for the Nasjonal Samling soon gave rise to a rumor that the party had been given a certain time in which to prove that it was able to convert the Norwegian people to the NS program. There was some basis for this rumor; it was well known that the occupying authorities, especially those of the military, were strongly opposed to Quisling. It was because of orders from higher up in Berlin that he was being shown any deference at all.

But the contact between the Royal Government in London and the home front had become better developed and extended since it was first established in July. Recent events of the war had clearly shown that the lack of defense preparations, which had been so acutely felt in Norway, had been common to all the democracies. The criticism of Norway's unpreparedness had accordingly disappeared. Furthermore, the war on the Western Front had caused Norwegians to feel proud of the sixty-two days during which they had fought the invader. Despite the billions they had spent on defense, neither France, Belgium, nor Holland had been able to hold out that long. And the Royal Government was carrying on the fight. This was of great importance. By means of the London radio the leaders in London kept the people informed on what war efforts Norwegians were making. It was at this time that the first volunteers began leaving the country—mostly young men who had received some training in aviation; now they were being drawn to the Norwegian air training center that had just been established at Toronto, Canada.

More important than the Royal Government's actual war efforts was the common knowledge that it was acting on full authority vested in it by a unanimous vote of the Storting. To the Norwegians, with their highly developed respect for democratic processes, this constitutional aspect of the situation took on almost sacred significance. No matter what one had previously thought of the Government headed by Johan Nygaardsvold, no matter to which political party one had belonged—every Norwegian recognized that the Nygaardsvold Government was Norway's legal Government and would remain so until its authority was revoked by a free Norwegian Storting meeting on free Norwegian soil.

It was on this foundation that the Norwegian home front was stabilized. It was on this foundation that all Quisling overtures were rejected. This was the moral that was consistently propounded in the underground newspapers which had sprung into being in the fall of 1940.

In the beginning these underground newspapers were only single sheets of paper, the contents of which were copied by readers and passed on to others. But their circulation was tremendous. The arithmetic was that of the simple chain letter familiar to Americans: the original "edition" was perhaps only ten copies, but it included a request that each reader prepare ten more copies and send them on to new readers. The request was repeated in these copies, and ten times ten times ten eventually mounts up to thousands and hundreds of thousands. Later the secret newspaper activity became better organized, and during the spring of 1941 a couple of the papers began appearing in printed form.

The London radio had steadily been increasing in popularity. It kept people informed on conditions in the world abroad, and it provided compensation for the incomplete or corrupt news coverage in the Nazi-controlled Norwegian papers. It also brought talks by members of the Royal Gov-

ernment, by Winston Churchill, and by President Roosevelt.
The latter were relayed by short wave from London.

President Roosevelt became tremendously popular in Norway during the fall months of 1940. It was the Germans who
saw to that. The presidential election in the United States was
followed with an interest more intense than any Storting election had ever produced.

One of the main arguments used by the Germans in their
efforts to make Norwegians understand that there was no escaping the New Order was to insist that America would never
get into the war. This contention ran like a red thread through
everything the press was permitted to publish about American
conditions. All speeches and statements by isolationists were
played up with big headlines, and when Wendell Willkie and
Franklin D. Roosevelt opened their campaigns Willkie immediately became the favorite of the German authorities. To
what extent the Germans believed Willkie represented isola-
tionism is impossible to say, but it was certain they feared the
re-election of Roosevelt.

The result, at any rate, was that Roosevelt became the Norwegian favorite. They would have chosen him if for no other
reason than to disagree with the Germans. But they did it also
because, in the average Norwegian's judgment, it was only
with the United States' active participation that the war could
be won—at least in the discernible future. And thus for the
time being nothing on the London radio was more popular
than the rebroadcasts of Roosevelt's speeches.

When the elections had been held and Roosevelt had been
assured his third term, the German propaganda boomeranged.
The Germans had obviously pinned great hopes on Roosevelt's
defeat. But Roosevelt had won. Thus Roosevelt's victory was a
victory for the Allies. That was the conclusion reached by the
Norwegians, and they celebrated the event as a serious blow

to German plans and as new proof that the development of the war was proceeding in the right direction.

Along with the broadcasts from London the underground newspapers helped greatly in cementing the Norwegian home front. And in the fall of 1940 a new morale builder appeared. A secret broadcasting station, which soon became known as the "Liberty Transmitter," began to operate inside the country's boundaries. It was on the air quite regularly a couple of times a day, and the fact that now and then it remained silent only increased its popularity. When Nazi authorities tried to upset confidence in the station by declaring that it was situated in England and not in Norway, the Liberty Transmitter replied by sending out accurate reports on the prevailing weather in Norway—something that could only be done on the spot because all newspapers were strictly prohibited from mentioning weather conditions.

The Norwegians' sentiments towards the Germans found many forms of expression. Nasjonal Samling placards were torn down as quickly as they were put up. Instead, the opposition decorated walls and board fences with their own "placards."

All kinds of insignia were adopted to indicate the bearer's attitude. Ordinary wire paper clips were worn on coat lapels and were taken to mean "Stick together!" They were also placed on the ears of cats and dogs belonging to Nazis. The advertising slogan, "100 per cent Norwegian," cut from milk cartons, served the same purpose. A match placed in a buttonhole with the red end showing meant "flaming hate." Red stocking caps were the last word in fashions.

Inscriptions on walls and fences also reflected the popular sentiment. Common ones were: "Long live the King!" "Down with Quisling!" "Out with the swine!" "We want our Government back!"

The Nazis staged a counterstroke. Detachments of the *Hird*

were sent out to tear the prohibited insignia from coat lapels. That led to fights and street riots in various parts of the country. These collisions were especially serious in Oslo. They occurred on the streets, in schools, in parks, and in restaurants.

After two months conditions had become so critical that on November 28 Propaganda Minister Goebbels arrived in Norway to make a personal inspection of the situation. The immediate result of the visit was a large number of arrests, but the Norwegians interpreted his visit as partial verification of the rumor that Quisling had been given a limited time in which to prove his ability as a leader.

The resistance continued. Fist fights became more frequent and more violent. So did acts of sabotage, and reprisals. The Oslo–Bergen railway was again and again put out of commission at various points. On one occasion it was found that saboteurs had been at work at ten different points on the railroad at the same time. The Germans announced that damage was due to "natural causes"—namely, a storm—but they nevertheless conducted mass arrests because of it.

During October, November, and December an especially large number of arrests were made of people who, it was charged, had insulted the "honor" of the German Army. On a single day, December 4, thirty-four persons in Ålesund were arrested for that reason. Many were also arrested on suspicion of carrying on espionage for the Allies. The British fliers appeared too well informed on everything the Germans undertook to do, especially along the coast.

At this time the first concentration camps were established, one near Bergen and one near Oslo. They were soon filled to capacity.

At the end of the year the German Gestapo had between nine and ten thousand of its agents in Norway. That is to say, there was one Gestapo agent for every three hundred Norwegians. At the same time the army of occupation totaled between three and four hundred thousand men—more, in proportion to population, than the Germans maintained in any other occupied country.

Probably the most effective—even though comparatively innocent—weapon used by the Norwegians at this time was their inherent sense of humor. Much of it was directed at the speakers which the Nasjonal Samling sent out to all parts of the country.

At one place the NS speaker found as his only audience two black cats. Outside the hall, however, a large crowd had gathered. These people politely explained to the speaker that the two cats had protested against attending the meeting, but that they had been chased inside so that the speaker would not be entirely alone.

At another place the NS speaker actually found two persons in attendance when he appeared on the platform to begin his speech. He launched immediately into an angry attack on those who had stayed away.

"I suppose those idiots are sitting at home listening to the London radio!" he bellowed.

One of the listeners pulled out his watch and exclaimed:

"That's right, it's almost time for London!"

Thereupon both men got up and hurriedly left the hall.

The humor was not all good-natured. At Trondheim, Bergen, and in other towns German police had to be summoned to protect *Hird* detachments. At Moss the loud-speaker apparatus was dynamited to bits, and the meeting hall was stoned. At Fredrikstad in the middle of November someone tossed a bomb at Quisling in an attempt on his life.

Towards the close of the year the Nasjonal Samling ceased sending out speakers. The attempts to win people to the New Order by means of persuasion had failed.

The Nazis themselves admitted that a home front had been

formed, and *Fritt Folk* angrily attacked this "front of class-war youth and spoiled papa-boys" as well as the new "partnership of the top hat and the workers' cap!"

How the front was being directed remained unknown to both the Germans and the Quislings, nor did the Norwegians themselves know who their leaders were. They knew only that at one place or another orders and directives were being given, and they regarded it as their duty to obey them. The underground newspapers had clearly established the home front's program: absolute solidarity among all Norwegians for the duration of the occupation, and action in all quarters in order to drive the invader from the country as soon as possible.

The battle cry had been supplied by the arrested Trond Hegna when he wrote: "No Norwegian is for sale!"

6. LAWLESSNESS BECOMES THE LAW

"WE COME AS FRIENDS" was the slogan of Germany's mighty million-man Army as it attacked a nation of three million Norwegians. "We come as friends," said the "Vienna children" as they entered the homes of their former foster parents, guns in hand. "We come as friends," said Reichskommissar Josef Terboven as he assumed supervision of the occupied territories. "The German people extend an open hand to their Norwegian brother-people with a wish for co-operation and understanding."

There is scarcely any doubt that the myth about the superiority of the Nordic race strongly influenced the German National Socialists in their efforts to nazify Norway. Their method of procedure in Norway was quite different from that employed, for example, in Poland, where the *Herrenvolk's* laws prevailed from the very first hour.

Norway was to be the great experiment in Hitler's New Order. Here the ideas were to be put into practice. Here they could count on finding understanding and sympathy for the theory that the Nordic peoples were predestined to serve as leaders for the world; in Norway explanation and guidance, rather than violence and force, would produce that solidarity with the Germans which a sentimental ideology had for years been preaching to German youth.

It was unavoidable, of course, that the Norwegian nation would have a minor position in the Greater German *Lebensraum,* but it was to be accepted voluntarily by the Norwegians themselves. Naturally, a certain degree of "correcting" would be necessary now and then. By nature, the Norwegians were austere and self-confident. They were strongly patriotic. They cherished freedom. They did not like militarism or authority. They were uncommunicative and reserved. They were slow to think and act, and also suspicious of strangers. And they had sympathy for England. That there existed a complete lack of understanding of National Socialism's goals was not catastrophic. That was simply due to the lack of education. And it was also due to the conscious propagandizing which Norway's Government had been carrying on for years under orders of the British Secret Service. All these, however, were matters that would adjust themselves with time or, if necessary, with the aid of forceful persuasion.

That, in rough outline, was the German policy towards Norway in the spring and summer of 1940. It was the substance of secret instructions given all German soldiers in Norway. The Nazi propaganda in the press and on the radio followed this general line. And it served also as the basis for the "negotiations" which the German authorities demanded and got in June and September. The fact that the policy did not succeed must have come as colossal defeat to the ideologists of National Socialism.

The *Führerverordnung* which formed the basis for Reichskommissar Josef Terboven's activity in Norway, and which was issued on April 24, 1940, was also composed with such a plan of action in view. In its text the decree was unassailable. It was written entirely within the spirit that characterized the Hague Convention of 1907, which produced definite, internationally accepted rules for government in occupied territory. It unconditionally pledged respect for the Norwegian Constitution and the country's laws.

However, it soon developed that the Hague Convention, in common with all other international agreements which Germany has entered into down through the years, was of no significance whatsoever the moment it conflicted with Hitler's plans.

And while Germans continued to hammer and hammer at their favorite melody, "We come as friends," the actual events spoke a different language. Not only the German authorities but also the German private soldiers were doing their share towards awakening a united Norwegian opposition. Not least effective in this respect was the striking change in the conduct of German soldiers that accompanied the enthusiasm stirred up among them by news of the German victories on the Western Front. Up to then many Norwegians had looked upon the big-eyed, tart-devouring, Baedeker-equipped "tourists" with a forbearing smile, but after the fall of France they suddenly saw them in a new light, for at one stroke the modest and would-be ingratiating "protectors" were changed to loud and big-mouthed representatives of the *Herrenvolk*.

It was of little help that the occupying power procured the largest display window on Oslo's main thoroughfare to exhibit a large portrait of Adolf Hitler, surrounded by snapshots of the *Führer* patting puppies and little children on the head. The only legend for the exhibit was a haughty, although partially concealed, sneer, printed in huge letters: "BUT, OF COURSE, YOU KNOW SO LITTLE ABOUT HIM!"

Little by little, the Norwegians got to know him fairly well. The numerous arrests during the summer and fall, the setting

up of concentration camps, the persistently worsening conduct
of the soldiers, the mounting number of attacks on defenseless
women, and last but not least the fact that Quisling's *Hird* had
been turned loose on a defenseless population—all these factors
ended once and for all whatever illusions the Norwegians
might have entertained with respect to the Germans' spirit of
friendship.

Simultaneously a gradual change was taking place in the
Germans' official attitude, a development that reached its
climax in Terboven's September speech and in the decrees that
followed it. Between the occupying forces and the Norwegian
judicial system there slowly developed an ever-increasing tension.

The establishment of the so-called People's Court was the
first definite encroachment on the Norwegian system for meting
out justice. The very existence of this court was in clear conflict with all the principles upon which Norwegian judicial
procedure was based. And it was also in conflict with all international law.

The Norwegian courts tried to keep functioning, even though
it did mean frequent brushes with the Nazi authorities, but
there was no doubt that matters were approaching a crisis. On
November 14 arose a situation which long had been anticipated. On that day the occupying power, through the "Constituted" Minister of Justice, issued a decree giving the Nazi
authorities the right, at their own pleasure, to dismiss or appoint mediators, jurymen, and witnesses. The courts were to be
brought definitely under Nazi control. The practical result of
the decree would, of course, be that the Nazi-controlled Department of Justice would at all times see to it that Nazis were
assured the necessary influence in all court decisions.

In a letter dated November 19 and addressed to the Department of Justice, the Norwegian Supreme Court protested
firmly against this encroachment. The protest stated, among

other things, that "this decree grants the Constituted Minister and the Department of Justice permission to interfere with the composition of the courts in a manner which is in open conflict with those principles upon which our court system is founded. The decree also transgresses the limits of authority for a constituted minister serving as the representative of the occupying forces, according to the Hague Convention of 1907 . . . according to which an occupant must respect the laws which apply to the country provided no absolute hindrances stand in the way."

Naturally, it was clear to the members of the Supreme Court that the letter was a direct challenge to the occupying power. Reichskommissar Terboven himself had appointed the "constituted ministers" as his personal representatives inside the Norwegian governmental administration. But it was also clear to the Supreme Court that the Norwegian governmental apparatus had been knocked to pieces by the September events and that only by dealing firmly now did it stand a chance of halting the developments which since that time had been moving steadily towards complete lawlessness.

The Supreme Court claimed, therefore, that the independence of the courts was clearly established in the Norwegian Constitution, which the Germans were duty-bound to respect, according to both the Hague Convention and the *Führerverordnung* of April 24. It stated further that "to maintain this independence is of fundamental importance to the certainty of justice."

The Germans were apparently in no hurry about replying.

Meanwhile developments throughout the country took a more critical turn. Fights between the *Hird* and the civilian population became everyday occurrences, and popular sentiment balanced on the brink of open revolt. From Trondheim and Bergen, from the towns along Oslo Fiord, and from inland districts came reports of bloody battles. A detachment of the *Hird,* which had arrived in Drammen for the purpose of "cleaning up," was met by an angry populace which literally chased the Quislings out of town. Two of the *Hird* members were killed, and others were given a thorough beating.

In Oslo conditions were even worse, and during the first half of December there was scarcely a day when the German police did not have to come to the rescue of the *Hird.* The Norwegian Nazis were beside themselves, as was unmistakably reflected in their official newspaper, *Fritt Folk,* which wrote:

"We shall strike back so that they lose both sight and hearing. He who strikes us once shall be struck ten times in return. That is to be our rule. . . ."

Gangs of uniformed *Hird* men terrorized the streets. No one could feel safe. Any kind of ornament in a buttonhole could be interpreted as a "demonstration" or "provocation," a display of a "hostile attitude." At one place in the eastern part of Oslo a *Hird* detachment attacked a crippled musician who made a living by playing in courtyards. They knocked him senseless because he had played "provocative melodies." Workers from a near-by factory rushed out and rescued the musician from the ruffians.

The development reached its peak on December 14 and 15 when street riots between the *Hird* and the civilian population occurred in downtown Oslo. During these battles the Norwegian police "forgot" their orders to protect the *Hird.* One result of this was that a policeman was "taken prisoner" by the *Hird* and literally kicked to death.

It was in the midst of this atmosphere of jungle warfare that the Supreme Court fought out its battle with the occupational authorities, and these events scarcely served to alter the justices' conviction that something had to be done to halt the downhill trend. Matters were not improved, either, when the Gestapo, early in December, arrested one of the Supreme Court's justices, Emil Stang.

On December 7 the Nazi authorities decided to force the issue. On that day Reichskommissar Terboven addressed a letter to the Supreme Court declaring that the Court did not have the right to pass on the validity of the laws and decrees which he or any of the "constituted ministers" had issued or intended to issue.

The letter precipitated an immediate crisis. The Supreme Court's answer came on December 12. In a letter signed by all its members, with the exception of Justice Stang, who was under arrest, the Supreme Court stated:

> The Reichskommissar has declared that neither the Supreme Court nor any other Norwegian court can express itself on the validity of legal precepts prepared by the Reichskommissar or the constituted ministers, since it befalls the Reichskommissar exclusively to decide which measures serve to promote the public peace and the public life in Norway.
>
> We want to set forth that, according to Norwegian law, the courts have the *duty* of trying the validity of laws and administrative decrees. Under military occupation the courts must, in our opinion . . . take a stand on the validity, as fixed by international law, of the decrees issued by the occupying power's agencies.
>
> We cannot subscribe to that view of the courts' authority which is expressed in the Reichskommissar's letter without acting in conflict with our duties as justices in Norway's Supreme Court.
>
> We therefore find it impossible to continue in our offices.

Naturally, no mention of the Supreme Court's action was permitted in the Norwegian press; but the time was long since past when people were dependent on the regular newspapers. Almost before the ink on the signatures was dry, the underground newspapers published the complete texts of the letters that had been exchanged between the court and the Reichskommissar. The London radio, which by then had extensively developed its contacts with Norway, was also Johnny on the spot—so much so that Terboven first learned of the Supreme

Court justices' threat to resign through BBC broadcasts from London!

To the civilian population, whose patience had been worn to the vanishing point by the *Hird's* scandalous conduct and by the brutality of the occupation troops, the Supreme Court's action came as a mighty relief. It was silently cheered far and wide.

Finally the question had been raised in all its fullness—the question of whether Norway was to be a nation of law and order, or not. The German reply was awaited with great tension. The fact that the Supreme Court's action had received the unconditional endorsement of the Norwegian Attorneys' Association and of the Norwegian Justices' Association gave it additional weight.

The German reply was not long in coming, and it was immediately apparent that the Supreme Court's action had not succeeded in forcing the occupation authorities to yield. Therefore the Supreme Court justices, on December 21, assumed the consequences of their action by ceasing all activity, despite all kinds of threats from the German authorities, who demanded that the justices remain in office until a new Supreme Court could be appointed.

The finishing touch had been applied to a development which long had followed a definite and invariable direction. It was established that Norway under German occupation was no longer a community of law and order, that the country no longer possessed a free and independent judicial system, that Germany's interests were above Norwegian law.

The myth of German friendship for Norway had been buried for good. The experiment of "peacefully" imposing the New Order on Norway had collapsed in ruins. The theory of the Nordic race had gone bankrupt.

The Norwegians, for their part, took the Supreme Court resignations for what they really were—a tremendous victory for the home front and for democratic reasoning. The occupying power's encroachments could not be halted. Quite the opposite, the Nazis' methods for the future would in all likelihood increase in ruthlessness. But, at any rate, the encroachments could not expect the approval of Norway's proper judicial authorities. The Supreme Court, the country's highest arbiter, had passed its judgment on nazism.

In the midst of all the misery and grief, the single purpose shone more clearly than ever before.

III. THE HOME FRONT
ON THE OFFENSIVE

1. THOU SHALT OBEY GOD MORE THAN MAN

EARLY IN OCTOBER 1940 a number of church people gathered in Oslo for a meeting. They arrived in the city quietly and unnoticed. Quietly and unnoticed they went about their affairs, and a few days later they quietly and unnoticed returned to their homes.

Naturally, the Germans knew that a meeting was taking place, but they attached no special importance to it. These mild-mannered and soft-spoken persons could certainly harbor no evil intentions. At any rate, they would never venture to undertake anything which could bring themselves and the Church into difficulties. It was, in fact, a little comical that people should meet to discuss spiritual and abstract matters at a time when force had taken the place of the spirit. Presumably the Nazis figured that they might as well let the church people amuse themselves while there was still time. "As long as they are playing with their own toys they will not be interfering with us."

Nor were any orders issued to the newspapers prohibiting

them from publishing the brief little communiqué which proved to be the only tangible result of the meeting and which, without fanfare, announced that a "Christian Council" had been formed. In a time when world politics and military matters dominated one's thoughts, this communiqué seemed only a pale ghost of the days of old.

The Germans knew nothing of church life in Norway, and therefore they did not grasp the significance of what had happened. They did not realize that in all quietness there had occurred a revolution right under their eyes. They were in blissful ignorance of the fact that the occupation, plus the favoritism shown Quisling, had brought about something that years of negotiations and honest effort had not been able to produce— the formation of a solid Norwegian church front.

Norway's official religion was Evangelical Lutheran, and the country had a State Church which included nearly 98 per cent of the population as members. The remaining 2 per cent consisted of Catholics and members of other free or "dissenter" groups.

Within the State Church there had for a long time existed serious strife between the exponents of liberal and those of orthodox Christianity. During peacetime this dissension had frequently taken on bitter and irreconcilable aspects. However, at the meeting in October the church people cleared the decks. Just as the political parties had done in August, the two factions within the State Church as well as all the other Christian groups and organizations now agreed to put all old issues aside. No matter what had divided them in peacetime, such things were minor matters now and had to give way to the all-important one: the defense against their common enemy, godlessness.

This event, which less than a year before would have created a sensation in all newspapers, was now dealt with in four or five brief sentences. But the Norwegians had long since learned that they could no longer count on finding the more important news under the big black headlines. They clipped out the little item and hid it away as new evidence of the solidarity and interdependence that the occupation had created.

Ever since the first clumsy attack made soon after Terboven's September speech, the Church had been left at peace, generally speaking. To be sure, the Oslo radio no longer broadcast any divine services, but life in the congregations had gone on as usual. The churches had continued to be a refuge where the shouts of battle could only faintly be heard and where people gathered to seek strength and assurance from something beyond the here and now.

But now there had come a direct interference with the activities of the clergy, and it was an intrusion that struck at the heart of things. In a decree dated December 13 the Nazi authorities had suspended the pledge of silence which Norwegian law required of all clergymen. The decree was supplemented with a decision that ministers who refused to break their pledge of silence, when being questioned, could be imprisoned and in that way be forced to reveal what had been told them in confidence.

The decree evoked a unanimous protest from the entire Norwegian clergy. The result, however, was negative. The decree was retained, and the Nazi authorities declared that when "interests vital to the State" were at stake, neither written nor common law could stand in the way. At the same time they pointedly emphasized that the Church would be left in peace only on the condition that it did not concern itself with politics.

But what was politics in a time such as this? Or, more correctly, what was *not* politics?

Also for the men of the Church it was difficult to draw the line.

The snow lay three feet deep and the cold was more severe than in many years that Sunday in early February 1941 when people set out for church. But the icy wind brought color to the pale and hard-bitten faces; woolen scarves and heavy coats shut out the chill. People went on foot, because automobiles and gasoline were things that had belonged to a happier day. They met at crossroads, formed groups, and the discussion was lively as they continued on their way. Small clouds of frozen breath trailed the groups on the church paths; people were talking freely, confident that if a German soldier should appear he could be spotted a long way off. And in passing him the churchgoers would swing far to the side in a wide semicircle.

Inside the dimly lighted church it was warm and pleasant. And as the pews filled, the large, naked room came to life. Soon came the rumbling tones of the organ, and singing filled the air. The church service ran its course. Devotions at the altar, followed by more singing of hymns, and then the minister mounted the pulpit. His familiar face was serious and drawn when he put the Bible aside and brought forth a document.

There was not a sound in the church. After a long pause he began, his voice calm and clear:

"I shall read for you a pastoral letter from the bishops of the Norwegian Church."

There was a little restlessness down among the pews. People changed their positions in order to hear better, cleared their throats. Then it was quiet again, breathlessly quiet. The minister's voice resumed, calm and confident:

"We gratefully acknowledge the fact that the Church and all Christian societies and organizations, generally speaking, have been able to carry on their spiritual work up to the present.

"But signs of a growing unrest and anxiety are nevertheless becoming more and more evident. Can the Church sit quietly on the side lines while the Commandments of God are being set aside and while many other events are taking place which dissolve law and order?"

Thus did the Norwegian Church serve notice that it had taken sides in the battle. The Nazis had thought they could appease the nation's spiritual power by leaving it alone. They believed this factor in Norwegian life could be neutralized simply by refraining so far as possible from challenging it. But by this pastoral letter the Church was proving that it had no intention of remaining silent in the face of injustice and force.

Clearly and unmistakably, the bishops explained the Church's position on the great, burning issue of the day. Convincingly and unconditionally, the Church stepped into the front line of battle. The letter disclosed that the bishops, in consultation with the country's other religious organizations, had sent a document to the Acting (or "Constituted") Minister of Church and Education on January 15. The text of this document and appendages were included *in extenso* in the pastoral letter.

The bishops began by emphasizing that the Norwegian Church was part of a nation based on law and order and that its confession presupposed that the State, through its agencies, would maintain the law and justice upon which a divine order depends. They maintained that from the Church's point of view the State was obliged to accept and feel bound by those legal and moral pillars which form the Church's foundation—the Bible and the confession of faith.

The bishops pointed out that recently there had arisen serious doubt as to whether the State felt itself thus obligated. They referred to three circumstances which were inseparably associated with each other, and which could not but be taken as signs that the State was not only failing to prevent encroachments but, quite the opposite, was consciously allowing them to go on. "There are signs that the system of justice itself is being dissolved in its basic factors," said the letter. The three circumstances which the bishops had referred to were the *Hird's* shameless conduct, the resignation of the Supreme Court, and, last but not least, the interference with the ministers' pledge of silence.

The bishops pointed to the events that had taken place at the Oslo Business College on November 30, when the *Hird* had beaten both teachers and pupils in such a way that many had to be given medical attention. They also recalled the *Hird* slogan which had appeared in the Nasjonal Samling's official newspaper that same morning, and which included the threat: "He who strikes us once will be struck ten times in return."

"If a community approves such a rule and does not see to it that law and order are united, then it has violated all the important prerequisites of a constitutional society," the bishops declared. And they continued by mentioning other examples —an attack on the president of the student organization at the Norwegian Institute of Technology at Trondheim on November 29, an attack on an errand boy in Oslo on December 11. They told how this errand boy, who was only sixteen years old, had been carried away in an automobile in the evening and taken into a cellar where members of the *Hird* stripped him of his clothing and whipped him.

They criticized the authorities for not having brought these matters into the courts. Instead, they charged, the authorities had sent out an order on December 14 calling upon the police "actively to join forces with the *Hird*."

"The revolting nature of the single acts of violence is such as to make them a problem involving the security of society as a whole," said the bishops, who also directed attention to a circular letter sent out by the Department of Domestic Affairs ordering all public officials "positively and actively to support the *Hird*." The circular letter stated that all who did otherwise would be making themselves guilty of "actions hostile to the State" and would be subject to severe punishment.

"If such a system should prevail the Church's servants will feel the lack of any basis for guiding the conscience of the people in so far as respect and confidence in the law of the land are concerned," said the bishops.

They also stressed the fact that the Supreme Court had felt itself forced to discontinue its work, and declared that this would inevitably create profound insecurity within the Church.

"The Minister of Church and Education will also understand," continued the bishops' letter to that official, "that the seriousness of the situation will not diminish when we emphasize that violence and that a spirit of hate are developing among the people. Not the least important is the way such things affect growing youth. The training of Christian character is by law assigned to Church and school, and this constitutes one of the Church's main tasks. Therefore, when the Department of Church and Education, in a bulletin dated November 12 and addressed to all school officials, advises all responsible schoolmen to guarantee upon their honor that they will give positive and active support to every resolution and decree issued by the new authorities, then we view the whole matter as approaching a conflict of conscience in the very essence of our profession."

Finally the bishops pointed out that the attack on the ministers' pledge of silence was the equivalent of tampering with the blood stream of all church activity and that the pledge of silence was not only established by Norwegian law but that it was accepted in all churches of all times in all countries.

The pastoral letter stated further that the Department of Church and Education had failed to reply to the original memorandum. Three of the bishops, led by Bishop Berggrav of Oslo, had therefore been delegated by their colleagues to call upon the department head and to impress upon him the serious character of the document.

This official's reply was received on February 1 and was included in full in the pastoral letter. It assured the Church anew that it would be given a chance to "work in peace," but no mention was made of any of the points set forth by the bishops except for an attempt to excuse the attack on the pledge of silence. Instead came a new threat: "The Church is not the only institution in need of peace to fulfill its mission; the State itself needs it. We hereby most sincerely warn the Church against any acts that may increase the unrest of our people. Thoughtless action now may result in serious consequences for the Church."

It was deathly quiet in the church. Only the minister's voice was to be heard—strong, clear, and calm. And it grew in strength as he approached the final paragraphs of the bishops' pastoral letter:

When the authorities permit acts of violence and injustice, and exert pressure on our souls, then the Church becomes the defender of the people's conscience.

One single human soul is worth more than the entire world.

The bishops of the Church have therefore placed on the table of the Acting Minister certain facts and official communiqués concerning the governmental administration, which, during the last few months, in the view of the Church, are against the law of God. They give the impression that revolutionary conditions are abroad in our land, and that we are not living under the rules of foreign occupation whereby all laws shall be enforced as far as is compatible with the occupation forces.

The Church is not the State, and the State is not the Church. In worldly matters the State may endeavor to use force against the Church, but the Church is a spiritual and sovereign entity built on the word of God and on its unity of belief. Despite all its human shortcomings, the Church has been given divine authority to spread God's law and gospel among all peoples. The Church can therefore never be silenced. Whenever God's commandments are deposed by sin the Church stands unshaken and cannot be directed by any authority of the State.

From this rock of faith we beseech the authorities to strike out all that is contrary to God's holy writ on justice, truth, and freedom of conscience, and to build only on the foundation of the divine laws of life.

We also beseech our people to avoid acts of force and injustice. In an internal struggle all individuals and groups must be guided by this moral law. He who promotes hatred or encourages evil will be judged by God. The Holy Bible says: 'Do not repay evil with evil, but overcome evil with good.'

Above all of us stands the One who is Lord of our souls. In our congregations we now perceive a ferment of conscience, and we feel it our duty to let authorities hear clear and loud the voice of the Church.

The pastor had finished. Calmly he folded up the document. Then he pronounced the benediction and left the pulpit.

When the service was over people rose and left the church even more quietly than usual. At the door the winter's cold rushed against them. Outside it had begun to snow.

The Germans had prohibited the reading of this pastoral letter, yet it was read in hundreds of Norwegian churches. For safety's sake, the bishops had printed it as a handbill and succeeded in sending out 40,000 copies before the police confiscated what was left. The underground newspapers also reprinted the complete text of the letter, and it was read in full over the London radio. Not a single person in Norway was ignorant of its contents.

All religious organizations in the country had aligned themselves with the bishops, and thus the pastoral letter became the expression of everything that the Norwegians felt and thought about the Germans and Quislings. It became something far more than a mere religious document. It became a national battle cry which had the support of all classes of the people.

And for the first time the Germans began to understand what really had happened during that quiet meeting of church people in Oslo in October 1940.

2. THE RANKS ARE CLOSED

THE BOMBED AND BURNED TOWNS still lay in heaps of ruins in the landscape. Kristiansund and Elverum, Bodö and Narvik, Steinkjer and Namsos—all these places which less than a year before had been living, busy centers of Norwegian enterprise were now dead memories of a time when the country was "unprotected" and free.

The snow lay like a vast cloth spread over the lifeless remains. A stench of rot still rose from the ruins.

Not a single new house had been built. The people were still living where they had first sought shelter during those terrible days when hell rained down upon their homes.

By wintertime people in Bodö were trying to keep alive by living in tents. At Narvik thousands of people were leading a wretched existence aboard small fishing boats. Both of these towns lie north of the Arctic Circle.

Norwegian architects had long since completed plans for the reconstruction. These plans had to be submitted to the Germans. The occupation authorities then sent the plans to Berlin for approval. They never came back.

The occupying power apparently had more important matters to look after than that of providing shelter for Norwegian civilians. Barracks and airdromes were to be built, Norwegian natural resources were to be exploited. The voracious maw of the German war machine had to be satiated before anything would be done for the civilian population.

The Germans blamed it on the shortage of material. Despite Norway's abundant forests, it was not possible for any private person to buy more than 500 kroner ($125) worth of building materials. But there was plenty of material for the German projects—airdromes, fortifications, railroads, and highways. All means of communication and transportation were, of course, under the control of the occupying forces.

The Germans also blamed the shortage of labor. In this they were quite correct. There had gradually developed a serious shortage of skilled and unskilled workers.

During the first few months of the occupation unemployment mounted to tremendous heights. Many industrial plants were destroyed during the war. People were left without jobs or income.

A more important factor, however, was the German plundering which had been carried on systematically and methodically ever since the first day of the invasion. Geographically Norway is a country that is forced to depend to a considerable extent on the import of both capital and raw materials. The country did have large stock piles on hand when the German attack came, but little by little these stores diminished and serious shortages developed. One of the first of these was the shortage of coal for industry. The paper manufacturers were especially affected by this and were compelled to curtail drastically their activity in order to save on fuel. That was in the summer of 1940. Later the textile industry suffered the same fate. There were few industries that managed to maintain production at the normal level. Transportation, too, encountered great difficulty.

It is necessary to cast back to the conditions which had existed earlier. During the early summer of 1940 two thirds of the workers in the paper mills were unemployed and three fifths of the construction workers were out of jobs. Four fifths of all those still employed by industry were working only part time.

To begin with there had been no shortage of glowing promises from the occupying forces. Norway was to get all it needed of coal and oil, iron and other metals, machines, tools, and food. But it soon developed that the Germans were not able, or else did not wish, to fulfill their promises. It is difficult to say to what extent this was due to lack of desire and how much of it could be blamed on inability. But as far as the laborers were concerned the practical result was that they were given the choice between starving to death and going to work for the occupying power. At first it was only vagabonds and other riff-raff who would accept "German jobs," despite the fat wages being offered and paid. Later, when unemployment became acute, many respectable workers were forced into German employment.

As soon as the occupying power no longer had difficulty in obtaining the necessary labor for its numerous plants and projects, it forced into effect a radical reduction of wages. The occupying power had thereby returned to its basic policy, which had been given clear expression on October 18, 1940, by Dr. Carlo Otte in an article which that eminent Nazi had written for *Deutsche Schiffahrtszeitschrift Hansa*.

"Through the lowering of prices, of real wages, and thereby of living standards," wrote Dr. Otte, "it is hoped that the co-ordination of the Norwegian economy in the European Economic Order will one day be achieved."

By Christmas 1940 the level of prices in Norway was from 30 to 40 per cent higher than the pre-war level, although wages were the same as or lower than those paid before the invasion. The situation had become critical for the laboring classes.

In October 1940 the workers were given unmistakable proof that the Germans intended to adhere rigidly to their policy. At that time the National Labor Federation and the Norwegian Employers' Association began negotiating over the question of a cost-of-living wage increase. The employers proved more than willing, and the pay boost was agreed upon. But the Germans refused to approve the agreement reached by the employers and employees. When on October 28 a Federation committee adopted a resolution demanding that decisive steps be taken towards the maintenance of the standard of living, the Germans immediately prohibited the group from making the resolution public.

The laboring class, along with all other groups of the people, was seething with an indignation that found expression in many ways. But the one felt most keenly by the Germans was the slow-down strike, which caused such obvious yet "unexplainable" declines in production and delays in construction.

The attempts to nazify the Federation, according to the plan launched by the September coup, ran up against a wall of opposition. To be sure, the Nazis had placed their men in the top positions of the organization, but they made no headway whatsoever in the various trade-unions and among the men at the places of work. Even their success at snatching control of the leadership was gradually nullified; the men whom the Nazis had squeezed into office found themselves ostracized, ignored, and soon all but forgotten. The workers were just as persistent in brushing aside all rapprochement by the Germans as the Germans were persistent in disregarding all demands for wage increases. Thus a plan to set up a so-called "German Cultural Institute" for workers was sabotaged so thoroughly that the venture never reached inception. The Institute idea originated in the Reichskommissariat, and its purpose was "to further the good relations between the occupying power and the Norwegian working class" through instruction in the German language and lectures about the German "Labor Front." The Germans felt this worthy enterprise should be financed jointly by the Labor Federation, the Employers' Association, the Reichskommissariat, the city of Oslo, and the nation's Government. The Institute was stillborn.

Much the same thing happened when the Nazis decided that German films should be shown at union meetings. The moment the lights went out, union members would get up and leave the hall.

And when the "Constituted" Minister of the Nazi Department of Domestic Affairs tried to force public officials and workers to declare their loyalty to the Nasjonal Samling, the unions immediately produced a counterstroke: practically 100 per cent of the employees replied by letter that the request did not concern them. These letters were identical, word for word, and they arrived in such numbers that the Department stopped opening them.

The Nasjonal Samling's attempt to send speakers out to address workers on the job also met with failure. Everywhere they ran into difficulty in obtaining listeners, despite the fact that lectures were scheduled in the midst of working hours and workers were ordered to attend.

To a large extent these and similar actions by the workers were spontaneous, but behind them stood prominent trade-union leaders who gradually became the leaders of the opposition. A mighty forward stride in the direction of united action was made at Christmastime in 1940 when an underground newspaper called *Free Trade-Unions* appeared for the first time. This small and unprepossessing sheet soon became the most widely read underground paper in Norway. The editors were, of course, anonymous, but it was soon plain to the workers that those responsible for the little paper were union men of clear vision and a strong sense of duty. *Free Trade-*

Unions became widely circulated, and through a well-organized distributing system it now reaches into all corners of the country.

This underground paper championed a program which, in all its simplicity, made the choice clear for laborers. It demanded that the Federation should assume its natural position in the Norwegian home front as the country's largest and most influential organization. It demanded a battle against the Germans and nazism. It made it clear to the workers that even though it was important that the organization be preserved for social and national progress, this principle should not be maintained at any cost; for if the Federation was a weapon in the hands of the workers, it could just as well serve as weapon in the hands of the Nazis. If the latter should come about, and if the Nazis should turn this weapon against the workers, then, said *Free Trade-Unions,* it would be up to the workers to smash their organization to bits. "The organization must not fall into the hands of the enemy."

During this period of uncertainty and restlessness, the workers were able to capitalize on the fact that there was dissension in the Nazi camp. Relations between the occupying power—especially the military authorities—on the one side and the Nasjonal Samling on the other had never been good. To be sure, their goals were the same, but they were constantly at odds over means of attaining them. The Germans' desire to nazify the labor movement was no less earnest than Quisling's, but the Germans held to a more long-range policy, and the Reichskommissar did not care to strike until he was entirely sure of success. Germany was still at war, and it was important to maintain order within the production apparatus.

Thus arose a situation that enabled the Federation, at least to a certain extent, to play the occupying power and the Nasjonal Samling against each other. This provided a much-needed breathing spell which the Federation used for establishing order within its own ranks. And it also led to a paradoxical situation; in certain instances, the Nasjonal Samling took sides with the workers against the Germans, as in the case of the Federation's demands for wage adjustments. In other instances, the Germans prevented the Quislings from taking too drastic measures against the workers.

This was the case at Christmas 1940, when the Nasjonal Samling made a serious attempt to get the entire secretariat of the Federation dismissed and replaced with dependable Nazis. By that time the Quislings had found out that the September coup had failed. They saw that the Federation was rapidly recovering from that first blow, and that it would soon be strong enough to strike back—unless the present trend was checked.

At this moment the Federation was playing up to the Germans, who were concerned over the drop of production in industry, and this proved wise. On January 9 the Federation's president was summoned by the Reichskommissar—it was the first time he had been asked to report directly to Terboven—and the result of this meeting was that the Federation was assured that it would no longer have to concern itself with politics. This meant that for the time being a halt had been called to the Nasjonal Samling's constant attempts to interfere with the trade-unions.

The open break, which the workers themselves were sure would come sooner or later, had been temporarily postponed. The period of comparative labor peace that followed made it possible for the leadership to make the necessary preparations for the ultimate showdown.

The time was well used. Not least important was the fact that the co-operation between the Federation and the Employers' Association was extended in a thousand different ways. Just as the Nazis had previously accomplished the seemingly impossible in bringing the various religious groups into a firm, united front, they now achieved another miracle by welding capital and labor together. Naturally, the old differences between employers and employees over wages and working conditions could not be locked up and put away on the spur of the moment. In spite of that the Employers' Association—which still had not been subjected to any direct attack and which still possessed its old, Norwegian leadership—and the Federation quickly reached an agreement to settle all differences without the aid of the Nazis. Before the war Norway had had a law covering labor conflicts. Among other things, this law established a Labor Court whose duty it was to pass judgment on all questions regarding the interpretation of existing contracts between labor and management. Judges of this Labor Court had been dismissed by the Nazis and replaced by Nasjonal Samling members. It did not take workers and employers long to agree that no disputes should be brought before this new Court.

Simultaneously the Federation and the Employers' Association set to work at solving a number of problems that had been made acute by the occupation and by all the difficulties that had followed in its wake. Together they organized a "Vacation Office" which organized inexpensive vacation trips and summer holidays for workers. Together they tackled the problem of providing better food for workmen on the job—a problem made doubly serious because of the increasingly rigid rationing. In addition, the Employers' Association adopted a program embracing vocational training, health promotion among workers, guidance for workers in making better use of leisure time and vacations, extension of social legislation, and many other worthy endeavors.

All in all, there was not much basis left for the Nazi propaganda about a "people's fellowship without class struggle." If there were any workers who wondered whether it was right for labor thus to join forces with its old "enemies," employers and capital, then *Free Trade-Unions* supplied the answer:

"The question of a free Norway is not limited to either employee or employer, socialist or conservative. It is a matter which concerns the entire people. The only possibility of building up a free labor movement is in a free country."

3. "THE BOAT TO ENGLAND SAILS AT TWO"

"YOU HAVE BEEN LISTENING to the news from London."

The voice in the loud-speaker was still. Then the national anthem crescendoed into the room. The group around the radio arose and stood at attention while the familiar, beloved melody ran its course.

As the last strains died away the room remained quiet for a moment. Then the discussion began, and there was much to be talked about. There was the situation on the war fronts. There was the question of when America would get into the war. And there was the inexhaustible subject—the possibility of an invasion of Norway.

A spirit of intimate confidence prevailed. The fifteen or sixteen persons in the room knew each other and depended on each other. Some were elderly, some were young boys and girls. A couple of them were businessmen, one was a pastor, one a carpenter, and another a taxicab driver. Conditions had thrown them together; bridges had been placed over all those gaps that in normal times had kept them apart. It was one of the thousands of sessions being held every evening in all parts of the country.

The windows of the room were covered with black-out paper. Not a ray of light found its way out into the darkened streets, from which occasionally the tramping sound of heavy soldier boots came.

"Oh, if a person could only get out and take part in it!"

It was a young boy who spoke from his place on the floor, his voice full of earnestness.

"Arne and Sven have left," he went on. "They vanished nearly a week ago. Nobody knows how they got away, but their parents got word yesterday that they had made it all right. Arne is joining the Army, and Sven is going to be sent to 'Little Norway' in Canada to be trained as a pilot."

He lay on the carpet and stared into the fireplace. The flickering flames cast shifting shadows over the youthful face.

"Nobody knows where the letter came from. There was no stamp on it. Somebody had put it in the mailbox near the door. Oh, if one could only get away!"

"What is it you would like to do out there? Isn't it just as well to stay here at home?" It was the pastor's voice. He sat in the dark of a corner so that his face was only a pale shadow in the dim light.

"What I'd like to do!"

The boy raised himself to his elbows. His voice was almost angry.

"What I'd like to do?" he repeated. "Fight, I suppose. Do something useful! I'd become a seaman, soldier, pilot. They certainly could use me for something or other. What are you driving at, Pastor? Don't you think it's right to fight?"

Now he was sitting up. His face had become hard, almost suspicious. He had known the pastor ever since he was a boy.

He had been baptized and confirmed by him. It couldn't be that the pastor was a . . . that is, that the pastor couldn't be relied upon?

The calm, mild voice sounded again in the darkness:

"No, I'm merely asking. It is, of course, a serious decision to make. Deciding to go away, I mean. War is not a game, and if one is caught trying to get out of the country, you know the result. You get shot."

But now the boy was on his feet. He could scarcely control his anger; his voice quivered with suppressed wrath.

"And if I do get shot, what then? I'm not afraid! At least I would have tried. But to stay here, and to see what's going on here . . . Today there was another fight at the meat shop. People had been standing in line there since five in the morning. And just before the shop opened at eight o'clock, two German trucks pulled up and carried away every scrap of meat in the place. Fru Haug and Fru Berntsen were arrested because they struck one of the soldiers. Anders Berg was knocked unconscious and had to be taken to the hospital. He's got five children and is out of work."

The boy was all but crying. He walked back and forth across the floor, swinging his arms helplessly.

"I would like to get away, too." This time it was a young girl who had spoken. She sat on the sofa beside a young man, and neither had previously uttered a word all evening.

"Yes, I certainly would like to get away," said the girl again. "They must be needing nurses or office workers or something. Seamen who get torpedoed need medical attention. Maybe I could be a stewardess aboard a ship."

She turned to the young man beside her.

"Sverre and I have often talked about how we could get away, haven't we?"

He nodded.

"Yes," he agreed, then continued: "If one could only get in

touch with those people who arrange such trips. It's easier for those who live on the coast and have boats of their own. For them it's just a matter of getting started. But we need help to get to the coast—money for counterfeit papers, and so on."

The pastor spoke up again, his voice still calm and mild.

"It seems to me," he said, "that you should set out on an Easter holiday trip. It's grand up in the mountains now. Snow and sunshine. I know of a little hut off to the west where you can stay. I was talking with four or five young people about it this morning. They're starting out early in the morning. You don't know them, but that doesn't matter. They're fine young people and I'm sure you'll like them. Why don't you pack your rucksacks and go along? Tickets and passes will be taken care of. The train leaves at eight-fifteen in the morning."

The pastor cleared his throat. "Then you won't have to worry about plans to get away for a while. And now it seems to me a little food would taste pretty good!"

"Oh, I had almost forgotten about that!" It was the hostess' voice. She rose and turned on the light, and the enchantment that had filled the room was gone immediately.

"Anne, won't you come along to the kitchen and help get things ready? I can't wait to see what all of you have brought along to eat. It seems to me I saw a little coffee in the pastor's package!"

A few minutes later she returned with cups and plates. Then the food was placed on the table. Each one had brought along a share of the refreshments. The rationing was strict, and it was no longer good manners to arrive at a party empty-handed.

The guests took places around the table, and the conversation was lively. But in a corner the two boys and the girls were engaged in a conference of earnest whispers. Shortly afterwards they quietly disappeared out the door. Nobody noticed them leave. It was, of course, only natural that young people wanted to be off by themselves.

When the train pulled out of the station the next morning one of the coupés was occupied by eight young men and two girls. They were wearing sports clothes; on the shelves heavy rucksacks were heaped together. In one of the corners stood the ski poles, and in the baggage car lay ten pairs of skis. All ten of the youngsters—for scarcely any of them could be considered grownups—poked their heads out the windows and waved. Far down on the platform stood a dark-clad man waving in return. His face was calm and mild, and clear eyes twinkled behind his glasses.

When the train veered to pass under the bridge, he turned and started for the station with short, hurried steps. The young people closed the windows again and settled in their seats. Soon they had the portable phonograph going, and cheerful music sounded from the coupé. Four or five German soldiers sat not far away, and there was envy in their eyes as they watched these happy, carefree young folk laugh and enjoy themselves. Several times the Germans tried to start a conversation, but nobody paid any attention to them; and when they tried to sing a little on their own, the chorus around the phonograph quickly drowned them out.

The train rolled on and up through the valley. Outside the snow-clad landscape glided past the windows. There was farm after farm with large, well-kept buildings. Norwegian flags fluttered from flagpoles. In former years the flag was displayed only on Sundays and holidays.

The valley grew more and more narrow, and the mountains higher and steeper. Late in the afternoon the train paused at a small station far above the timber line. Vast, white plateaus extended as far as the eye could see.

It was already growing dusk, and by the time the young people reached the hut night had fallen. But it was not snowing. Far above, a myriad of stars shone out of the black heavens.

They were unstrapping their skis when the door of the hut opened and a hulking figure loomed against the light inside.

"Who's there?"

The voice was deep and rumbling, and the words were spoken in the dialect peculiar to this region.

"We bring you greetings from the pastor," said one of the boys, a serious-minded fellow who had automatically become the leader of the little expedition.

The voice at the door was still deeper:

"You'd better take off your skis and come in. I've got a fire going, and you'd maybe like a drop of coffee."

They tramped into the hut and took off their rucksacks. The flames in the fireplace cast flickering, eerie shadows on the walls, but it was warm and pleasant, and soon all ten freed themselves of their heavy jackets and were gathered around the table. The man set cups of steaming coffee in front of them, and soon the conversation was in full swing.

The coffee and the warmth of the room at length brought drowsiness to the young travelers. The big stranger had not had much to say; he had merely been sitting in his chair watching his guests with clear, penetrating eyes. But finally he spoke up:

"I guess we'd better see about getting some sleep. We've got to get up early and put a lot of distance behind us to-morrow."

The boat lay in a little bay. It looked small and insignificant at first sight. Just an ordinary, weather-beaten fishing boat. But the long and strenuous ski trip had been hard on the muscles, and it felt good to relax on the narrow benches in the tiny cabin.

It had begun to grow dark as they neared the boat, and they could scarcely see more than their hands in front of them as they stumbled aboard. Other people were here ahead of them—many others. They heard their guide speak to a man on the pier:

"I brought three more than we agreed—a girl and two boys. The pastor sent them."

A voice answered, laughingly:

"Well, we're going to have a load, all right! But we can't be so particular about that nowadays. And, of course, it's only for a couple of days."

The voices were lost in the dark.

It was warm and crowded in the cabin, but after a little everyone found a place. All together there were twenty-seven of them, and space for feet was at a premium. Nobody could see anyone else, and no one dared to speak aloud. Soon the whispering also died away. Only the slow splash of the water against the sides of the boat could be heard.

On the deck above heavy boots tramped back and forth. Then chains rattled, and soon the motor began to pound. The boat trembled a moment, and everybody knew it was free of the pier. The boat rocked a little as it got under way.

Voices were heard from up on the deck. Some men laughed. A husky voice was heard clearly:

"Those Germans turn out fine gasoline. I borrowed six cans of it for this trip."

When day began to break, the boat was far from shore. A strong wind had sprung up, and the sea was running white. There was snow in the air.

Light began to creep into the cabin, too, and gradually the faces became discernible. The travelers looked around and became acquainted with one another. Most of them were strangers to one another. For the most part they were young boys and men of military age, but there were also some young women and a middle-aged man who had brought his wife and two children along.

"The Germans got suspicious," he chuckled, "and there was no use keeping it up any longer. A week ago they took my house away from me. We've been living in a hut up in the mountains waiting for a boat."

The wind grew stronger, and the little craft was tossing heavily.

"Swell weather!" grinned the skipper, when he came down to have a look at his passengers. "The Germans won't be out flying today. They don't like storm and fog. Tomorrow we'll be there!"

Slowly the boat headed westwards. The seas washed over the foredeck, and the wind howled in the rigging. Down in the cabin it was warm and stuffy, and the two children were sick. There was no chance to prepare any food, and apparently no one felt fit to volunteer as cook. They slouched down and allowed themselves to be tossed entirely at the will of the boat and the storm.

Suddenly there was an outburst of activity on deck. Someone shouted, and all at once the boat lay over on its side while the helmsman turned it into the wind. Down in the cabin the passengers were thrown from one side to the other in a tangled mass. Rucksacks, ropes, and eating utensils rained down on them.

Then, just as suddenly, the boat was on even keel again, and everything was as before.

The passengers below heard the helmsman's voice:

"That was a close call! Missed it by a foot at the most, I'll bet. Look at that big black devil, would you!"

The people in the cabin looked at each other. Nobody said a word. It was not necessary to say anything. Just a foot more to port and everything would have been over. The North Sea was full of drifting mines.

The next morning sea gulls screamed as they swirled wildly around the mast. The boat was nearing shore. The Norwegian flag was waving from the masttop. A little later the roar of an airplane was heard, and that led to more moments of suspense. But it was a British plane, not German, and a little later a trawler appeared on the horizon. The fishing boat was towed in through the mine fields, and a few hours later it was alongside a pier. The Norwegian consul was there to greet the newcomers. He shouted to the skipper:

"Right on time, as usual!"

The people in the cabin could hear the skipper cackle with satisfaction.

"It's a good thing to be right on time!" he called back.

Not long ago Norwegians in London organized a club for those who have sailed across the North Sea in fishing boats. Today that club has more than 10,000 members. No meeting of the club has drawn a 100-per-cent attendance. That will have to wait till after the war, because North Sea travelers are now scattered all over the world—wherever Norwegian war activity is taking place. Some have continued on across the Atlantic to Canada, where the Royal Norwegian Government has training camps for its Air Force, Army, and Navy. Some have entered the Norwegian army forces in Great Britain and Iceland. Some are stationed at Norwegian naval bases in South Africa and Australia. Others man Norwegian warships in the Mediterranean. And still others serve as seamen in the Norwegian merchant marine, which is the third largest of those belonging to the Allied nations and which plies all seven seas for the Allied cause.

And some never reached their goal.

Somewhere in London a crude little rowboat is being preserved. It is guarded as a sacred relic, because eventually it is to be taken back to Norway, where it is to have a place of honor in the country's Museum of Shipping. In this little boat two Norwegian boys rowed 450 miles through turbulent seas in order to offer their services to their country.

Then there were the five young schoolboys who had never been outside Norwegian territorial waters. They stole a boat from the Germans. They also stole gasoline. They set straight out to sea. In the middle of the North Sea their engine went dead. None of them knew anything about repairing engines, but as if by a miracle they got it running again. A pocket compass told them in which direction they were heading. Near the British coast they spent a whole night cruising haphazardly about in a mine field. But the boys had no knowledge of the danger they had been in until they were safe ashore.

There were the two Oslo lads who started out far up in Oslo Fiord with an old six-meter sailboat, a regatta craft. They sailed out the fiord. They "acted dumb" when they were hailed by German patrol boats. They stopped at small towns along the fiord to buy provisions, a little here and a little there. Upon reaching Lindesnes they headed out to sea.

"It was only the two of us," they said later, "and there really should be four or five men to handle a six-meter. We'd have been in trouble if the weather had gone bad—but it didn't, and that's that!"

There was, too, the boy who later was shot down in an air battle over France. With two friends he left Norway in a small boat. A German plane found them and chased them back to shore. They had to abandon the boat and hide in the woods. A week later they got hold of another boat and set out anew. Again they were discovered by a German plane, which sprayed them with machine gun bullets. The helmsman was shot through the head and died instantly. Another got a bullet through a lung and slowly bled to death. The third youth continued the trip, and four days later he arrived in the Shetland Islands. He went on to Canada, where he received his training as a pilot. Then back to England and to active duty with the Royal Norwegian Air Force. He died in France.

There are thousands of such accounts.

And somewhere in Scotland Norwegian fishermen have formed a wartime community of their own. Hundreds of modern, sturdy, and well-equipped Norwegian fishing boats have crossed the North Sea. Many a Norwegian fisherman, faced with the prospect of being forced to work solely for the Germans, took wife and children aboard his boat and struck out for freer air. Eventually there were so many of these that the Royal Norwegian Government had to appoint a Director of Fisheries to supervise their activities. These fishermen are making their contribution to the Allied cause. Fish make good and healthful food, and soldiers must eat.

The exodus across the North Sea has never been completely halted. On some days hundreds of volunteers have arrived. On others only small boatloads of three or four men have come in. The number has varied with the season of the year. The Germans keep close watch over the Norwegian coastal areas, and it is not easy to get through to those outlying ports from which the boats set out. Getting started does not mean that the dangers are past; there are still the German planes and patrol boats to think about; and floating mines hold certain death for those who run upon them.

But the Norwegian coast is long and jagged, and the Germans, many as they are, cannot have a man in every little bay or inlet. During the night people hoist sails and steal away among the isles and skerries. They bring with them greetings to the external front from the home front. And they bring other things with them, too—information of all kinds. There is not a cannon, not an airport in Norway which has not long since been indicated on the war maps in London.

"The boat for England leaves at two," say the people in Norway.

4. THE WHITE, THE STRIPED, AND THE BLACK

IT WAS ONLY a typewritten message on a small slip of paper. But there were hundreds of thousands of copies of it scattered all through the country. The message was read in homes and workplaces, on the large farms in the broad and open areas as well as in the weather-beaten huts of the mountain folk, in the workers' homes and in the factory owners' private villas. Here is the message:

Norwegians: On April 9 we shall commemorate those who fell in the war against the invaders. We shall not do so by open demonstrations, which only bring reprisals in return. But we shall nevertheless do it in a way which will give the Nazis something to think about.

During the half-hour between two and two-thirty o'clock on April 9 we shall pay tribute to our fallen countrymen. Stay indoors during this half-hour. Do not show yourselves on the streets or in public places. Streets, business places, and trains are to remain empty during the half-hour dedicated to our fallen.

Housewives: Do not do any shopping during this half-hour. Stay inside and make sure your children do the same.

Businessmen and office workers: Do not use your telephones and do not answer any telephone calls during this period. Avoid waiting on any people who venture to burst in during the half-hour of silence which is to be our way of honoring the memories of those fallen.

Students and pupils: During this half-hour do not answer any question which your teachers may venture to ask you.

Workers: Do all you can to take part in this action.

No one should go outdoors for the mere purpose of seeing how deserted the streets are. *You can rest assured they will be quiet.* Rather, stand by the windows and look out. Our own people will be in control of the situation.

During the half-hour the wind might easily cause flowerpots to fall from ledges and onto the heads of those who show themselves in the streets.

Remember our goal, and stick together!

It was only a typewritten message. No one knew where it originated or who had given the order. And no one asked. The message contained an order, and it had to be obeyed. A whole year under Nazi domination had taught the Norwegians that the only way to stand up to the occupying power was to stand together. Through bitter experience they had learned the truth of Benjamin Franklin's dictum: "We must all hang together, or assuredly we shall all hang separately."

During the winter months the home front had become firmly welded together with a united and permanent leadership. It had developed like a vast cell structure, and only those who shaped and directed it had any knowledge of its details. Nobody knew who the leaders were, but their orders nevertheless were followed. That was because it was clear to all that the orders were right and for the good.

After the initial confusion following the invasion had been overcome and the home front had become stabilized, the

Nazis succeeded only once in creating disorder in the ranks. This setback, great and painful though it was, was nevertheless turned into good, simply because it taught an important lesson. Yet it was a defeat nonetheless.

For a hundred years Norway had had local government. Residents of municipalities elected a council to govern them. On December 21, 1940, the Nazi Department of Domestic Affairs issued a decree which with one blow put an end to this institution. The *Führer* principle was to be introduced into municipal administration. The authority which formerly rested with the popularly elected council was to be transferred in its entirety to the mayor. The mayor was to be appointed by the Department after consultation with the provincial governor and the Nasjonal Samling *Führer* in the province concerned. Aiding him, the mayor was to have a council appointed by the same procedure. But the council members were to have no right to vote. The mayor, as the local *Führer,* was to listen to the council's suggestions, but he himself was to make the decision in all matters, great or small.

The Department's decree was a crushing blow at one of the pillars of the Norwegian social structure, and the blow was met with various thrusts and counterstrokes, but not by a united front. The regular provincial governors, who still retained their offices, tried to the utmost to save the administration. They saw the danger in the decree, but they believed the most effective countermeasure would be to keep the Nazis out of the mayoral positions. Therefore they urged loyal Norwegians to continue as mayors or to take over as mayor wherever possible. Other Norwegians insisted that the New Order had to be fought by all available means. They demanded that the mayors resign and turn over the administration, in chaos, to the Nazis. They knew that the Nasjonal Samling would not have enough people to fill the vacant offices. In some districts the provincial governors' appeal was followed. In others, the reverse was true. And the Nazis could not conceal their malicious delight. They had succeeded in causing a split in the home front.

It was several months before the consequences of this defeat were neutralized. Not until spring, when the provincial governors resigned from their offices in protest, did the Nazis find themselves in the quandary they should have been in around New Year's—they were left without mayors.

But the home front was an apt pupil, and in the course of the winter it organized an endless series of offensive actions that caused the Nazi front line to waver dangerously. The development towards complete chaos within the Norwegian community proceeded at a steadily accelerated pace. And the home front did not go out of its way to avoid using totalitarian methods when it was a matter of maintaining solidarity within its own ranks.

The Norwegian language soon produced three clear distinctions: the "white," the "striped," and the "black." The white were the good, patriotic Norwegians. The black were the Quislings. The striped were the fence sitters and the vacillating who did not really know where they belonged.

The winter of 1941 became a fight between the whites and the blacks over the striped. The Quislings coaxed and threatened. The Norwegians only threatened. The Nazi-controlled press hammered away at the hedgers—flattered them, courted them, tempted them with high-sounding and big-paying positions and with a share of the fruits of victory.

"There's no time to waste," wrote *Fritt Folk*. "Soon the gates will be closed. Soon the party will be accepting no more members. It may well be wise to have your membership in order when the war is won."

Repeated over and over again, in the press and on the radio, was the old, standard refrain of the Nazi orator:

"The only path to Norway's freedom and independence leads through the Nasjonal Samling."

There were those who faltered and gave in. They soon found themselves ostracized. Old friends knew them no longer; old acquaintances passed them on the street with no greeting but a cold, penetrating stare. Black businessmen and shop-keepers found their trade falling off sharply. Owners of book-shops who displayed the literature of the New Order in their windows discovered that their patrons had disappeared. News-papers that displayed a too great willingness to run the Nazis' errands lost their subscribers and advertisers, and in the end had to close up shop.

A public official in a small town outside Oslo was known to be on the verge of joining the Nasjonal Samling. One morn-ing, as he was setting out for work, he discovered that some-one had laid a path of evergreen boughs right from his door-step to a near-by cemetery. He did not join. In a village in northern Norway a businessman had yielded to pressure and joined the party. The same day he received an envelope con-taining a rifle bullet and a slip of paper with the message: "This time you get it this way!"

Lists of the names of all those who were black were circu-lated in all towns and rural districts. These lists were also read over the London radio. Those whose names appeared on the lists were done for—they were permanently excluded from contact or companionship with Norwegians.

The number of the striped had never been great, and as the winter wore on it virtually vanished. Almost all of them had lined up with the whites. A few filled in between the stripes and became black.

The Nasjonal Samling never attained a membership any greater than 1 per cent of the total population, and Quisling has never permitted publication of exact figures.

In due time the blacks were marked, isolated, and neutralized. There was no use, however, in trying to escape the fact of their existence. They composed a "foreign body" that had got into the Norwegian system; but the foreign body had been incapsulated and was no longer infectious. People resigned themselves to that, and consoled themselves with the firm conviction that the thing could be removed by a simple operation when the time was ripe.

The Quislings were well aware of their defeat, and they tried to reach their goal by other means. In April 1941 members of the home front got hold of a circular letter sent out by Erling Kvadsheim, Nasjonal Samling *Führer* for the province of Rogaland. The letter was dispatched to London and read over the radio there. It follows:

If for certain reasons it is not possible for you openly and officially to support the Nasjonal Samling and to join in as a member of the movement, there will be an opportunity for you to help through our so-called "Contributing Circle." The participants in this circle pledge themselves to make a regular monthly contribution or to donate a larger amount once and for all, without thereby binding themselves in any way or assuming obligations of any kind whatever.

For paid-in contributions members of the "Contributing Circle" will get a receipt card, and their names will be entered in a locked and confidential card file. If a participant should later decide to join the Nasjonal Samling officially, the time he has been a participant of the "Contributing Circle" will be credited to him as full membership.

He who has sacrificed for Norway's cause in this time of destiny will be rewarded by the great things to come. But he who refuses to sacrifice cannot expect to receive help.

Simultaneously *Fritt Folk* carried on a strenuous campaign for new subscribers, but the campaign produced diminishing results. The paper therefore found it advisable to start a contest. According to the *Fritt Folk* of March 22, 1941, three prizes were being offered:

> 1st Prize: The person who by April 5 has obtained the greatest number of new subscribers will be sent a large, framed portrait of the *Führer* [Quisling] signed in the *Führer's* own hand.
>
> 2nd Prize: The next best subscription getter will receive *The Book about Quisling* with the *Führer's* inscription.
>
> 3rd Prize: The best subscription salesman in the Nasjonal Samling's Youth Organization will be invited by the *Führer* to spend a whole day with him.

Apparently not even these tempting prizes produced the desired result. The names of the winners, if any, were never made public. Later all public servants in the country were compelled to subscribe. *Norsk Meldingsblad,* an official publication carrying information about all vacant civil service positions as well as all governmental notices and announcements, was in due time suspended as an independent publication and made part of *Fritt Folk,* thus assuring the latter of some readers— at least of the public notices.

Efforts to enforce the rule that Quisling's picture be placed in all public offices, schoolrooms, and in the University of Oslo also met with failure.

At the University the sentiment had always been strongly anti-Nazi. Of the institution's more than 4,000 students, only about thirty were members of the Nasjonal Samling. Among the faculty members only one man—Klaus Hansen, professor of medicine and for many years chairman of Oslo's Norse-German Society—had fallen in line with the Nazis. The rest stood firmly with the majority of students. In the spring of 1941 when the Nazis threw out the old board of examiners in the law school and named a board composed of Quislings, the law students simply refused to appear before the new board. In this the professors backed up the students, and the

Nazis had to undo their work. The same thing happened when Quisling's picture was to be hung; the students and professors threatened to go on strike, and the Nazis were again forced to give in.

It was the same way in the schools. School strikes flared up again, and despite the fact that the Nazis seemed determined to force obedience—even to the extent of arresting a number of teachers and expelling many pupils—they were in the long run compelled to yield on the point of Quisling's picture. A number of other orders also created disturbances in the schools. Late in the spring a *Hitler-Jugend* exhibition was arranged, and headmasters were ordered to visit it along with all the pupils of their schools. The pupils went on strike, and it was at this time that the Nazis established their "reform school for children who have displayed an attitude hostile to the State."

There was no longer anyone who listened to the Oslo radio, so no one cared about the propaganda being broadcast there. As far as the newspapers were concerned, the opposition was also comparatively quiet. People had to read some sort of newspaper if they were to keep posted on new rationing regulations and other official orders. Besides, the Norwegians had learned to read the newspapers in their own way, and the journalists—whose position was clear to everybody—did their best to bring out the truth between the lines. The orders and instructions given to newspaper editorial staffs had become well known to the people through the underground press.

But the home front went into determined action when the Nazis began earnestly to use the movies as tools of propaganda. A boycott was begun in the middle of January, and the idea spread like wildfire. Within fourteen days the receipts at Oslo movie houses, which were owned and operated by the municipality, dropped by about 80 per cent. Only the Germans and Quislings continued to attend movies. In Flekkefjord and a number of other towns the movie theaters had to shut down. No American films had been shown since the beginning of the occupation. One of the first things the Germans had done was to close the Norwegian offices of American moving-picture concerns, and it was declared in the newspapers that "the stream of smut and gangster idolization coming from Hollywood" was to be ended once and for all. The Norwegians were to be made to understand that the names of the real movie stars were "no longer Greta Garbo, Charlie Chaplin, Melvin Douglas, and Bette Davis, but Paul Hörbiger, Georg Alexander, and Willy Fritsch."

The Norwegians refused to learn.

During the spring months strife arose between the Nazi authorities and the Norwegian actors. The Nazis, who knew well enough that people no longer listened to the Oslo radio, had decided to try to lure them into listening by forcing well-known actors to take part in the broadcasts. Strong pressure was exerted on a number of actors to get them to appear, but they refused. They claimed the right to decide how they were to use their leisure time, and they said they did not care for any extra work. In mid-May the affair reached a crisis, and at an extraordinary general meeting held late in May the Norwegian Actors' Association voted to strike. On the same day the theaters in Oslo, Bergen, and Trondheim had to cancel all performances. The Germans replied by arresting the association representatives at all the theaters, and at the same time prohibiting a number of the country's foremost actors from again appearing on the stage. But the actors stood firm, and the strike lasted several months. In the end the Nazis had to withdraw their demands. The home front, which had supported the actors in every possible way—including financial, since the actors had been enjoined from drawing on their bank accounts—quietly marked up one more victory.

Meanwhile the occupying power had established its own

Deutsches Theater, which put on its performances in Oslo's famous National Theater, and which also went on tour to other leading Norwegian cities. This theater received scant support from the people of Oslo; for the most part it was German soldiers who attended the performances. When the German actors visited Trondheim, they were greeted with a pleasant surprise. Hours before the performance was to be given the house was completely sold out! There was a cheerful tension backstage as curtaintime drew near. But eight o'clock came and went . . . eight-thirty . . . and still not a seat in the theater was occupied. The tension turned into panic when the Germans finally realized that they had been tricked. German police were sent out to restaurants, and eventually they succeeded in rounding up about fifty soldiers. With them as an audience the play began.

Trondheimers were jubilant.

The boycott of everything bearing the German or Quisling taint was complete. It applied to individuals and to the Nazis as a whole, and it was not limited to ignoring Quislings on the street or to getting up and leaving when German officers or men entered restaurants and other public gathering places. The daily *Fritt Folk* was finding something to complain about. Now it was Nasjonal Samling members who were being persecuted! "Party members are being deceived at working places!" wailed the newspaper. "Housewives belonging to the party are not being waited upon in stores. We suggest establishment of private food shops for party members."

In April the Nazi Department of Church and Education sent a circular letter to all clergymen and congregational councils in the country. "Members of the Nasjonal Samling," said the letter, "are being frozen out of the religious organizations in Norway, from communion and from the divine worship. Yes, doubt has even been openly expressed as to whether one can be a Christian and at the same stand as a member of the Nasjonal Samling. . . . The Department is constantly in receipt of cries of distress from Christians who say that as soon as they become members of the Nasjonal Samling they are 'finished' in the [religious] societies."

The position of Nazis in religious groups was made no easier when the Nazi Department of Church and Education sponsored the publication of a new catechism for school use which had a reference to Quisling woven into the explanation of the Fourth Commandment. The little book was placed on sale on May 23, and Norwegians quickly became incensed over the following:

"If Norway is to become a good home, everyone must be aware of his responsibility. Consideration for the people must be above all other considerations. Community benefits must precede private benefits. Above all we are obliged to be obedient to the *Führer* and the state leadership. To oppose authority and the State is to oppose God's order, and it leads to punishment."

The loyal Norwegian's relation to the Nasjonal Samling was clear. So also was his relation to the occupying power. During the winter months the contact between the home front and the Royal Government in London had been further improved, and a complete news service by way of the London radio had been organized. It seldom took more than two or three days for word of any important occurrence in Norway to reach London, where it would immediately be broadcast back to Norway. Even secret or confidential documents intended solely for Nazi eyes reached London almost as soon as they did their intended destinations. There appeared to be a spy in every public office. *Fritt Folk* raged, and the Germans raged, and finally Quisling issued an order to the effect that all important documents emerging from the party leadership should be numbered; the recipients were ordered to keep the documents under lock and key and to be prepared to produce them at any time a checkup was made so as to be sure none had gone astray!

The occupying power acted even more drastically. During the winter and spring thousands of arrests were made throughout the country, and the number of concentration camps grew so that by midsummer there were sixteen scattered about Norway. In April, Heinrich Himmler, head of the Gestapo, came to Oslo, and his visit was the occasion of 350 arrests in the capital alone. Those arrested represented all classes and ranks of the population, and it was plain that the Germans' methods were based on the hope of finding a few large fish among the small when the nets were hauled in. They were especially interested in killing off the underground newspapers, but one of these, *Et Fritt Norge*, replied to the threats with these words:

"The editors of the underground newspapers can never be arrested. These newspapers are edited by the entire Norwegian people."

The home front had long since halted assaults on individual German soldiers; when a man in Trondheim stepped out of the dark and flung a bottle of acid into the face of a German soldier it constituted a rare occurrence. Experience had established that such attacks resulted only in the most brutal reprisals.

The front therefore concentrated on more important problems. The first and foremost of these was to halt all Nasjonal Samling efforts to gain control of the social machinery. The second was to retard German war activity as much as possible. Workers had long since introduced the highly effective slowdown technique into industry. At a shipyard in Fredrikstad workers succeeded in extending the time "necessary" for building a whaling boat from one month to five. On German fortifications the workers followed a self-imposed rule: "Six hours for the King and two for the Germans."

Open acts of sabotage were another part of the front's program. German cables and wires were cut in such a way that the alarms would fail to sound when British planes approached. Telephone lines were destroyed. Railroad tracks and equipment were constantly being tampered with. The Germans struck back by imposing large fines on communities as a whole. Arendal had to pay 20,000 kroner, Trondheim 40,000, and Stavanger headed the list by being forced to pay all of 5,000,000 kroner ($1,250,000) in "collective fines." When this proved ineffective the Germans resorted to the arresting of hostages, a practice which was also adopted for discouraging activities other than sabotage. Their planes and patrol boats had not been able to halt the exodus to England, so now they began arresting the parents of those who had set out. On one occasion no less than seventy-four hostages were arrested at Ålesund, where the urge to migrate had been especially noticeable. When these hostages were to be transferred from the city, an enraged crowd of 5,000 people gathered to protest. Fighting began, and eventually German soldiers had to be called to hold the throng in check.

A particularly brutal outburst of German punitive measures resulted from the Norse-British raid in the Lofoten Islands on March 4. On that occasion more than 300 Norwegians accompanied the raiders back to England as volunteers, and Reichskommissar Terboven personally supervised the punishment of those who remained behind. A large number of men and women were taken to a concentration camp near Oslo as hostages, and more than 100 homes on the islands were burned down. The wanton destruction ceased only when the fishermen of Lofoten threatened to quit fishing if peace and order were not restored. The little fishing village was also fined 100,000 kroner by the Germans. It was paid within a few days, and entirely through contributions that poured in from all parts of the country. The Norwegians had learned to stand together.

It was only a typewritten message on a sheet of paper. But it contained an order, and the order was obeyed. From two to two-thirty o'clock on April 9, 1941, all Norway was as quiet as death itself. Aside from German soldiers and a few Quislings there was not a person to be seen anywhere. House-wives stayed inside and drew all curtains. No children played outdoors. In shops and offices all activity was suspended. School children were spared from answering questions, because both pupils and teachers had remained away from school. In factories the machinery continued to run, but no one made use of it.

It was the first anniversary of the German invasion of Nor-way, and the Germans marked the day by doubling their regular guard everywhere. But neither soldiers nor police found anything to do. Around them was only silence—a heavy, threatening silence that not even the spring sun could mollify.

It was only a slip of paper with a typewritten message. But both the whites and the blacks, the Norwegians, the Germans, and the Quislings, knew that some day a similar slip of paper would be passed out—but with another order on it. On that day the silence would be broken.

5. BEHIND THE ONE STAND MANY

THREE TRUCKS, traveling at breakneck speed, swung onto the main highway between Oslo and Drammen. With motors roaring they sped through Baerum, past Asker, and on up the gradual incline east of Vardaasen.

People along the road turned and stared at the racing trucks. They discerned the brown-shirted uniforms of the *Hird* and the red-and-yellow banners of the Nasjonal Samling flapping from the radiator caps. They spat after the cars in disgust.

When the trucks reached the level plateau where, from Vardaasen, one can look out over the greater part of the Asker district, they turned sharply to the left. Before them lay a group of large, modern, hospital buildings. It was Dikemark Asylum, the largest institution in the country for the mentally ill.

In the open courtyard the trucks came to a stop, and thirty uniformed Quislings jumped to the ground. Marching in single file, they forced their way through the main entrance. The civilian guards were pushed aside, and the *Hird* headed straight for the director's office. But the director was not in; his secretary said he was busy with a patient and could not come right away. The *Hird* forced its way into the sickroom and arrested the doctor then and there.

A few minutes later the motors were roaring again. With gears grinding, the caravan moved out of the gates and headed back towards Oslo.

Dikemark Asylum is owned by the Oslo municipality, and, under the direction of the world-famous psychiatrist Dr. Rolv Gjessing, it had become a model institution which annually attracted numerous research commissions from all parts of the world. On April 25, 1941, the hospital and its director were drawn into a controversy that resolved itself into a struggle of principles between barbarism and civilization. Dr. Gjessing, who had always been the spokesman for science and free research, suddenly emerged as the symbol of all the forces opposing nazism. When the conflict finally ended some months later as an unconditional victory for the nation's doctors, it came to be regarded by Norwegians as tantamount with the demonstrations effected earlier by the Supreme Court and the bishops of the State Church.

The "Gjessing affair," as it was later referred to, began March 28 when Dr. Gjessing received a letter from the Nazi Department of Domestic Affairs stating that a man by the name of Camillus Wassdal had been engaged as head nurse at the hospital, replacing the former head nurse, a Mr. Myrvold, who had reached the retirement age on July 1. Dr. Gjessing replied by sending the Department a statement concerning Wassdal's lack of qualifications for the position. It concluded with these words:

"It would probably be an impropriety to assume that the Nasjonal Samling permits party considerations to supersede the professional. This would of course conflict absolutely with what has been professed untold times in the party's program and upheld in its press. I must therefore suppose that the appointment of Wassdal was due to lack of knowledge of his qualifications for the position of head nurse."

A few days later Wassdal returned to the hospital after a vacation. Here he learned for the first time of his appointment; he readily admitted that he was unqualified for the position and that he had never applied for it.

Dr. Gjessing wrote again to the Department, declaring that "it is a little difficult to imagine that it is the central administration's intention to burden us with a man who entirely lacks the necessary qualifications for the position of head nurse, and who, in addition, is mortally afraid to take the job."

But the days passed and no answer came. After fourteen days Dr. Gjessing received a letter from Wassdal, and the letter reflected an attitude altogether different from that which the man had maintained previously. It was obvious that he was acting on instructions from higher up. Wassdal declared flatly that he would assume his new position beginning April 21. Having said that, he proceeded, "as representative of the Nasjonal Samling and as head nurse," to issue orders for various changes in the hospital's work schedules.

Thus a comparatively unimportant personal matter had assumed the proportions of a political battle over principles. When Dr. Gjessing persisted in opposing the Wassdal appointment, the *Hird* took matters in its own hands and arrested him on April 25.

But when the Nazis went after Dr. Gjessing they succeeded only in stirring up a hornets' nest. Not many days passed before the Norwegian medical profession launched a counterattack. During the days immediately following the Gjessing arrest, doctors and hospital staffs held a couple of meetings in Oslo, and on April 28 the Nazi Department of Police received a letter, signed by the city's sixteen "head" doctors, which stated quite simply that if the wrong were not righted at once the whole medical profession would go on strike.

This letter pointed out that Dr. Gjessing had been set upon while treating a patient, that he had been arrested by persons who had no authority to do so, and that no warrant had been issued for his arrest. The doctors declared:

A public servant has been gravely disturbed in his work. He has been removed from a position of unusual responsibility, and in addition this has happened without his being given a chance to make provisions for a successor, etc. An asylum with 800 patients and a staff of 400 workers has abruptly been deprived of its leadership. A human relationship, which in all civilized countries is regarded as among the most delicate, has been violated— namely, the relationship between doctor and patient.

This is a revolting breach of the simplest rules of justice, and it therefore cannot be tolerated in an orderly community. The undersigned head doctors naturally take it for granted that those guilty will be severely punished. Further, we must place an absolute demand that the authorities instantly take steps to protect the sick. We also require guaranties for the safeguarding of the tranquillity which is the foundation for all hospital work.

The tone had changed since those days of confusion that had immediately followed the invasion. Now it was the Norwegians who were doing the dictating and making the demands. Now it was "the conquered" who were making the threats. The letter continued:

The hospitals have always remained outside political strife. And they have in the same conscientious way treated patients belonging to all political parties, trades, and professions. If considerations other than these become determinative, or if able employees are dismissed from their positions for political reasons, it will lead to a decline of the professional standard and efficiency of the hospitals, which in turn will have incalculable effect on the health and lives of patients. The head doctors have the full responsibility for the work done in their divisions—including the work done by the subordinate personnel, doctors, and nurses. The head doctors therefore have the right to demand that the authorities make appointments and promotions in accordance with the mentioned basic principles so that the work always will be done by those best qualified professionally. If these basic principles are not followed, then the head doctors cannot assume the responsibility for the operation of their respective divisions. In such event, we should consider ourselves compelled to seek severance from our duties.

Almost in passing, the doctors concluded:

It may be added that our reserve doctors, assistant doctors, and interns share our view in this matter unconditionally.

But this apparently casual postscript gave the matter great significance. The Nazi authorities found themselves face to face with the prospect of seeing a couple of thousand doctors leave their work in protest. The crisis was acute. The head doctors' threat was given still more weight when doctors, nurses, and all other hospital workers, in all parts of the country, warned that they would follow their lead. A unanimous protest against the encroachments by the administrative leadership of the municipality of Oslo, and a similar letter from Bishop Eivind Berggrav, made the situation still worse for the Quislings.

Through the underground newspapers and the London radio, the "Gjessing affair" had become known throughout the country, and by May 7 Quisling found himself forced to speak out in self-defense. On that day *Fritt Folk* appeared with an angry article under the headline: "English-sick Head Doctor Commits Illegal Acts and Is Removed." The article set forth:

The liar center in London has been busy telling about the "martyrdom" of the head doctor and director of Dikemark Asylum, Dr. Gjessing.

Ever since April 9 of last year Gjessing has been engaging in an activity far beyond that which a public official should allow himself to undertake. He has declared that he will not tolerate members of the Nasjonal Samling. He has to the best of his ability sabotaged the decisions of the state authorities and otherwise has in every possible way demonstrated that his heart is in London. The Director of Public Health states that it will not do to have a man such as Gjessing in public office. . . . London-dictated chicanery against Nasjonal Samling members and others who do their duty will not be tolerated.

The stand thus taken was sharp and absolute, but nevertheless the Quislings had to give in and release Dr. Gjessing from arrest.

The medical profession did not content itself with that. The threats to strike were continued, with the head doctors directing the action and serving as spokesmen for doctors, nurses, and all other hospital workers. They gave the Nazi authorities until June 25 to come to terms. Meanwhile they attended to their duties, but they also made preparations to put the strike into effect if the Nazi reply was not forthcoming.

The Nazis realized the danger that threatened, and they could see there was no escape. It became a matter of concealing the defeat as much as possible. So a commission was appointed "to explore the situation," and a few days before June 25 the result was made public. Dr. Gjessing was completely vindicated, and the commission's report stated that "no criticism can be made concerning Dr. Gjessing's direction of Dikemark Asylum." The commission also stated that those Nazis "who have acted against Dr. Gjessing have made themselves guilty of improper conduct."

The following day another automobile moved along the main road to Drammen. It traveled more slowly than the three trucks on April 25, and people along the highway had no difficulty in recognizing the erect figure of Dr. Gjessing in the back seat. They waved to him, and he smiled in return. The car turned in at the big iron gates, and the director was again the director.

A few minutes afterwards Camillus Wassdal sneaked out the back way. A while later he returned again—as a patient.

6. NO ROAD LEADS BACK

FORTY-THREE SOBER-FACED men and women were seated in the Storting's assembly hall. They were not members of the Storting, but they sat there as representatives of the Norwegian people—although on somewhat different premises and under entirely different conditions than was the case with the 150 Storting members who filled the room in former years.

All doors and windows were being guarded by German soldiers. They stood with legs apart, their black shoes glistening, and stared emptily into space. The steel helmets gave the motionless figures the appearance of statues molded in bronze. A swastika hung behind the president's chair.

It was absolutely quiet in the hall. Nobody talked, not even in whispers. The forty-three sat in their seats and looked straight ahead, each one lost in his own thoughts.

Perhaps they were recalling the old days, days not much more than a year behind them, when this hall was the nerve center of Norwegian life; when free men stood up and exercised free speech, when large and small matters were presented and discussed in an open interchange of opinions; when the count of ballots was decisive; when representatives of a free press sat in their gallery observing and listening to everything that was done or said in order later to convey complete reports to the voters; when the Norwegian flag, and not the distorted swastika, fluttered in the breeze over the building's roof.

Outside it was summer, but the shimmering June daylight was shut out by the heavy curtains that had been drawn over the windows. The street noises from below could be heard only faintly.

The breathless silence lay heavily over the room.

Suddenly there was a small commotion near the door. The guards brought their feet together with a sharp clicking of heels. A bark from the captain of the guards. Weapons clattered.

"Heil Hitler!"

"Heil Hitler!"

Reichskommissar Josef Terboven strode into the room. Behind him marched a number of bemedaled officers. In their wake followed two of the "constituted ministers." The latter seemed uncertain and nervous in the face of the wall of silence rising from those in the hall.

The Reichskommissar ascended the stairs to the president's chair. The slim figure seemed a bit stooped, and the small eyes glittered behind the glasses. He studied the people seated before him.

Josef Terboven knew his strength. He was an old hand at this sort of thing. He had made opponents far stronger than these forty-three average persons weak and submissive. He knew all the tricks. Had he not in his day brought Fritz Thyssen with all that man's wealth and connections into Hitler's domain? Then how could it be that he should so strongly feel the displeasure of those forty-three calm glances which so emotionlessly followed the least of his movements?

There was a brief pause while he fumbled nervously with

his papers. Then, with a snarling voice, he began. And at once the strange enchantment was broken.

Epithets hailed down on the forty-three. Insult followed insult. Such language had never before been used in the old and revered assembly hall of Norwegian Storting members. The victims sat there motionless, allowing the storm to rage over them.

For a half-hour or more Reichskommissar Terboven gave his wrath free play. Then, suddenly, he stopped. He straightened his shoulders. His voice became still more cutting. He looked like a bewildered, apoplectic teacher facing a class of unruly boys. He pointed a long and nicotine-stained finger at his audience:

"Will the following gentlemen be so kind as to come promptly to the front of the room as I read their names?"

There was a brief moment of suspense. Then came the first name:

"Acting president of the National Labor Federation, Ludvig Bueland."

Bueland rose slowly.

"Hurry! Didn't you hear what I said?"

Ludvig Bueland took his place at the front of the room, and the voice continued:

"General secretary of the Norwegian Medical Association, Dr. Jörgen Berner. President of the Norwegian Municipal Association, Torbjörn Henriksen. Chairman of the Norwegian Postal Association, Oskar Röine. President of the Norwegian Commercial Association, Paul Frank."

The five stood in a row at the front of the room facing the Reichskommissar.

Once again complete silence reigned.

Then the voice barked out anew:

"Gentlemen! You yourselves know what your sins have been. You will be given ample time to think them over!"

The Reichskommissar gave a signal. A squad of Gestapo men came forward. The five were taken away as prisoners.

The Reichskommissar collected his papers and dismissed his audience with a gesture. The German soldiers withdrew from the doors where they had stood guard. Thirty-eight persons were still sitting in their chairs as if turned to stone. At the door Terboven turned and cast a glance at them. Then he shouted: *"Heraus!"*

The sun blinded them as they emerged. The midday papers had just reached the street. They were dated June 18, 1941, and they reported that relations between the occupying power and the Norwegian people were marked by friendliness and mutual confidence.

Developments within the Norwegian administration had been following a straight and sure course towards complete chaos ever since Reichskommissar Terboven had turned the power over to the Nasjonal Samling in his speech of September 25, 1940. The Quislings' numerous attempts to force themselves into the leadership of the State, municipalities, and organizations had produced disturbances and strife. The *Hird's* raids had cost blood and misfortune. And the conduct of the occupation troops had time and again sent public indignation to such heights that only the utmost patience on the part of the opposition leadership prevented open revolt.

At the same time the home front had felt its power increase. Through common, united action the people had won victories that added to their self-confidence and to their hope that it was all worth while. Time and again the pressure of the opposition had forced the Nazi authorities to back track. This served to encourage new attacks.

On April 3 twenty-two of Norway's leading organizations had sent the authorities a letter of protest against a practice that the Nazis had introduced in connection with the selecting of applicants for civil service positions. The so-called Nasjonal Samling's Personnel Office for Public Service had been systematically overlooking a person's professional qualifications in their efforts to place party members in all public offices and positions. The organizations had called the Reichskommissar's attention to the fact that this practice was in direct conflict with his own promises that everyone could feel secure in his position, and that no public servants were obliged to join the Nasjonal Samling.

The letter was never answered. Therefore, on May 15, the protest was repeated, and this time the letter was signed by forty-three national organizations. This time the protest was expanded in such a way that it summed up all objections to the entire governmental administration since the beginning of the occupation. It was a letter of complaint, and it made no pretense of being diplomatic. But the purpose of the protest was not to smooth over the difficulties. It was an offensive over a wide front, a proof that the war in Norway was by no means ended even though the home front had no tanks, planes, or cannon with which to fight.

The language used was frank and unreserved. The letter stated in part:

It was with great uneasiness that the Norwegian people last September looked forward to the Nasjonal Samling's assumption of the responsible task which the occupation leadership had entrusted to the party, namely, to look after the civilian administration of the country under the supreme leadership of the Reichskommissar. The question which at that time was naturally asked all over the country was this: Will the party and the men who now assume this leadership build upon our people's ancient traditions of law and justice; and will they build upon our civil servants' honest determination to do their daily work conscientiously as they have done heretofore, exclusively on pertinent foundations and not upon the basis of partisan politics?

Regrettably, it is not to be denied that an entirely different course has been followed. The constituted ministers have in a number of cases issued decrees and reached decisions which are in open conflict with international law, with Norwegian law, and with common Norwegian conceptions of justice. . . . These measures have to a great degree broken with our laws' concern for individual security. . . . The *Hird's* conduct has led to disturbances and riots, and we have lived to see the police forced to remain passive in the face of obvious acts of violence on the part of the *Hird* in schools, in other buildings, and on the street. The last case of this type that we shall mention was the kidnaping of the director of Dikemark Asylum. . . . Further, we point to the constantly repeated attempts by the Nasjonal Samling to seize power and privileges for itself which in our judgment are not authorized. . . . We mention in this connection that the public servants of the State and municipalities are to a large extent being subjected to strong pressure in order to get them to join the Nasjonal Samling and that they are threatened with dismissal if they do not do so, despite assurances that no one shall be forced to join the party against his convictions. Loyal and conscientious public servants have been dismissed or suspended because they have not been in good grace with the party. We also constantly see proof that membership in the Nasjonal Samling has been made of decisive importance in connection with placements and promotions and that professional qualifications have been relegated to secondary importance. . . . Orders to join the party or to work actively for the party's progress, accompanied by threats or other pressure, will be taken by the overwhelming majority of Norwegians as a conscious attempt to make them compromise with their consciences and to veer away from that which they believe to be right and just.

It is plainly noticeable within all groups of the population that all this has led to a mounting restlessness which greatly impairs the regular daily work and thereby injures the country. The restlessness and irritation have recently been approaching the point of indignation.

It was this letter that Reichskommissar Terboven had lying on the table in front of him while he raged at the forty-three men and women who were assembled under German police guard in the Storting hall on June 18, 1941, for the signatures of these forty-three were on the letter. The Reichskommissar was fully aware that these forty-three persons represented a united people fully as much as had the one hundred and fifty Storting members who used to convene regularly in this very hall.

He knew—or, if he did not know it, his "specialists" could have told him—that the forty-three organizations which had signed the protest were powerful and still capable of delivering telling blows. And by scanning the list he could have assured himself that all the country's classes, trades, and professions were represented there. He knew also that when an organization bore a name such as the Norwegian Dental Society or the Norwegian Nurses' Association, then the word "Norwegian" in the name meant that the organization was nation-wide in scope. In a small country such as Norway there was no room for competing organizations within the same profession. There was no use in looking for two parts to play against each other. Every one of the names on the document before him obligated thousands, and in some cases tens of thousands, of individuals.

The list was long. It began with the National Labor Federation, which consisted of some 350,000 members. It continued with the Public Officials' National Association and the Civil Service Association. Then came the others: druggists, engineers, agricultural students, architects, telephone and telegraph employees, lawyers, doctors, teachers, nurses, clergymen, dentists, customs officials, artists, scientists, and so on. All organizations with members in the public service participated in the action.

And on May 16—the day after the protest had been sent— the country's eighteen provincial governors demonstrated their support by submitting a similar protest. Unanimously they demanded that the rules for appointment to public positions be revised.

Two completely different philosophies stared each other in the face that June day in the Norwegian Storting hall. They were as incompatible as fire and water. On the one side were power and compulsion, represented by Reichskommissar Terboven's lean figure and by the black-clothed, armed Gestapo soldiery. On the other side were the people—the living, breathing, and toiling people—who still believed, resolutely, in freedom and justice and democracy.

It was within four walls in Norway's capital that the two faced each other. Only a few feet of floor space separated them. And yet it was as if there lay a universe between them—a yawning chasm that no bridge could ever span.

Josef Terboven met the calm, defiant stares with eyes that were furtive, nervous. With his barklike voice he tried to break down the wall of contemptuous and ominous silence.

But the stares would not relent. The wall could not be crushed.

Reichskommissar Josef Terboven, Adolf Hitler's personal representative in Norway, the crusader for the New Order, stood face to face with the people. For the first time he had met the home front, the enemy which he had for a year been trying to crush, which seemed only to grow with every blow that fell on it, and which seemed to have boundless resources.

Was he thinking of all those whom he had ordered arrested and rendered harmless? Was he wondering how it happened that new leaders always turned up? Could there be an error somewhere in the theory? He had taught his subordinates that every show of resistance could be broken by eliminating the leadership and that the masses, as such, are inarticulate, that they can be shaped and directed by the one who gains control of the nerve centers.

Again he glanced up from his papers. The same staring, imperturbable faces. The same patient, irreconcilable silence. He straightened his shoulders, opened his mouth, and snarled.

There had been many stages in the Nazis' campaign to nazify the Norwegian people and thus win them for their own. It was a long, uphill march. One struggled on. Just one last rise in the road—then success! But at the top stood a new opponent, and beyond him was a new height to be climbed as soon as the opponent had been struck down. Then the same thing over again, and again. Endlessly.

The road became steeper and constantly more difficult to travel. The precipices more abrupt and ghastly.

On and on. Close your eyes and keep moving. Don't look down! For God's sake, don't look down!

But somewhere the road ends. Sometime one reaches the brink of the precipice, the end of the road. And then what? Should one jump? Or should one crawl back again?

There is no road back.

Terboven's words could not be mistaken: the Norwegian people had scorned Germany's open, outstretched hand. They had rejected all well-intentioned attempts at co-operation in a peaceful and tolerant spirit. A shameless and defiant letter had swept the very foundations from under *der Führer's* friendly attempts to lead the people along the right paths. There was no escaping the consequences.

"*Meine Herren!* I regret to report . . ."

All scientific groups shall be immediately dissolved.

All other organizations shall be assigned "commissar leaders" who shall see to it that the organizations are not used for illegal activity.

All public servants who have signed the letter shall be removed from their positions.

Once and for all there is to be an end to insults.

And, to begin with, these five gentlemen are being arrested and will be placed in solitary confinement so as to get a chance to contemplate their sins.

"*Heraus!*"

The occupying power set to work immediately. On the same day that the meeting in the Storting hall took place, the Gestapo appeared at the annual meeting of the Locomotive Engineers' Union. This was taking place in Valdres. The union's president was arrested while he stood on the platform, conducting the session. Shortly after the Gestapo had taken its prisoner away, the union unanimously re-elected him as its president!

During the days that followed all the others of the forty-three signers were arrested, one by one, and locked up at Möllergaten 19—the Gestapo prison in Oslo. But the members of the organizations were ready to take up the fight. They knew now that there was only one course for them to pursue—namely, that of scuttling their organizations before they could be used against them by the occupying power. As weapons in the Norwegians' own fight they had served well; but that time was past.

Norway's Farmers' Association was not among the organizations that signed the joint protest, but as far as this group was concerned the problem was already solved. After its president had been dismissed and arrested early in March, the organization simply ceased to exist. The Nazis were left with an empty shell. An organization without members is no organization. It is a name, but a name without sense or significance.

During the summer the Nazis' collection of such empty shells mounted steadily. As the Nazi-named "commissars" appeared, the directing boards of the organizations withdrew of their own accord. This action was the cue for mass resignations from membership. On July 1 the board of directors of the Norwegian Attorneys' Association resigned. On July 3 the organization's general secretary quit his post. A few days later there were no members left. On July 14 the Norwegian Architects' Association followed the same procedure. After it came others, like beads on a thread: the Norwegian Engineers' Society, the Association of Pastors of the Norwegian Church, the Norwegian Commerce Association, the Norwegian Justices' Association, the Norwegian Dental Association, the Norwegian Medical Association, the Norwegian Nurses' Association, the Housewives' Association, and all the others.

Postal employees were kept busy handling the flood of letters that poured into the organization offices. The letters came from all parts of the country, for these were not local organizations with only a handful of members. The nurses' group, for example, had 3700 members, all of whom resigned. The more than 2,000 doctors belonging to the Medical Association did the same, and so did the architects, engineers, pastors, and the others.

The reasons for the withdrawals were always the same: there was no desire to remain as members of organizations that would be forced to run the Nazis' errands.

The Nazi authorities tried to put a halt to the mass resignations by means of a public decree directing the main post office in Oslo to cease delivering mail to the forty-three organizations that had participated in the protest action, and ordering that all letters addressed to them should be returned to the senders after a fourteen-day period. The decree was a futile gesture. Within a month the action was complete. The authorities were buried under empty shells.

But they were also buried under vast wealth. All the scuttled organizations had been financially well off. They had their various funds and bank accounts; they owned buildings and other real estate. None of this could be saved by the members. It was spoils of war falling into Nazi hands. But the Nazis would gladly have forgone the wealth if they could only have got the members. It was the members they wanted, and they did not get them. Once again it was the single purpose holding true.

The country's provincial governors, who had supported the protest, were also ready to face the consequences of their action. Only six months earlier they had felt sure that the situation could be saved if loyal Norwegians could retain the local mayoral offices. That was when the Nazi authorities had attacked municipal self-government. Now developments had reached a stage where they themselves forced the issue. During the summer they were removed, one by one, from their positions. Upon withdrawing, they left the administration in complete chaos.

But they, too, had their eyes fixed on the single purpose which ran like a red thread through the ruins of the official system that they themselves had helped to build and protect.

7. LABOR IN REVOLT

NINE MONTHS HAD PASSED since that September day when the Nazis attacked Norway's largest and most powerful organization, the National Labor Federation. The coup had succeeded, but during each of the following nine months things had happened that served to weld the labor front more firmly together. The laboring class was the backbone of the people, and the invaders had not been able to break it. It was the workers and the people of humble circumstances who had been hit hardest by the occupation. Those with the least means were the ones who had paid most dearly through a reduced standard of living and forced labor.

The victory that the Germans had won in September was Pyrrhic. The Germans realized it themselves. Therefore on more than one occasion they applied the brakes to the Nasjonal Samling when the party sought to speed up the nazification program.

As for the Federation, it had exploited the antagonism between the occupying power and the Nasjonal Samling to consolidate its own position. The leadership was aware of the direction developments were taking, and it also realized that sooner or later they would lead to a showdown between the

Federation and the Nazis, probably an open break. Today it may seem strange that this break did not come earlier. There were, to be sure, powerful men within the Federation who disliked the situation and wanted to hoist their true colors early in the winter. This group, however, constituted a minority within the Federation as well as within the various member unions. The democratic processes prevailed. The same line had been followed ever since the so-called negotiations in the summer of 1940. The political education that the people had been through during the last hundred years demanded that all honorable means be given a trial before resorting to open battle. That was the line the Administrative Council had followed. And the Supreme Court. And the Church. And the University, the schools, the provincial governors.

There was no cowardliness in this. Nor was it a form of surrender. For a struggle had been carried on all the way, and resistance continued. It was only a question of means. The goal was always clear.

No doubt the occupying power profited from this situation in the beginning. It avoided the chaos which would have been the inevitable result if all Norwegian groups and enterprises had at once forgotten democratic procedures and plunged into open conflict. The Germans thus managed to maintain a semblance of orderliness in the administration and at the places of work. For the most part it had been the Germans who said when and whether a break was to occur.

But not all the gains fell to the Germans. The fact that the development was permitted to follow its natural course, and that all attempts to halt the nazification process by legal means eventually proved futile, completely precluded any divisions or serious dissensions within the ranks of the home front. The various common-sense solutions had been tried. The Germans themselves had supplied the proof that there was no use trying to negotiate with Nazis.

The Administrative Council had played itself out. So had the Storting members when they declared themselves willing to negotiate with the invaders. The results had been depressing. But the strange thing was—and to the great bewilderment of the Germans—that the home front had emerged from these defeats stronger than ever. The setbacks were in reality necessary to the united opposition, which had steadily grown stronger. The encroachments and broken promises had disposed of all possibilities of compromise, and the humiliations suffered only served to nurture hate and scorn for that which was proudly called the New Order.

The opposition had formed itself as a line of defense around all that had been created, built up, and held dear for hundreds of years—a defense that never yielded an inch of ground without struggle. And this opposition had scored successes, both large and small. The greatest victory was that the New Order had in this way been stripped to the skin, exposing all its vile and ridiculous features. In the eyes of everyone the picture grew steadily clearer, until an entire people was shouting as did the child in Hans Christian Andersen's fairy tale about the Emperor's new clothes:

"But he's naked!"

And naked it was. Neither written words nor spoken could conceal the ugly nakedness.

The meeting in the Storting hall on June 18 was the drop that caused the pitcher to run over. What happened there provided conclusive proof that open conflict was not to be avoided. And this time it was the home front that set the time for the break. The Germans were forced over to the defensive, and it was almost three months before they could decide on how to handle the situation. The organizations acted promptly and without hesitation when the crisis came. This held true for every one of the forty-three groups that had signed the letter of protest.

The National Labor Federation's showdown with the occupying power was of particular interest not only because it was the largest and most influential of the groups, but also because its break was the final touch of a long and irresistible development.

In common with all the other organizations, the National Labor Federation had to the end sought to safeguard its members' interests and property. The laboring class had greater interests at stake than any other. It had taken many years of toil and strife to attain the position in the Norwegian social structure which the laborers' organization occupied at the time of the invasion.

But the end of the rope had been reached. With right, the laborers were questioning the value of an organization that could not give its representatives even the simplest form of protection, that could not prevent such things as that which happened on June 18. For negotiators to have been arrested when summoned to confer with their opponents was entirely without precedent in Norway. It was such a grave breach of established principles of negotiation that there could be but one answer. The situation could not be tolerated.

The Federation had adjusted itself to conditions under the occupation as far as it found so doing consistent with the interests of its membership. But its efforts to co-operate had been met with broken promises and deceit, by encroachment after encroachment. Even the most cautious-minded realized that if the break were not made now it would be too late.

The underground newspaper, *Free Trade-Unions,* succeeded in expressing more clearly than ever before the workers' thoughts and feelings, when it declared:

Fortunately, members and officials understand the situation, and the Federation's members know what they have to do. The opinion is spreading more and more throughout the entire Federation that, in view of conditions as they now are, no honorable worker can refrain from severing his membership if he is to be true to his conscience. Therefore the policy of refusing to pay dues and resigning from membership is spreading like an epidemic in the unions and at the workplaces. This is right. The policy will be understood and followed by the hundreds of thousands who are proud of their organization and who, neither calmly nor unmoved, would see it fall into the hands of the Nazi mob. Rather than see that happen, they will apply their own hand to the matter. They know that some time the Federation will rise again and become what it once was: a free trade-union movement with the right and the ability to protect the lot of the working people.

That was how the National Labor Federation came to assume its natural position of leadership in the Norwegian home front.

On the same day that the meeting in the Storting hall was held, June 18, the occupation authorities demanded that the Federation appoint new presidents for those trade-unions whose leaders had that day been arrested. The demand was rejected.

The Federation then set to work preparing its plan of battle. On June 30 the cards were placed on the table before Reichskommissar Terboven in the form of a letter from the secretariat of the Federation. It stated that neither the members nor the various associated unions could adjust themselves to the New Order to the extent of sacrificing their own reasons for existing. The letter ended by saying:

After having carefully considered the situation, we have inevitably reached the conclusion that this point has been reached. . . . If the authorities cannot co-operate in providing satisfactory possibilities for the operation of the Federation, there will no longer be any reason for us to retain our offices.

The letter also included an unconditional demand that the arrested officials be immediately released and allowed to resume their former functions.

Simultaneously with the sending of this letter to the German authorities, tens of thousands of copies of it were distributed at workplaces, where union representatives and chairmen of the local unions explained the situation that had arisen to the workmen. At the same time the plan to refuse payment of dues was made known to all union men.

The Federation's decision to call for a final reckoning with the occupying power was received enthusiastically by the workers. To the Federation headquarters came thousands of letters supporting the leadership in the action taken. *Free Trade-Unions* was again the true spokesman of labor when it stated:

The secretariat has the support of all officials, from the highest to the lowest, and of all alert and loyal members. The organization's thousands of members stand as one man behind the demand that has been made, and they know what their duty is if and when the Germans strike. Nobody can say how our opponents may choose to strike. They may, as has been their custom, resort to arrests and dismissals. They may install Nazi commissars, and they may use this as an excuse for establishing, by decree, a "labor front" with compulsory dues, etc. But whatever they do, they will not succeed in breaking our solidarity. If the Nazis liquidate our free trade-union movement, the officials and members will be found outside the organization. No official, no member is for sale. No one is going to compromise. This is the hour of destiny within our organization. In this critical situation we shall all stand our ground.

No German reply to the letter was immediately forthcoming. But the Federation gave the Germans no peace; it insisted on an answer. The course had been laid out; now it was win or lose.

The occupying power proved evasive. On July 14 it notified the Federation that trade-union matters no longer would be handled by the Reichskommissariat's so-called "Social and Labor Department." They were to be the province of a special "Directorate for Labor Organizations," which was a subdivision of the Department of Social Welfare under the leadership of a Nasjonal Samling member.

The Federation had its answer to this ready the very next day. It was short and to the point:

So long as it has not been made clear to what extent the Federation will be assured tolerable possibilities for future operations, there is, in the opinion of the secretariat, no reason for the Federation to enter into co-operation with the newly created Directorate for Labor Organizations.

But still no reply came from the Germans. Obviously they were in doubt as to how to handle the situation. The establishment of the new directorate was intended only as a distracting maneuver. The purpose was to gain time so that they could get a better idea of what means would be the most effective in conquering the Federation. Eventually the new directorate was dissolved without ever having begun to function.

But the feeling among the workers, as well as among the people as a whole, was running high. This sentiment had been given extra stimulation by the fact that Russia had entered the war. People could see daily how the campaign against the Soviets had come as a blow to the occupation soldiers, and the new development gave fresh hope to the masses for an early end to the war with an Allied victory. New measures of compulsion aimed at the working people also contributed to the indignation. On July 12 the occupation authorities issued a decree providing for the drafting of workers for "especially important labor projects and industries"—obviously projects and industries important to the German war machine. At the same time workers engaged in a number of trades and industries were prohibited from leaving their jobs. The increasing difficulties on every hand—not the least of which was the food situation, which had grown steadily worse and was nearing the point of desperation—did not help to alleviate the indignation.

Under all this pressure the Germans produced their reply on July 30. The Federation's president and its legal adviser, Viggo Hansteen, were summoned to a meeting in the Reichskommissariat. Present at the conference were Reichskommissar Josef Terboven and Wilhelm Rediess, chief of the Gestapo in Norway. The Germans demanded an explanation of the Federation's stubborn attitude with regard to the newly created Directorate for Labor Organizations.

The meeting had a dramatic prelude. It began with the Reichskommissar's reading aloud a long statement in German wherein he called attention to the fact that the letter sent by the secretariat on June 30 had caused great annoyance. He demanded that in the future such requests be made orally, since letters might easily fall into the "wrong hands" and be used by the opponents of nazism.

This was another reflection of the Germans' indignation over the fact that the London radio was always so well posted. The secretariat's letter to the Reichskommissar had been read in full over the London radio, which always managed to keep informed almost up to the minute on everything that happened; it even broadcast the minute details of the various meetings and conferences.

The Federation's representatives stood firmly by their demands, although they were met with open threats. Terboven reminded them that he had the means to ward off any action by the Federation. There was a storm brewing, and the two labor representatives were in no doubt about the seriousness of the situation when they left the conference. That made it all the more surprising when, on that very afternoon, not only the arrested labor officials but also all of the forty-three persons who had signed the protest of May 15 were released from prison.

The workers interpreted the freeing of these people as a victory. Unlike their leaders, the workers did not realize the gravity of the situation and therefore deduced from the action that the Germans were giving ground. They declared that now was the time to strike. They demanded action. Bold and threatening language was used at all workplaces and in local unions. The spirit among the workers was aggressive and bitter.

But in uttering their threats, the Germans had been in earnest. Open terror was not far off.

IV. THE FIRING SQUAD

1. STORM WARNINGS

THEY CAME FROM EVERYWHERE. They came by streetcar, by bus, and by subway. But most of them came on foot. The July evening was still and clear, and a little exercising of the legs was more of a pleasure than a trouble. Besides, it cost nothing to walk, and in times such as these it was difficult enough to make the money stretch without wasting any of it on luxuries.

It was after six o'clock, but the sun was still high over the Holmenkollen heights. A ghost of a breeze stole in from Oslo Fiord and caused the trees of Frogner Park to sigh softly. It barely wrinkled the water of the lake on which the familiar swans still reposed in casual contentment.

The people represented all classes of society: laborers and businessmen, office clerks and light-haired girls, and elderly couples who for years had taken their evening strolls along the pathways of the park. They arrived singly, in pairs, or in groups, and they came from all parts of the city. They filled the walks and lawns and became a throng which gradually gathered around a central point—a statue of Abraham Lincoln.

It was July 4, 1941.

No celebration committee had summoned this meeting. The newspapers had not mentioned it. Nor had the radio. No colorful placards had urged people to attend. But from one place or another an announcement had been sent out. Typewritten on small slips of paper, it had been circulated among workmen and in offices, and it had been whispered from mouth to mouth.

People by the thousands and tens of thousands had obeyed the instruction. By seven o'clock the large and venerable Frogner Park was a sea of humanity. The evening sun forced its way through the leaves to add its warm rays to the wealth of color.

A man stepped forward from the crowd—just an ordinary man in a threadbare suit. Nobody knew him, and he did not give his name. Nobody uttered a sound as he jumped up onto the pedestal of the statue.

Then he began to speak. The man was no silver-tongued orator. The words he used were simple and direct; the calm confidence with which he uttered them gave them substance and power. He talked about freedom and justice, about democracy and popular government, about all those ideals and principles which Abraham Lincoln represented and which for hundreds of years had been part of the Norwegian national heritage. He was a man of the people and he addressed himself to the people. His voice carried far out among the listeners, and where it could not be heard the words were relayed in whispers to the outermost fringe of the crowd.

Then he raised his arms, and, gesturing for the others to join in, he began singing America's national anthem. Some of the people knew the words, others did not. But everybody knew the melody, and like a wave rising steadily the song surged, ever louder, towards the heavens.

Quietly the man vanished again in the crowd. He was one of the many, and there was where he belonged.

But Abraham Lincoln remained there on his pedestal. It seemed for a moment as though he were nodding approval to this great gathering of people, for he, too, was one of them— a man of the people.

All voices then joined in Norway's national anthem, and once more song crescendoed towards the heavens.

And at that moment the Gestapo automobiles roared through the gateways and into the park.

It was not long before fists were flying.

When Germany attacked Russia on June 22 the harassed Norwegian civilian population took on new hope. A year of encroachments and humiliations had produced a burning hatred for everything German; the news that Hitler had taken on still another foe made Norwegians more determined than ever to continue the resistance.

If the Germans ever believed that they would be able to use their war against Russia as a means of distracting atten- tion from their own actions in Norway, it did not take them long to find out that they were mistaken. If they ever thought their "crusade against Communism" would persuade the Nor- wegian people to rally enthusiastically behind the German war machine, their disappointment must have been keen.

The Fourth of July demonstration in Frogner Park, which brought tens of thousands of Norwegians together to observe America's Independence Day and at the same time to pay tribute to the ideals of freedom, was only one of many tes- timonies produced. It was probably not owing to coincidence alone that this demonstration occurred at the same time as a widely publicized Nazi rally in University Square. This Nazi affair had been advertised days in advance through the press, over the radio, and by placards, and yet it attracted a crowd of only 2,000 or so—including Quislings, German civilians, and the German soldiers who had been ordered to attend.

The Nazis had wanted the people to come, but the people had preferred to gather around the statue of Abraham Lincoln.

The German crusade propaganda was centered around the planned formation of a so-called "Norwegian Legion" which was to fight with the Germans against "the enemy of humanity and Christianity." The attempt to recruit such a legion met with utter failure, and in the light of previous bitter experiences the Germans should have known that it would. The first attempt to enlist Norwegian soldiers had been made as early as January.

At that time a so-called "Regiment Nordland" was to be formed, in order to give right-thinking Norwegians a chance to take up arms for the German cause. Announcements regarding the regiment were played up in the papers. Quisling, under bold headlines, proclaimed that in this way Norwegians would "win back their military renown." There is no doubt that the Nazi authorities felt confident of great results. This was indicated by the optimism with which they set about renting elegant offices in all the larger cities and employing huge staffs to take care of the flood of volunteers. But few, if any, volunteers appeared. They stayed away despite all the Germans' fat promises. The appeal for recruits stated that Regiment Nordland was to serve as a means for creating a Norwegian nobility, a real nobility that was to form the backbone of "the New Norway." All who volunteered and served a couple of years in the Regiment Nordland were to be assured large farms as their reward, and they were to be granted German citizenship along with their Norwegian.

Special emphasis was placed on attempting to lure young men by playing up the adventurousness of war. A decree was issued giving minors the right to join the regiment and to set out for the war without the permission of their parents. Students were promised academic advantages if they would join. When such measures failed to produce results, the age limit was raised in the hope that older men would welcome the chance to fight with the Germans.

The tremendous recruiting campaign was a complete fiasco. All together about 300 men joined the regiment, and most of these were drafted from Quisling's *Hird*. This meant that Norway would be rid of these ruffians, and no tears were spilled on that account.

A later effort to create a Norwegian section of the German *Waffen-SS* resulted in a similar failure. About ninety to one hundred men—drawn mainly from the thin ranks of the *Hird* —pledged their allegiance to Quisling and Hitler and thereupon donned German uniforms.

The campaign to form a "Norwegian Legion" was the third, and probably the last, of these attempts. It got under way just a week after the Germans had attacked Russia. Despite high-pressure advertising, it, too, collapsed.

Reichskommissar Terboven had himself launched this drive. After the experiment with the Regiment Nordland, it was plain enough to the Germans that no appeal from Quisling could start any mass movement. In a radio address, which appeared simultaneously in the newspapers, Terboven announced that *der Führer* had fulfilled the wish of the Norwegian people by agreeing to the formation of a Norwegian Legion which was to fight on the Eastern Front under Norwegian leadership.

"With all my heart I am at this moment with the Norwegian people," declared the Reichskommissar, "and my most sincere wishes accompany them on their march towards a great future." The speech was drowned out by an outburst of scornful laughter from one end of the country to the other.

But the Germans set to work with their customary and methodical aggressiveness. The propaganda machine was shifted into high gear. A few days later, when Finland was drawn into the war, systematic attempts were made to re-

awaken the sympathy which had gone out to the little neigh-
boring country during the winter war of 1939–40.

First the Germans appealed to the clergy to support the
"crusade against Christianity's enemy." The men of the
Church, however, were not to be confused. Of the country's
thousand or more pastors there were only twenty-six who
signed their names to an appeal in behalf of the Legion, and
these twenty-six names had long since appeared on the lists
of traitors published in the underground newspapers. The
seven bishops of the State Church, who happened to be in
session at this time, refused steadfastly to endorse the appeal
despite threats and pressure. Nor did an appeal directed to
labor make the desired impression. It gathered a dozen signatures, but once again these were names that had long been
black-listed. An appeal from "trade-unions and associations"
was taken for what it was—a counterfeit. The directors of the
unions and associations involved had not been consulted beforehand, and when they protested they were arrested.

To be sure, there was a good deal of sympathy and understanding among the Norwegians for Finland's difficult position,
but for the time being the people of Norway had their hands
full with their own difficulties, and therefore Finland's fate
was naturally enough of secondary importance. *Norway was
at war with Germany.* No peace had been agreed upon. Only
the legal Government could negotiate a peace. The Norwegians
were convinced this could never occur until nazism was
vanquished. German propaganda could not confuse the people.
They had long since become immune to German influences.

At this time the home front was more active than ever before. Among other things this activity took the form of extensive sabotage directed against all German military efforts.
Innumerable mysterious fires occurred in all parts of the
country. German warehouses went up in smoke. German
cables were cut. At the Gullaug ammunition factory an ex-

plosion caused heavy damage. The same happened at a plant near Kristiansund. Railway tracks were put out of commission. Street fights and indoor rows occurred almost daily between the civilian population and the occupation troops.

Underground newspapers flourished, and printed placards made their first appearance. These came into such extensive use that the Oslo police set up a separate department whose sole function was that of removing anti-Nazi posters.

Simultaneously the V campaign was spreading like wildfire throughout the land. In Norwegian the V stands for *Vi Vil Vinne,* i.e., We Will Win. The Vs blossomed out on walls, fences, and telephone poles everywhere. People greeted each other with the V sign; they whistled and sang the "three shorts and a long."

As a counterstroke the Germans launched their *Viktoria* campaign. People laughed at it.

German placards bearing the inscription "Germany Winning on All Fronts" were put up in town and country. The people of Bergen printed placards of their own which they affixed under the German boast: "Does not apply to Bergen and vicinity!"

The "Legionnaires" who ventured to show themselves in the street were regularly found the next day beaten almost to death. German soldiers, who had long been left in peace, now began disappearing in mysterious ways. Simultaneously persistent rumors began to circulate that an invasion could be expected in the fall. The frequent British-Norwegian raids along the coast put new life in these rumors.

The food situation, which had grown steadily worse, increased the bitterness towards the Germans. After a winter of scarcity the Norwegians had welcomed the summer with great expectations. They anticipated that vegetables and berries would add luster to their dreary diet. But after the war with Russia had begun, German plundering became still more thorough. Potatoes and vegetables, berries and fruit did not reach the Norwegian homes. These foods were confiscated by the Germans. Milk was also growing more and more scarce, and even fish was rationed in Europe's foremost fish-producing country.

There was a storm brewing, and the restlessness spread to the occupying power, which resorted to drastic countermeasures. The number of arrests mounted. The Gestapo was particularly active in northern Norway. Death sentences were pronounced and carried out, and a closer watch was imposed on fishing boats. Simultaneously so-called "factory guards" were established for industry; these were small groups of workers who were held responsible for any acts of sabotage that might occur.

But these German measures were not able to quell the optimism that was growing with almost dangerous speed. Towards the end of July of 1941 the spirit of the people had reached such a point that the Germans found it necessary to adopt even sterner measures. They systematically set to work to create the pier against which they expected the storm flood to crush itself.

The first warning came on July 31, when Reichskommissar Terboven issued a decree giving him "the right" to place the country under "a state of civil emergency" at any time. The decree was published in all Norwegian papers. It meant that the Reichskommissar was free, on any pretext, to leave it to the SS and German police to resort to court-martial to maintain or re-establish peace and order, without regard for Norwegian laws. The decree stated: "The court-martial pronounces the death penalty or life imprisonment or imprisonment for not less than ten years." Also: "Death penalties are executed on the spot by shooting."

The language and the tone were quite different from those of a year before, when the catch phrase was "We come as friends." Now the slogan was extracted from the old German song:

Und willst du nicht mein Bruder sein,
dann schlag Ich dir den Schädel ein.

In English: "If you will not be my brother, then I shall bash in your skull."

The moral was simple and easy to understand.

2. "DER HENKER" APPEARS ON THE SCENE

REINHARD HEYDRICH'S REPUTATION had not yet reached Norway. People knew his name and knew also that he was Gestapo Chief Heinrich Himmler's most trusted man, but his earlier accomplishments were hidden in the atmosphere of mysterious hush that characterized all Gestapo activity within the Third Reich.

It therefore caused no particular alarm when the man with the narrow, brutal face emerged from a plane at the Fornebu airport near Oslo one day early in September 1941. Himmler himself had been in Norway earlier. So had Josef Goebbels and other Nazi "greats." Usually such visits were followed by new waves of arrests and new acts of terror. People realized well enough that Reinhard Heydrich had not arrived on a pleasure trip. But they still had their eyes fixed on Wilhelm Rediess. It was the brain under his black cap, with its skull insignia, which up to now had been directly responsible for the Gestapo's brutality. And there were so many other things to occupy the thoughts these days. *Der Henker* vanished in a flood of uniformed "guests" without drawing much attention.

The day after Reichskommissar Terboven had issued his decree pertaining to "a state of civil emergency" another was made public. This was on August 1, and the new decree provided for the confiscation of all radio receiving sets in coastal districts. The Reichskommissar ordered that all radios in those areas be turned in to authorities by four o'clock in the afternoon of August 7.

This decree did not come as a surprise, but it was nevertheless a severe blow. The thrice-daily broadcasts from London were the last ties that the average man had with the outside world, and they had to an ever increasing extent become the high lights of each passing day. They represented the counterweight to the Nazi propaganda. They took the life out of the puffing headlines in the Nazi-controlled newspapers, which daily reported overwhelming German victories on the war fronts. They kept people informed of the Royal Norwegian Government's activities, of the Norwegian merchant marine's important contribution, and of the steady growth of the Norwegian armed forces. They were a constant source of new courage and new hope, and they assured the oppressed that their cause was not being forgotten. Excellently informed as the London radio was, it also confirmed for the people of the home front that the outside world knew what it was doing and appreciated its contribution. It gave the home front new courage and pride to realize that the world was watching its struggle.

But even though the disappointment over losing radios was great and the blow severe, there was still a bright side to it. Had not the Nazi authorities in this way made an admission to the opposition? Had they not voluntarily bid farewell to their best means of spreading propaganda, the radio? Had not the Quislings for more than a year been bragging that the mounting interest in the New Order was clearly indicated by their increasing radio audience? Why should it then be necessary to confiscate the radios? How would people be able to listen to the Oslo radio's Nazi propaganda from now on?

The Germans' task of confiscating radios was comparatively simple. For many years all broadcasting in Norway had been government-controlled. This meant that there was no advertising on the air, and, in order to finance the broadcasting, all listeners were obliged to pay an annual tax on their radio sets. In Norway it was impossible to buy a radio without at the same time registering as a listener. Whatever advantages this arrangement possessed in normal times, it was certain that in this time of crisis all the advantages lay on the side of the occupying power. The Germans had the lists of listeners, and each was compelled to account for as many radios as the list indicated were in his possession.

But the Nazi press had been paying too much attention to the London radio, and the home front had made its preparations. Thousands of illegal radios had been obtained during the past year, and on the very day the decree went into effect "radio newspapers" began to appear in every part of the country. These carried in condensed form the world news as broadcast by the London radio, and to make it easier for listeners to get the news on paper the broadcaster would repeat important items in concentrated form and at slow, dictation speed. Simultaneously the underground newspapers extended their activities to allow for news reports. Thus the Reichskommissar decree was to a considerable degree wasted effort.

But the decree had another and far more important aspect: it strengthened the rumors of an imminent invasion. It was the radios in the coastal areas that had been confiscated. What else could this signify but a fear that the coastal population would, upon instructions received by radio, co-operate with the invasion troops?

Other events of this period tended to confirm the suspicion.

The Germans were constantly striving to fortify their military positions along the coast. Large forces of soldiers were being removed from inland districts and stationed along the coast. Work on fortifications was speeded up. New planes arrived almost daily from Germany. Large cannon were set up everywhere that an invasion attempt was at all thinkable, and the patrolling of the skerries was much more painstaking. At the same time an increasing number of Norwegian fishing boats was being requisitioned and armed.

What was still more significant, a large-scale evacuation of the coastal population was begun. A new wave of arrests was in the upsurge. The evacuation was enforced with a hard hand. People were routed from their homes with little or no warning and without permission to take along more than their most necessary belongings. At Kleven, near Mandal, the entire population had to leave house and home and head for the interior. All people living near the naval base in Melsomvik were ordered to move. The same thing happened at Stavern, Ulvik, Hardanger, Laksevaag, near Bergen, and Orlandet, near Trondheim.

In order to speed up the evacuation the Germans in many instances set fire to farm buildings, and simultaneously large surrounding areas were requisitioned for use as airports. This was particularly true at Jaeren and Lista, in southern Norway, where about 400 small farms had to be abandoned in order to make room for German "military projects."

Not that these events had any depressing effect on the people. Far from it. They served only to increase the optimism. The rumors spread and grew, and gave birth to new rumors, new optimism. Plainly the hour had arrived, and people girded themselves for what might come. Weapons of which the authorities had no knowledge were polished and made ready for use. In the homes rucksacks stood packed and handy. Everything was ready. Quislings who dared to show themselves in public were soundly thrashed; speakers sent out by the Nasjonal Samling to appeal for peace and order were stoned. In the factories production sank to an all-time low, and the workers were talking big.

The Oslo stock market also reflected the optimism. Despite the fact that practically the entire Norwegian merchant marine remained outside Norwegian waters, shipping stocks continued to rise steadily. During the days following the Roosevelt-Churchill Atlantic conference they climbed 35 per cent. The Nazi newspaper *Fritt Folk* raged because "the Norwegian people so clearly indicate their faith in a German defeat."

On Saturday, September 6, bombs suddenly fell in Oslo Harbor. The attack came as a surprise to the Germans, and the air-raid alarm did not sound until the British fliers had finished their work and were on their way home.

That night the planes returned, and the German defenses spouted with activity. Searchlights sent their beams heavenwards in search of the night raiders, and the anti-aircraft guns barked. Mines and bombs were dropped on the harbor area, and a German tanker was set afire.

People swarmed in the streets, and enthusiasm ran high. This was the first time British planes had appeared over the capital since April 1940, when they attacked the Fornebu airport steadily for three weeks. When a new air attack was made on Sunday morning, September 7, people were convinced that large-scale military operations were in the making.

In the course of the night a British bomber had been shot down at Holtekilen, just outside Oslo. Thousands of people hurried to the spot to pay tribute to the daring airmen. Three of the fliers were saved, and these were taken in cars to the Baerum hospital. The ride was nothing less than a triumphal procession. People had gathered along the road with flowers and other gifts. Hurrahs rose on every side. German soldiers had to be called out to disperse the throngs.

The next morning, Monday, September 8, the newspapers carried unveiled threats against the Oslo residents for the manner in which they had conducted themselves during the raids. The Germans were perturbed over the possibility of new Allied operations, and there was no mistaking the spirit that prevailed among the Norwegians. It was at the boiling point.

On this Monday milk rationing was commenced in Oslo. The regulations provided that children and the sick should receive a somewhat smaller amount than what they were accustomed to, but that adults were to be allowed only what might be left over after the rations had been made. Beginning with that day the serving of milk at workplaces was to cease.

The camel's back promptly collapsed.

From week to week, from month to month, the living standard had been declining. The difficulties of obtaining the foremost necessities of life occupied the people's thoughts and hours. Lines formed in front of meat shops at four or five o'clock in the morning, and housewives were constantly on the hunt for food of any kind. As the tea and coffee had disappeared (in early September 1941, the coffee ration was ten grams a week), milk had taken their place in the daily diet. It was nourishing, and to a certain extent it answered the craving for fats, which had grown steadily.

But now the milk was being taken away. The people knew exactly where it was being taken. It was no secret that the munitions factories used vast quantities every day for the production of glycerin, and that unsalted butter was being used for grease. Indignation among the workers was intense. What was a workingman going to live on? Meat was not to be had, the fish was of poor quality and strictly rationed, and the sticky, black bread had no food value.

The reaction was spontaneous. When the workers received no milk for their breakfasts, they served notice that work would not be resumed until the milk was restored. It was the iron and metal workers in Oslo who started this spontaneous and unpremeditated strike. The employers and the workers' representatives did all in their power to provide the milk. But none came. The workers dropped their tools, stopped their machines, and went home. Large industrial plants, such as the Akers Mekaniske Verksted, which was under direct German control, were suddenly paralyzed by the workmen's action. Within a few hours all Oslo knew what had happened. The workers kept in touch with each other, and the strike spread from plant to plant. By midafternoon practically all factories were empty.

The next day, Tuesday, September 9, the workers were back at their places, ready to resume work. But breakfasttime came, and there was no milk. The workers again dropped their tools and went home. By now the iron- and metalworkers had plenty of company. Workmen at breweries and textile factories, printing plants and tobacco factories joined in the strike. Even office workers took part in the walkout.

German officers appeared at a number of factories and tried to persuade the men to go back to work. The workers listened to them, then walked away. Outside a number of plants German soldiers and Norwegian workers became involved in violent fighting. Many Norwegians were arrested.

The National Labor Federation and the various unions were outside the action. The strikes represented a spontaneous action of the workers themselves. They were the result of a bitterness towards the Nazi authorities that had been increasing steadily, and this indignation was undoubtedly stimulated by the rumors of an impending invasion.

But the Federation's leadership had, through its own bitter experiences, learned to know the Nazi authorities for what they were. The Federation leaders knew what means the occupying power had available for putting an end to the strikes.

They knew also that the Germans would not hesitate for a moment to make use of these means.

Early Tuesday morning the president of the Federation and its legal adviser, Viggo Hansteen, were summoned to a conference with Reichskommissar Terboven. The latter demanded that the Federation see to it that the strike ended immediately. The threats made by the German official could not be mistaken. The Federation's leadership was convinced that everything would have to be done to prevent the threats from being put into effect. A number of meetings and conferences were held during the afternoon, and with German assurances that everything would be arranged in the best possible manner the strikers yielded and agreed to return to their jobs. Work was to be resumed the following morning, Wednesday, September 10.

But in an office in the Storting building a lean man with close-set eyes and a weak, sadistic mouth had assumed command. The black uniform with skulled lapels further emphasized the pale, small face. Reinhard Heydrich, *der Henker,* issued his orders.

During the days that followed it was his law that prevailed, *der Henker's* law. In the evening of September 9 a state of civil emergency was declared in Oslo, Aker, Asker, and Baerum. The Gestapo had assumed control of the administration, and court-martial had been introduced.

3. THE WEEK OF TERROR

IT WAS a little before five o'clock in the morning, and it was not yet light. A gray, heavy September sky seemed to be bearing down on Oslo, and there was a trace of rain in the air. Or probably it wasn't rain, but only the last wisps of the mist that had lain over the fiord during the night.

The streets were deserted, and the blacked-out house windows stared like blind eyes into the gray dawn. Out to the east the morning sun still struggled vainly to break through the fog.

Then suddenly there was life in Oslo. Small patrol cars with armed German police whizzed around the corners and raced through the streets. Now and then they stopped long enough for a couple of men to smear paste on house walls with fat brushes; others would press freshly printed posters against the pasted area, and car and men would speed on to the next stop. This was the Germans' way of announcing the state of civil emergency. Later the announcement was repeated in radio broadcasts.

Other cars followed the poster brigade. These were larger,

and they were manned by fully equipped soldiers with helmets and fixed bayonets.

The entire police organization of the occupying power was in full activity. Like an octopus the Gestapo extended its tentacles to encompass the city. Automobiles roared through the streets; the brakes shrieked as they rounded corners and came to a sudden stop at a gate. Then the soldiers would hop out and vanish into the house. They hammered on the doors, and when these were not opened quickly enough they forced the locks. Men, half asleep and half dressed, were summarily arrested and dragged to the waiting cars, where the soldiers tossed them in like cattle carcasses and then crawled in themselves. With a grinding of gears the cars continued on their way.

Down in Möllergaten 19, Oslo's main prison, the Germans were in charge. The place was as busy as a railroad station in the midst of the rush period. Cars came and went, and there was no time to close the heavy gate from the time one car left until another pulled up with a new load. German soldiers stood on guard in the streets surrounding the prison. Machine guns were set up on the street corners. Piles of hand grenades lay on the walks beside the guards.

In the prison yard the captives were thrown out of the cars and herded through the long corridors, which were soon overcrowded. Each was subjected to a brief questioning. Then the prisoners were placed in cells, and, despite the fact that four or five men were stowed away in each one-man cell, it was not long before Möllergaten 19 was overfilled. It is not a large prison; Norway had had no need for large prisons.

The Germans took over all other jails in the city, and there were also two concentration camps near the city—Grini in Baerum and another in Hakadal—to which prisoners were taken.

The most dangerous of the prisoners were taken to the

Gestapo headquarters in Victoria Terrace where the Norwegian Government's Department of Foreign Affairs had been housed in the days of peace. The large buildings had long since been remodeled to serve their new purpose. Here Reinhard Heydrich ruled with an iron hand.

Within two or three hours the raid was finished. The hurly-burly traffic of police cars disappeared, but the street scene was still dominated by armed German police and German soldiers. Now and then an armored car, bristling with machine guns, sped through the streets, and motionless, helmeted German front-line soldiers were posted at all strategic corners throughout the city.

Behind the lifeless windows people had long since been stirring. For the first time in many months the Oslo radio was being tuned in, and thus the people obtained an explanation of what had occurred during the early morning hours. At regular intervals the following announcement was read over the air:

Reichskommissar Terboven has declared a state of civil emergency to exist in Oslo and the surrounding districts as of today. This step has been taken because communistic and Marxian elements within the National Labor Federation—and particularly the Federation's leaders—have during the past few days attempted to disturb the working peace by launching strikes. The German police chief, Rediess, has accordingly prohibited strikes. Inhabitants are not permitted to appear out of doors from eight o'clock in the evening until five o'clock in the morning. All means of transportation, with the exception of railroads, shall cease operating by seven-thirty o'clock in the evening. Restaurants, cinemas, and theaters shall close at seven o'clock. Meetings and demonstrations are prohibited. All radios in Oslo and vicinity must be handed over to the local chiefs of police. Anyone who displays unwillingness to conform with these regulations will be brought before a court-martial.

There was not much time left for the regular programs on the Oslo radio on Wednesday, September 10, 1941. At brief intervals the Germans thundered their commands into the ether. The Gestapo continued to operate just as drastically and effectively as earlier in the morning, although perhaps not so conspicuously. No home was safe, and no doors were left unlocked in the Norwegian capital that day. At any moment the doorbell might ring, at any moment a lock might be hammered loose with a revolver butt. Then someone would be taken away. Nobody knew why all the people were arrested or where they were being taken. They only vanished to an unknown fate. It was as if all evil forces had been set free simultaneously.

The workers were ready to leave for their jobs when the raid commenced. Setting out, they were bewildered by all the goings on. Just the evening before they had received the promises and assurances of the Germans, and on this day the strikes were limited to a few scattered places. In reality the strikes had been discontinued before the state of civil emergency was declared, and there was nothing in Terboven's decree to indicate that its effect was to be retroactive.

But even though the factories were quickly surrounded by armed German soldiers who mounted machine guns at all entrances, and despite the fact that according to the decree the state of emergency had been declared in order to halt these strikes, it quickly became clear that the real purpose was to deliver a crushing blow to the Norwegian home front, one that would finish it once and for all. Fright and terror were to be spread to all classes and groups, and the claim that "communistic and Marxian elements" were to blame was only an excuse.

Early in the morning of September 10 the directors of the Norwegian Employers' Association were dismissed and arrested. The board was replaced by a Nazi from the ranks of the Nasjonal Samling who for the time being was to take charge of the organization's interests. At the same time another Nazi was placed at the head of the National Labor Federation. In this way these two influential organizations were to be paralyzed.

During the days that followed the ax fell also on other organizations and institutions that could scarcely be accused of communistic sympathies. On September 12 the Nazis seized control of the University of Oslo, which had up to then been one of the opposition's firm fortresses. Dr. Didrik Arup Seip, head of the University and an eminent educator, was dismissed and sent to the Grini concentration camp. He was replaced by the "Constituted" Minister of Church and Education, Ragnar Skancke. On the same day the relief organization, the Nasjonalhjelpen, was taken over by the Nazis. Originally this organization was formed to direct relief work for Finland during the Russo-Finnish war of 1939–40. After Norway had been drawn into the war, the Nasjonalhjelpen, along with the Norsk Folkehjelp, had been occupied with aiding war-harassed Norwegians. Now the Norsk Folkehjelp was dissolved and its funds confiscated.

But the Nazis did not stop there. They were intent on a thoroughgoing cleanup, and no organization escaped. The Salvation Army could no longer be tolerated. It was dissolved, its leaders were dismissed, and its publication, *Krigsropet,* was suspended. The same thing happened to the Army's organizations for boys and girls. Dissolved also were the Norwegian Boy Scout and Girl Scout organizations, the Y.M.C.A. and the Y.W.C.A., and other similar groups. The International League of Norsemen, whose chief purpose had been to maintain contact between Norwegians at home and abroad, was taken over by the Nazis, who placed one of their number in charge of activities.

On September 10 radios in all homes had been tuned to

the Oslo station all day, and at seven-nineteen that evening the listeners received their first word of court-martial activities. At that time the following bulletin was read:

Höhrer SS und Polizeiführer, SS-Gruppenführer und General-leutnant der Polizei, Rediess, announces: The court-martial established in Oslo today has pronounced the following sentences:

1. Secretariat member of the National Labor Federation, Viggo Hansteen, to death.
2. Trade-union local chairman Rolf Wickström, to death.
3. Painter Gunvald Gregersen, to life imprisonment.
4. Helper Torbjörn Koppang, to fifteen years' imprisonment.
5. Lathe operator Toralf Kapstad, to fifteen years' imprisonment.
6. Lathe operator Ivar Saether, to ten years' imprisonment.

The death sentences were signed by me.

Since Reichskommissar Terboven rejected appeals for leniency, the death sentences were carried out late in the afternoon by shooting.

The announcement also contained a notice that the Nazis had assumed control of the Federation and the Employers' Association.

Immediately after this the "Constituted" Minister of Social Welfare, Birger Meidell, stepped up to the microphone. He appealed to laborers to continue their work. He emphasized that a state of war still existed between Germany and Norway and warned against acts that would compel the occupying power to resort to the sternest measures. Then followed the customary talk about bolshevists and communists who had through their agitation destroyed the good relationship that had prevailed up to then between the civilian population and the occupying power.

The Gestapo's announcement came as a shock. People had taken the state of civil emergency and the arrests calmly. Such things were not exactly new. But the death sentences placed

the events in a new perspective. To be sure, death sentences
had been pronounced and carried out previously during the
occupation, but up to then it was the German military authorities who had been responsible for the executions. The
earlier death sentences had been imposed for activities directly
interfering with the German war effort. Now it was the Gestapo
that manipulated the strings, and that set the picture in an
entirely new light.

When Oslo awakened the next day the city had changed.
It could not be recognized as its old self. Faces were sullen
and gray and troubled, and an impenetrable silence prevailed
in the streets, in offices, and at workplaces. There was no sign
of fear or panic. It was sorrow and bitterness that marked
all faces.

The spirit did not improve when it was learned that Viggo
Hansteen and Rolf Wickström had done everything in their
power to prevent the strikes. This made the Germans' crime
still greater. No one was in doubt as to why Hansteen had
been murdered. Although nominally he was only the legal
adviser for the Federation, it was he who had more and more
come to be leader within the movement against the Nazis. He
had been present at all negotiations with the occupation authorities, and his clear, young brain had plotted the course
for the opposition. It was to him that union representatives
would go when they needed help in a difficult situation.

Viggo Hansteen was one of the most promising young
lawyers in Norway. His academic record at the University of
Oslo was the best in the history of that institution. He spoke
German fluently, and time and again during the negotiations
he had proved that he knew more about German law than
did the Nazi authorities themselves. Intellectually, he was completely superior to his adversaries, and they knew it. He knew
it too. In confronting this clear-thinking man Josef Terboven,

with all his power, was reduced to the shrieking little parvenu that he really was. There is no doubt that the execution of Viggo Hansteen was an act of revenge.

The executions occurred late in the afternoon, and eyewitnesses have since told that, even in the face of death, Hansteen remained the stronger. When a Gestapo soldier approached to blindfold him and Wickström, Hansteen motioned the man away. Then he placed his arm around Wickström's shoulder and began singing the national anthem. The young laborer joined in, and they sang till bullets stilled both their voices.

That evening there came a heavy knocking at the door of the Hansteen home. The lawyer's wife answered and was confronted by two German soldiers. They tossed an armful of clothes and a small valise through the door. "These are your husband's things," said the soldiers. "He was shot this afternoon." Then they clicked their heels and disappeared.

Mrs. Hansteen was not permitted to see her husband, and no one knows where he and Rolf Wickström lie buried. All that remained were the clothes and the little handbag containing pajamas and toilet articles that Hansteen had taken with him when he was summoned by the Gestapo early that morning. It was customary to take along equipment for a prolonged stay (in prison) whenever one was summoned "to conference" with representatives of the occupying power.

On September 11 the Germans offered a defense for their actions in the columns of *Fritt Folk*. This was in the form of an editorial entitled "Two Salvos," which declared:

We find reason for emphasizing on this occasion that whoever has ventured to draw any bold conclusions regarding the humaneness and forbearance of the Reichskommissar certainly lacks a true understanding of German mentality. With German officials, as with all Germans, the claims of duty always cut straight through all human sympathy when the moment of decision is at hand. The Norwegian people have always been a compromising people. With our German brother-people there is no middle way. It is either . . . or . . .

Germany has been free to treat the Norwegian people as they deserved in view of the unneutral, hostile policy to which the Norwegians have adhered. Instead, Adolf Hitler has tried to win the friendship of the people of Norway. In this no means have remained untried. Germany gave our country the necessities of life and coal and saved it for a certainty from the danger of bolshevism. We all know what thanks the Reichskommissar has received for his efforts. It consisted of disgraceful demonstrations, insults, and direct molestation of German soldiers together with delight over every British bomb that killed Norwegians.

We stand today, Norwegians as well as Germans, under the iron laws of war. Norway's fate is closely bound to Germany's fate. If Germany goes under, we follow. If Germany wins, undreamt-of opportunities will arise.

During the following days the Gestapo kept on the move. Innumerable arrests were made, and the court-martial pronounced new sentences. On September 12 the vice-president of the National Labor Federation, Ludvig Bueland, was sentenced to death. Probably because Bueland had not been in Oslo when the state of civil emergency was invoked, and also because of the heightened indignation then prevailing, this sentence was commuted to life imprisonment. Long prison terms were being meted out on every side.

On September 14 two labor leaders, Harry Westlien and Josef Larson, were sentenced to death. On the same day Olav Gjerlöw, editor in chief of the conservative *Morgenbladet,* was sentenced to fifteen years in prison, and Frederik Ramm, another editor and one of the leaders of the Oxford Group Movement in Norway, was given a life term. A number of presidents of union locals suffered a similar fate. All of them were branded "communists."

Nearly 2,000 persons were arrested during this week of

terror in September 1941, and they represented all classes and groups of society. Besides laborers and labor leaders, there were businessmen, university professors, lawyers, and artists, men and women. The jails and prisons were overcrowded, and the persons arrested were subjected to the cruelest of treatment. A man who was arrested on the morning of September 10, and who later managed to escape to Sweden, gave the following account of the treatment accorded prisoners at the Grini concentration camp:

We were lined up and ordered to run up a hill immediately after we had been brought to the camp. The order applied to everybody, irrespective of age, ailments, or physical handicaps. While running we were supposed to sing Norwegian national songs, and the speed we made had to be "satisfactory." An officer had stationed soldiers all the way up the hill, and they struck us with revolver butts if we did not run fast enough. The officer followed on a motorcycle and took sadistic delight in striking everyone within reach. It was no ordinary dash that we had been ordered to make. We had to run two steps, then throw ourselves flat in the roadway, then rise and run two more steps and repeat the performance. At the top of the hill we were compelled to crawl on all fours past the German officers and soldiers. This punitive exercise continued for several hours, and many elderly prisoners collapsed from fatigue. The old prisoners in the concentration camp had to witness all this, and they had been warned that if they showed the newcomers the least sign of sympathy they would be placed in the dark cell or receive other disciplinary punishment.

When the punitive exercises had continued for two or three hours we were led into the prison, dead tired and low in spirits. But the rest did not last long. At one o'clock in the morning we were awakened and driven outdoors again. Then we were put through the same exercises again until four o'clock. We received no food at all the first two days. And all the while the German soldiers amused themselves by frightening us and striking us with their revolver butts. They showed the bullets with which they were going to "shoot" us. "Do you see this fine, sharp bullet?" they would ask. "It's a new type that we're going to try out on you. . . ."

The state of civil emergency lasted one week to the day. It was formally suspended at five o'clock in the morning of September 17. But on the day after that Reichskommissar Terboven issued two new decrees which in reality extended the state of civil emergency to all parts of the country. The first of these was to provide for "the safeguarding of business activity and peaceful labor conditions," and it stated:

Whoever disturbs or threatens business activity or peaceful working conditions by strikes, lockouts, damaging or rendering unusable industrial plants or equipment belonging to an industry by agitating others to act, by intentional reduction of working effort, or in any other way, will be punished by imprisonment or in serious cases by death.

The other decree established the authority of the "SS und Polizeigericht Nord" and extended the court-martial to all of Norway.

A few days later Reinhard Heydrich boarded a plane at the Fornebu airport just as inconspicuously as he had arrived. During the week of terror his name had not been mentioned publicly a single time. Nevertheless it was known that it was he who was manipulating the strings behind the scenes. He was the expert, the professional, who knew exactly how such a situation was to be handled. Many years of experience had taught him how to operate with arrests and firing squads.

It was Reinhard Heydrich who definitely put an end to the unsuccessful German experiment of trying to win the Norwegian people over to nazism by friendly means. He had turned a page in the book of history. No grass grew in his footsteps. Instead, wherever his foot had fallen grew the plants of hatred, thick and bristling. He had sown a seed which sprouted and bore fruit, the bitter fruits of hate.

Some months later when he met his fate along a Czechoslovakian roadway, his death served to strengthen those bonds that held the occupied nations together, the bonds with which nazism will one day be strangled.

4. THE LASH OF HUNGER

KARL JOHAN STREET, which is Oslo's main thorough-fare, runs from the East Railway Station, near the harbor, straight to the Royal Palace. Everybody in Norway knows this street, which is never referred to as a street, but merely as "Karl Johan." Midway between the railway station and the Palace is the Storting building, and midway between the Storting and the Palace is the University of Oslo, gracefully set back in a large, flowering park. Bordered by university buildings on three sides and Karl Johan on the fourth is University Square, which has now for more than two years served as stage and setting for many a strange performance by representatives of the occupying power. Here, on October 4, 1941, Reichskommissar Josef Terboven again set up his speaker's stand in the lee of the pillared hall of Domus Medias.

The square was decorated for a festive occasion, the German Thanksgiving Day. Flag poles had been placed and adorned with garlands. Large floral arrangements supplied a frame around the square. The swastika fluttered in the cool October sun. In long, straight, motionless lines stood the German soldiers while young German girls in national costumes hovered near.

A noisy army band struck up "Horst Wessel," and suddenly Josef Terboven mounted the platform. He spoke, telling again the same old story of how Germany had come to the protection of Norway, of *der Führer's* magnanimity and his earnest desire to co-operate, of the Third Reich's illustrious future as leader of "the New Europe."

But the speech also contained a warning to the Norwegian people, a renewed declaration of war against a nation that had been completely unable to understand the high-mindedness of *der Führer* and his representatives. The loud-speakers which were mounted around the square thundered the Reichskommissar's concluding words into the streets where Norwegians were going about their own errands. In brutal and shameless simplicity it was the *Herrenvolk* speaking:

"It is a matter of complete indifference to Germany and to the war Germany is fighting if some thousands or tens of thousands of Norwegian men, women, and children starve or freeze to death!"

Like a storm the shouts of applause rose from the listeners in the square:

"*Sieg Heil! Sieg Heil! Sieg Heil!*"

The German attack of April 1940 had found the Norwegian people unprepared and confused. The little nation of three million souls had no defenses with which to stand off Adolf Hitler's hordes. The Army was small and untrained, the Navy was far from adequate to guard the entire 2,000-mile coast, the Air Force was by no means able to compete with the legions of Messerschmitts and Heinkels that swarmed over the country.

Norway was not a military power and had never tried to become one. The mountainous, far-flung land posed other problems than that of building tanks and cannon. In a military sense the country was unprepared, but as far as food supplies were concerned it was ready. The war of 1914–18 had taught Norwegians once and for all what an easy victim of a blockade their country could be, and when war clouds began to gather over Middle Europe in the late 1930s the Government became busy.

Few countries are as dependent on imports as Norway, and in relation to its population the country carried on a very considerable foreign trade during the years of peace. Great amounts of grain and foodstuffs were imported annually, along with coal and coke, oil and gasoline, rubber, iron, steel, and other metals, and semifabricated and finished industrial products. Eighty per cent of the country's grain for flour had to be obtained abroad, and the fact that the country had had, during the years immediately preceding the war, a slight surplus of butter, meat, eggs, cheese, and other agricultural products for export was mainly due to the possibility of importing fodder. Agricultural production dropped catastrophically the moment it became impossible to import fodder.

The most important of Norway's products for export were wood pulp, paper and cellulose, furs, fish, and ore. But the exports did not nearly balance the imports, and every year the shipping and whaling industries along with the tourist traffic had to bring in nearly half a billion kroner in order to balance accounts.

With this in mind the Government had acted betimes to lay up a considerable stock of goods which might otherwise become scarce in time of war, such as grain, sugar, coffee, and other foodstuffs, and oil, gasoline, and coal. The stores were believed sufficient for at least two years if Norway, owing to a war, should become cut off from the outside world.

Besides the purely strategic advantages offered by the long Norwegian coast in the war against the Western Powers, there is scarcely any doubt that the main object of the German inva-

sion was to give Germany control of the Norwegian merchant
marine, the fourth largest in the world.

This failed. Only a scant ten per cent of the fleet was in
Norwegian or German-controlled ports at the time of the invasion and thus came under German domination. The entire
whaling fleet—the world's largest, and responsible for about
one third of the world's total production of whale oil—
escaped the clutches of the Germans. Nevertheless the spoils
gained in Norway were comparatively great. And the Germans
proved particularly adept at seizing everything they found.

Aside from the difficulties that arose during the two months
of open warfare in Norway, the civilian population noticed
little of the problem of supply during the early stages of the
occupation. A number of products had been put on a rationing basis even before the invasion began, but rations were quite
generous and the system had been put into effect chiefly for the
purpose of preventing hoarding. New rationing regulations
were not issued, these having been blocked by the Germans.
The Administrative Council, which had assumed control of the
civil administration of the country following Quisling's brief
period as Prime Minister in April, wanted to introduce rationing of a number of commodities. From the very start, the
Council was aware of the critical situation into which the
country had fallen. But the Germans said no. This may have
been partly owing to the German plan of seeking to "win" the
Norwegian people over to their side. Everything was to remain
as it was. The Germans had come as friends; the occupation
was a "peaceful act," and popular opinion was not to be
stirred up unnecessarily. Undoubtedly it was also owing in part
to the Germans' desire to give their soldiers a share in the
spoils. With their ample supplies of Norwegian money the
soldiers were to have the opportunity to make unrestricted
purchases in Norwegian shops.

But the decisive factor was certainly the Germans' confidence that the war would be short. It was not necessary to conserve. France was collapsing, and England was on the verge of doing so and would surely be ready to capitulate by fall. Germany would soon be wallowing in wealth.

During the first months of the occupation the system of plunder was not put into effect. To be sure, the Germans confiscated everything stored in Norwegian military warehouses, and that was considerable. By and large, however, that was the extent of the Germans' early plundering in Norway.

The first cream was skimmed off by the officers and soldiers, and they made a good job of it. To say that "they made themselves right at home" would hardly give an adequate picture of what happened. They came from a country where the people had preferred cannon to butter. And now they were suddenly in a land of milk and honey. Like a swarm of grasshoppers they swept over the land. The officers bought fur coats, jewelry, silks, and gold watches. The soldiers bought clothes, chocolate, silk stockings, and cameras.

They wrote home for money, more money. The rate of exchange between the German mark and the Norwegian krone gave the mark a far greater value than would have been the case normally. Never had the soldiers been anywhere where goods were so cheap. And the shipments to family and friends in Germany took on great proportions.

When it came to food the German troops carried on as if they had never before had a chance to eat their fill. In Oslo and other cities Norwegians were soon driven from the restaurants. Germans swarmed in and ate everything in sight. They ordered eight or ten fried eggs at a time, and cream tarts and chocolate were the true meaning of the term *"gefundenes Fressen."*

The Germans even carried their feasting to the city's parks, and it was a common sight to see them emerging from food shops with a package of sweet chocolate in one hand and a package of butter in the other. They would settle down at the nearest available spot, spread thick layers of butter on the chocolate, and eat it sandwich-fashion!

At first this frantic gluttony seemed only comical to the Norwegians. But as the results of it began to become apparent in the lines that formed in front of food shops and in the difficulties encountered in obtaining even the most essential goods, irritation and bitterness took the place of laughter. It was no longer amusing to see German soldiers "invading" large trays of tarts. It no longer provoked mirth to see the German officers combing the shops for everything of British origin and then buying it for themselves. In all its naked ugliness the situation was clear.

By the summer of 1940, conditions were already desperate in those parts of the country where the war had raged. Entire towns had been wiped off the map, entire villages lay in ashes. Large industries had been put out of commission. People by the thousands were homeless and jobless. The occupying power, which just at that time was preparing for an invasion of England, requisitioned a large part of the Norwegian fishing fleet. The fisheries were inactive.

It soon developed that the Germans either could not or would not fulfill their promises with regard to supplies. As the Norwegian stores of raw materials were used up or confiscated, industries were forced to close down, and additional thousands joined the ranks of the unemployed.

The merchant fleet, which in normal times brought supplies to the country, now stayed away from home ports. It was sailing for the Royal Norwegian Government in London, and it was the backbone and the shoulders of Norway's continued war effort. Its many and varied cargoes, however, were of no direct benefit to the civilian population at home. The country was shut off from more than half of its old markets.

The Administrative Council took steps to assure an adequate food supply for the coming winter. Parks and ornamental gardens were plowed and planted. Potatoes were to comprise the bulk of this emergency crop. Potatoes, together with fish, made a good and nourishing diet—though hardly imaginative—and winters are long in Norway.

When fall came, the Germans "borrowed" the 300,000 tons of potatoes by which the normal annual production had been exceeded. The efforts had been in vain.

Late in the summer of 1940 came the new rationing regulations. They were strict but not catastrophic. The average man received two kilograms of bread a week. That was little enough for the usual laborer, but it was still comparatively easy to obtain additional rations.

Next the Germans "borrowed" the larger part of the Norwegian grain stores, and the difficulties increased. It is true that the bread rations remained unchanged, but the quality of bread decreased steadily. The Germans paid back their "loan" with a small quantity of slack-dried rye which contained a large percentage of sprouting kernels. Later the flour was mixed with cellulose. During 1941 the rations were gradually lowered, and by the end of January 1, 1942, each person was being allowed one and four tenths kilograms of bread weekly.

Meat and eggs disappeared quite early in the fall of 1940. Since that time months have passed between each time a housewife has seen an egg. Norwegian meat shops had long been closed for all but a few hours a week. Cheese had disappeared. Butter rations, which in the summer of 1940 were forty grams a day, dropped in two years to half that amount. But these rations presuppose that butter or margarine was obtainable, which was by no means always the case.

There was plenty of milk to be had until Germany attacked Russia in June 1941. Rationing was then introduced, and a year later each person was being allowed one fourth of a liter of skimmed milk a day—when milk was available. Coffee, tea, and tobacco had completely disappeared. Chocolate was not to be had.

Fish and potatoes were long the salvation of the civilian population, but potatoes began to become scarce in the spring of 1941. This scarcity continued throughout the summer and fall, and by Christmas 1941 potatoes had also vanished completely from the markets. For a while turnips took the place of potatoes, but not for long. The turnips disappeared also.

Before the war, Norway was Europe's greatest fish-producing country, but the invasion led to immediate suspension of all fishing. During the fall of 1940 the industry revived somewhat. However, a large part of the Norwegian fishing fleet was powered by oil or gasoline, and the lack of these fuels, along with constantly sharpened German restrictions regarding boat movements along the coast, proved a tremendous handicap to the fishermen.

Despite everything, the fisheries have been maintained at least in part, and if, say, half of the production had been made available to the Norwegian people their food situation would have been comparatively good.

But the Germans had uses for the Norwegian fish, and they took it. It was estimated that about 90 per cent of the total catch went directly to the occupying power. Part of it was exported fresh to Germany, and the rest was salted or otherwise preserved at Norwegian factories, now German-controlled, or in plants which the Germans had erected since the invasion.

The major part of the herring caught was sent directly to the herring oil factories and from there to the insatiable maw known as the German war machine. Destruction of these herring oil factories had been among the most important objects of the British-Norwegian Commando raids along the coast.

As early as July 16, 1941, the Nazi-controlled newspaper

Fedrelandsvennen of Kristiansund contained the following news item:

Meat is not to be had in Kristiansund, and during the last days there has been no fish available, either. Yesterday most housewives had a desperate day. No dinner could be provided. And the situation today is just as critical.

In December 1941 the underground newspaper *Free Trade-Unions,* stated:

Potatoes are not to be had. The bread ration is inadequate. Workers are told to eat salted herring for lunch. Margarine is being rationed within the rations. Workers in the margarine industry have been notified that production will gradually cease, and that they had better be on the lookout for new jobs. Milk is becoming more and more scarce. Cheese has disappeared. Meat rations are being steadily reduced. Fresh fish is a rarity. Of eggs there are none. The workers are steadily growing hungrier. And then comes winter with its problems. Clothes are wearing out. The fuel supply, entirely in the hands of Germans and Nazis, proves wholly inadequate. Decrees providing for reductions and restrictions are everyday occurrences. There is no help to be got from electricity. That is to go first and foremost to the Germans for their barracks and other buildings.

The occupying power has found many ways of plundering the country of its foodstuffs. The requisitioning of canned goods, dried milk, condensed milk, coffee, tea, and such articles was simple.

It was somewhat more difficult to get hold of the farm produce brought to market daily. But here, too, the Germans succeeded, chiefly because Norway had built a modern system of trading centers. The Germans seized control of these centers, to which all produce was brought, and through them requisitioned the foods. Thus the enterprise which during peace years had represented a decided social advance became in the hands of the occupying power a mere tool used to drain the people. The Germans strengthened and expanded these marketing centers, always under the pretext that it would make possible a fairer distribution of goods. The result was that the Germans seized the lion's share for themselves.

It was only in the districts most remote from the centers that it was possible to keep produce from flowing to the market. This led to an intimate, underground relationship between town and farm dwellers, and this helped prevent hunger.

It was also becoming difficult to obtain clothes. The textile industry was one of the first to be hit by a shortage of raw materials, and it had to shut down. Then came the clothes-rationing regulations, more strict even than those prevailing in Germany. To buy an ordinary suit a man had to use up all his rationing points for five quarters (fifteen months) in advance. And what he got was a poor substitute, as far as cloth was concerned. Wool and cotton totally disappeared.

Before the war Norway had built up a fairly respectable shoe industry, but now this was entirely under German control. One example of what this meant was the fact that, shortly after they attacked Russia, the Germans requisitioned 500,000 pairs of sturdy "beksöm" boots—favorite footwear of Norwegians for skiing and other outdoor wear. Today Norwegians may buy a pair of shoes only after filing a special application. In the spring of 1942 the factories were making shoes with wooden soles and paper tops. Even these came under the rigid rationing.

An account of German methods of seizing industries could constitute a chapter by itself. The procedure in Norway was much the same as in other occupied countries. The Germans thought that the end justified any and all means. In some cases—as, for example, the great canning factories of Chr. Bjelland & Co., or Standard, Ltd., in Stavanger—the main owner was simply arrested and replaced by a German "manager." In other cases—such as that of Norsk Hydro—gentler methods were employed. The Germans, by pressure and connivance, bought up the Norwegian-held stock, confiscated that held by Frenchmen, and promptly assumed control.

The main idea was to gain possession of the property without paying out any German money. By the end of 1941 the occupying power had drawn about four billion Norwegian kroner from the Bank of Norway, and much of this was "invested" in Norwegian industrial enterprises. The four billion kroner, incidentally, represented nearly four times the total of the Norwegian Government's 1938–39 budget.

The Germans had also been pushing a far-reaching expansion of Norwegian electric power production. Thousands of Norwegian workers had been ordered to move from their old homes and to take jobs on the new projects. The object was to develop a vast German light metals industry in Norway. Owing to the shortage of materials and other difficulties, however, the Germans had thus far been unable to realize these plans to any considerable extent. Aside from this, the Germans had seized for themselves the entire Norwegian electrochemical and electrometallurgical industries.

In addition to the money confiscated from the Bank of Norway, capital for enterprises such as these had been readily obtainable through the control which the Germans exercised over Norwegian exports. Of all her old markets, all Norway had left were those within German-occupied or German-controlled territory. This "foreign trade" had been sorely simple to administer. The Germans made all the decisions; they decided what goods Norway was to export or import; they decided the qualities; they decided the prices to be paid or received.

The Germans had made no attempt to conceal their theories or purposes. In the daily paper *Deutsche Zeitung in Norwegen* and in the monthly magazine *Deutsche Monatshefte in Nor-*

wegen—both publications were started after the invasion—German specialists discussed in detail the possibilities of exploiting the natural resources of Norway. The articles were hardly to be considered enjoyable reading for Norwegians.

In July 1941 a writer by the name of Paul Herre indulged in some German dreams of the future. He declared that boundaries would have to be altered to correspond with German demands for security. "But," he said, "this matter of changing boundaries is by no means the most important." Then he continued by explaining how all Europe was to be reorganized socially, economically, and politically to fit the German pattern. This applied also to Norway. The living standard of the Norwegian people would have to be reduced, he said, to the mid-European level, which would mean a reduction by at least 20 per cent. The Norwegian fisheries would have to come under complete German control. The same was true for all Norwegian industry and shipping.

Up to now there had been little or nothing to prevent the occupying power from putting its ideas into effect—nothing except that the Norwegian merchant marine was out serving the Allies. With other Norwegian industries the Germans did as they pleased.

On September 2, 1941, a decree was issued in Berlin, and it led to a definitive phase of the occupying power's plundering of Norway. It prohibited future export to Norway of all goods the sale or production of which had been prohibited in Germany. Likewise it prohibited the export to Norway of all goods which could not freely be bought in Germany. The decree excepted only goods which it could be proved were of immediate importance to the German troops or the German administration in the occupied area. In reality the decree prohibited all export to Norway, at least that of food.

This decree came at a time when the "visits" of German

civilians to Norway had attained an overwhelming volume. These visitors had started arriving as early as the summer of 1940, but the real flood started in the spring of 1941. By the thousands and tens of thousands, young Germans and elderly ones flocked to spend their vacations among Norway's hills and valleys. No rations or travel restrictions applied to the visitors. Norwegians had long since lost their freedom to travel at will. The visitors came mainly from Hamburg, Bremen, Kiel, and other places exposed to British air raids, and authorities lost no time in providing them with places to live. At first summer homes, huts, and bungalows in the coastal districts of southern Norway were requisitioned for this use. Then the towns were raided for houses and apartments. In Oslo, Trondheim, Bergen, and other cities Norwegian tenants were summarily ordered to abandon their living quarters in order to make room for the visitors. These orders were categorical, and they stipulated that the Norwegians must turn their homes over to the Germans just as they were. The owners were not allowed to remove furniture or any other equipment. They were permitted to take with them only personal effects. The Germans had been careful in selecting the most modern sections of the various cities for the visitors. The owners were not compensated in any way, either for losses sustained or for inconveniences inflicted. Nor were they shown any other place to live.

The occupation authorities also saw to it that the visitors were accorded special service in the shops. At Jensen & Co., in Oslo, for instance, a special department was reserved for German civilians. It was always well stocked with goods that Norwegian housewives had not seen, much less been able to buy, for many months.

In the restaurants, too, the German civilians were entitled to special attention. This proved such a source of irritation, however, that the authorities eventually found it advisable to requisition a number of cafés and restaurants in the various cities and reserve them for German patronage. In Oslo some of the largest and most popular restaurants thus became German establishments with new German names, and no Norwegians were allowed inside the doors.

Among these visitors were numerous expectant mothers who were to spend the final months of pregnancy in Norway in order to give birth to new, healthy soldier material. An Oslo hospital and several buildings belonging to the Norwegian Agricultural College were in this connection converted into lying-in homes for the German women.

The German campaign against Russia led to a speeding up of the confiscation of all Norwegian property that could be of any conceivable use to the troops. The shipment of food and shoes to the front has already been mentioned.

When the fighting had been going on a couple of months and it began to grow clear to the Germans that the war would last on into the winter and that the snow would prevent the use of tanks, Norwegian farmers were forced to hand over their horses. In order to have feed for the requisitioned horses the Germans demanded vast quantities of hay. To get this, the occupation authorities sent out German patrols that called at every farm and saw to it that regulations were followed. The farmers' loss of their horses added a new handicap to agriculture. Tractors had long since been put out of commission by the lack of gasoline and grease, and a considerable part of the fall plowing had to be left undone.

Next the Germans cast their eyes on skis and skiing equipment. Not only did they snatch up everything found in shops or warehouses; they also required that large sections of the population hand over privately owned equipment.

On September 26, 1941, Reichskommissar Terboven issued a decree ordering the Norwegian civilian population to surrender woolen blankets to the Nazi authorities by October 3.

Punishment for failure to obey the order was to be three years' imprisonment or a fine of 100,000 kroner.

On October 15 came a decree ordering all Norwegian citizens, business firms, corporations, societies, and organizations that owned tents or tent canvas to deliver these articles to the Germans. In and around the larger cities it was also required that rucksacks be handed in. Also to be surrendered for the use of German troops on the Eastern Front were all privately owned windproof jackets or trousers, all ski pants and thick sweaters. The same punishment of three years in prison or a fine of 100,000 kroner was promised those who failed to obey this decree.

Still another decree appeared on November 29, and this provided convincing proof that the Germans had given up the last hope of winning the favor of Norwegians through their "good will" propaganda. This decree stipulated that "people who during the national emergency display laziness, indifference, or obstinacy, and who do not perform worthy labor, shall not share in the distribution of the means of existence and enjoyment in the same degree as those who exert their full working energy." Further, it provided for the issuance of "working cards" to be used in regulating the distribution of commodities in accordance with work performed. The nation was to be starved into submission to the New Order.

As usual it fell to *Fritt Folk* to make public the German comments. On the day this last decree was issued, that newspaper stated:

Today an unusually important decree is being issued by Reichskommissar Terboven. The decree is thoroughly National-Socialistic and is without parallel in Europe.

It is quite clear that Germany as the main provider and as the only helper in time of need also imposes its conditions and demands that the Norwegian people show a feeling of solidarity, thrift, and determination to assist in the best possible way to overcome the difficulties. We greet the new decree with honest joy, and we have the faith in our people to believe that they will not appear ungrateful, but will co-operate for the solving of a problem which is above all our own, namely, the unification of Norway. Those who *refuse* will have to take the *consequences* of their attitude and do without their share of available goods. Money and good connections will not be able to alter this situation. Parasites will not be given a place at the table. All Norwegians must choose between supporting the New Order or fighting it.

The open hand that Reichskommissar Terboven had declared he was extending to the Norwegian people in behalf of the German people only a year and a half before now firmly clutched the lash of hunger. The blows whistled through the air, leaving open and smarting sores which are never going to heal.

5. CAUSE OF DEATH: TYPHUS

THERE WERE TEN MEN AND A WOMAN. They had escaped from a German concentration camp in Norway and had managed to cross the border into Sweden. All eleven were worn out and deathly tired when a sentry on the Swedish side led them to shelter. Four or five thousand Norwegians had previously crossed the border in much the same way in order to place themselves at the disposal of Norwegian authorities in Sweden, so their arrival caused no sensation. At most it meant a new responsibility for the overworked Norwegian authorities, who already had their hands full. Taking care of four or five thousand men whose only desire is to get into active war service may at times be difficult enough in a country such as Sweden where communications with the outside world are so limited. Everybody wants to get to England in order to join the Norwegian fighting forces, but to get them there is more easily said than done, no matter how good the intentions.

But these eleven refugees were in a somewhat different situation than most others who had come across. For one thing, all of them needed immediate medical attention. All of them had been terribly maltreated, and it was only by mustering the last remnants of their strength that they had been able to reach the border.

Days passed before they had recovered sufficiently to be questioned. But when they were finally permitted to talk, these eleven persons opened the doors to a world so full of cruelty and horror that one might have suspected it could only be the product of a base and perverted imagination.

However, these eleven carried the proofs with them on their bodies. Lies could never erase the welts that had risen where lashes had fallen. The blue-green marks that remained where clubs and blackjacks had struck were real enough. And the eyes in those sunken faces still reflected the horror—a horror that can never be forgotten.

They were eleven living witnesses of the Gestapo's inhuman brutality.

Rumors had preceded the arrival of these eleven persons, rumors of cruel hearings in the dark cellars under Victoria Terrace, rumors of men and women being crippled for life or tortured into insanity. After the week of terror in September 1941, the rumors had become more frequent, more convincing. The underground newspapers described what was going on in prisons and concentration camps. But no names were ever included in the accounts; the papers explained that this was impossible because the victims were still in the hands of the Gestapo. So absolute proof was still lacking.

Not that anyone really questioned the truth of the rumors, or that they at least contained a kernel of truth. Terboven's revenge expedition to Lofoten after the Commando raid there was still fresh in the memories of the people. At that time about a hundred houses had been burned to the ground in reprisals against those who had aided the landing troops in their battle with the occupation soldiers. Hundreds of hostages were arrested and brought to Oslo for questioning.

Prisoners who were released from the prisons or concentration camps kept their knowledge to themselves. They had found out what the Gestapo was and is. They kept their mouths closed. But now eleven people had reached the other side of the border in still free Sweden, and the marks on their bodies provided proof of the truth of their accounts.

Swedish newspapers, which have loyally obeyed their Government's order not unnecessarily to invoke the wrath of the powerful neighbor to the south, found the accounts so creditable that they published them without reservations. The refugees had given their testimony under the obligations which always prevail when a witness is heard in a Norwegian court, and an experienced judge led the questioning.

She was a young housewife from Oslo, and she had been arrested at Christmastime in 1941. Her face was disfigured, and four front teeth had been knocked out. It was difficult for her to talk. Parts of her body were still black and blue.

She was a widow. Her husband had been sentenced to death and shot before she reached Sweden.

She was subjected to questioning immediately after her arrest, and the session lasted eight hours. All this time she had to stand at attention. Sometime during the night she was locked in a cell where she was permitted to sit on a chair. But every half-hour a couple of Gestapo soldiers entered. While they asked her questions they pointed a powerful flashlight at her eyes. At dawn she was led from the cell to a larger room where the questioning continued.

Her voice was unsteady as she continued her account:

The afternoon of the following day they locked me in a closet where there was barely room to stand upright. Gradually the closet grew warmer, and my legs ached. Then I lost consciousness, and I did not come to until I was being carried up some stairs by two Germans. I wasn't able to stand up. It was late in the evening by then, and I was brought into an office where I was given a little food and was allowed to sleep a few minutes. At four o'clock in the morning I was taken to another office, and the questioning began again. They tried to make me confess by threatening me, but I didn't say a word.

Then they ordered me to undress, and when I refused they tore off all my clothes. I stood there naked. One German held me while others kicked and struck me. Afterwards they made me march back and forth while they forced me to beg forgiveness in German and Norwegian because I had lied. They insisted I had confessed while I lay unconscious in the closet. That was a lie.

He was a young policeman from Oslo, and he had been arrested in the spring of 1941. On the day of his arrest he was taken to Victoria Terrace for questioning by the Gestapo. The grilling lasted nine hours without interruption. Present were Gestapo agents Fehmer and Hoehler and two other Germans.

Fehmer drew a revolver and said I would be shot if I didn't confess. He had a blackjack lying beside him on the table. Throughout the time I was being questioned the Gestapo agents sat around me smoking cigarettes and eating chocolate. I said nothing. Just before the session ended, Fehmer struck me across the mouth with the blackjack so that I lost four teeth. Later I got an infection in my jaw. But I didn't get dental care until six months later, and by that time the infection had spread so that 12 teeth had to be pulled.

In prison the former policeman had met an elderly businessman who had been struck in the face with clenched fists, hit over the head with a chair, and also kicked in the stomach.

His eyes were still bloodshot from the blows, and his head was badly swollen. I had to shave him, because he was unable to raise his arms.

The witness had also seen another prisoner who had been beaten during a questioning, and who had to have others help him when he wanted to wash himself or eat. The prisoner was scarcely able to talk, and he also suffered from cancer. Four of his fingers were broken, three on one hand and one on the other. On two of the fingers the nails had been pulled out. It was the Gestapo agents Fehmer, Hoehler, and Bernard who had had him in their treatment. They had also pummeled him with blackjacks until he fainted. And while he lay helpless on the floor they had jumped on his stomach, causing blood to emerge from both his mouth and his rectum. The prisoner himself believed that the flow of blood was caused by the reopening of the cancer.

Another of the refugees had also seen this prisoner.

I talked with him after they had brought him back to his cell. I went in there to take him food. By then he had collapsed completely and was begging the guard for a chance to confess. He was being taken back for a new questioning, but the moment he got out of the cell, which was on the second floor, he made a dash for a window in order to leap out. It was obvious that he had lost his mind. The guards got hold of him and dragged him back to his cell. I could hear the way he cried, and it was heart-rending. Later it became a matter of course that the guards took turns at entering his cell and beating him. Later on he didn't even cry. He only stood there, mumbling over and over: "Isn't Father coming soon?"

Six of the eleven refugees had met the prisoner called Y. B. in the Gestapo prison at Möllergaten 19 in Oslo. One of them recalled:

I saw Y. B. after he had been questioned. He was in bed and one cheek was torn and bleeding freely. One leg was badly swollen and looked like a chunk of raw meat. He had a broken rib and was blue, yellow, and red all over his body and head. He had asked the Gestapo to take him to a doctor but had received only abuse in reply.

The following day he was being taken back to the questioning cell but fainted on the way and had to be carried back to his cell. Shortly after I brought food to his cell. He was lying on the cot and a couple of Gestapo agents were questioning him. They weren't sober.

One after the other the refugees were brought in to give their accounts of what they had experienced. The testimony was recorded in full by stenographers. The judge, himself a refugee, led the questioning. The refugees spoke slowly and in low voices. The realization that they were free, that they had escaped from the hell of the Gestapo terror, had not yet fully dawned on them. On the judge's table lay no revolver. No uniformed guards stood near the doors. There was bright daylight in the room. Nobody harassed them. Nobody threatened them. They talked freely. Most of them had relatives in Norway, but they knew their names would not be revealed. Gradually they cast aside caution.

One of the fugitives, who had been arrested on suspicion of espionage, related the case of an elderly man from Oslo:

His cell was next to mine, but he had been at Möllergaten 19 several months when I was arrested.

One night in October I was awakened about two or three o'clock and was ordered into the corridor. It was half dark out there, and a man was lying on a leather sofa. At first I thought he was intoxicated, because he didn't stir and his clothes were sopping wet. He smelled bad, too. But when I looked at him more closely I understood what had happened. I helped the guard carry the man to his cell, where we laid him on his cot and left him there with his clothes on. The next morning I went over to have a look at him. He was conscious, then, but was entirely helpless. His entire body was stiff and sore; he couldn't eat; he could not lift a finger. He told me what had happened.

At ten-thirty in the evening he had been taken to Gestapo headquarters at Victoria Terrace for questioning. He had been led straight to a room where six Gestapo agents sat waiting for him. Among them were Fehmer, Hoehler, and Bernard.

Only one question was asked. When he answered negatively, he was accused of lying. The Gestapo made him sit down on a stool, and two of the Germans struck him with clubs while a third kicked him in the legs and cuffed him with his fists. When he fell from the stool under all the blows he was ordered to resume the seat, but while he was trying to drag himself up the agents struck him with clubs over the hands and arms.

"I had got only halfway up when I fainted," the man said. "They dumped a bucket of water over me and I regained consciousness. While I was trying to get up, they continued to strike me. One time Hoehler missed me and hit the stool instead; it was smashed to bits. A new stool was brought in, but I was still unable to get up. Then Hoehler grabbed the stool and struck me across the chest with it so that I fainted again. Once more they poured water on me.

"While I lay on the floor they twisted my nose and ears. After that they thumped my head against the floor. Another prisoner was brought in to watch, and he had to stay there during the rest of the session. They continued to strike me while I lay on the floor, and a couple of them who had no clubs kicked me wherever it suited them. I fainted for the third time. When I came to, Fehmer kicked me in the stomach while Hoehler pulled my shoes off and clubbed me across the soles of my feet. Bernard grabbed me by the hair and pulled me across the room. All the while a fourth German stood there shouting: 'Tell the truth, you damned pro-English crook!' After that they began heating wires over an open flame and said they were going to stick the red-hot wires under my fingernails. Then I lost consciousness for the fourth time, or made believe I did. I couldn't stand it any longer.

"I was thrown into a small adjoining room while the Germans held a council of war. A little while later Fehmer came in to see whether I was still unconscious. He kicked me so that I rolled over several times. Soon another man entered; each grabbed one of my legs and then pulled me across the room and down the stairs from the fourth floor. The back of my head kept pounding against the steps. When we got down, they dumped me into a car, where Fehmer said: 'He belongs in a hospital, but toss the swine off at No. 19.' That was how I got back here."

The last time I saw the man was three weeks after his visit to Victoria Terrace, and he was still unable to leave his cot. He needed help for everything. When I left the prison, the entire right side of his body was still paralyzed.

Three other refugees told of a prisoner at the Grini concentration camp in whom the Germans seemed to be particularly interested. They regarded him as a dangerous man.

One of them recalled:

The prisoner had been kept in a dark cell, and he was treated terribly. I talked with him once through the keyhole. I could barely see him lying on a bench in the middle of the cell. He was bandaged so that only his nose was visible. Hoehler had struck him across the arm with a club so that the bone had been crushed, and after that the Germans had poked red-hot wires under his fingernails.

When I asked him about it, he answered: "It was worst during the first hours, but fortunately I was unconscious during the last three or four hours so I noticed nothing."

He said they had twisted one of his legs all the way around, and had whipped and pounded him over his entire body.

"I'll never come out of this alive," he said. "Either I'll be shot or, I hope, I'll die on their hands."

My personal opinion is that the Germans will never let him out alive. He had been so maltreated that they wouldn't want it to become known. Kneller, the Gestapo agent who questioned me, said they had ways of making me talk and that I shouldn't figure on being alive after the treatment. He said they preferred that people who had seen the happenings in prison remain silent.

Fourteen days after I had talked with the man through the keyhole I saw him being carried out and placed in a German ambulance. He was so well covered that no one could see whether he was alive or dead.

The hearing of the refugees in Sweden lasted several days, and gradually the pieces were put together to form a comprehensive picture of German prison methods.

Soon afterwards came reports from Norway that confirmed the accounts given. Two Norwegian journalists, Erling Pedersen of Drammen and Henry W. Kristiansen of Oslo, died at Möllergaten 19. Relatives were never permitted to see the bodies. The Germans announced the cause of death to be typhus.

Lieutenant Kristian Aubert, one of Norway's most famous ski jumpers, was arrested and locked up in Möllergaten 19. He was subjected to torture for almost a week. Apparently the Germans thought that he knew something. After a week's imprisonment, Aubert died.

Tor Salvesen, also one of the country's foremost athletes, was arrested because he had concealed a friend in his home and would not tell what had become of him. He was arrested about the same time as Aubert, and, like Aubert, he failed to survive the torture more than a week.

The Germans announced officially that Aubert had died of "pneumonia with a blood clot," and Salvesen of "stomach ulcers with respirational difficulties."

But the families were never permitted to view the bodies. However, a few days later they received bags of ashes from the Gestapo along with a message that the cremation had taken place. And with each bag of ashes came a bill for 100 marks "to cover expenses."

6. THE PEOPLE'S GOVERNMENT

THE FEAR AND PANIC which the occupying power thought it could create through the state of civil emergency in September 1941 never materialized.

To be sure, the wave of hope and optimism that had swept over the land was crushed to froth and foam against the wall of violence and torture on which Reinhard Heydrich and his colleagues had ensconced themselves. But a new wave was already rising on the horizon. It grew slowly but surely into a mighty tidal wave that rolled forward untamably. The German reverses on the Eastern Front speeded it, and the United States' entry into the war gave it power which the home-front leadership succeeded in keeping under control only with the greatest of difficulty.

The occupying power, on its side, had made its choice and resorted to the only means it knows when it comes to holding a people in check: terror and more terror.

Although the state of civil emergency had not succeeded in taming the spirit of the people or in creating fear and panic, it had nevertheless accomplished one thing: the iron fist of the occupying power had smashed to pieces the fine network of underground connections that had tied the home front together. First, it was the German technique of mass arrests that produced results. The home front lost many of its most valuable leaders, people who during a year and a half of occupation had mastered the art of conspiracy. The Germans had cast out a net, and the catch was bounteous. It made no difference to the occupying authorities if the Gestapo "fishermen" could not tell the big ones in the net from the little ones. The result was the main thing. Everybody arrested was locked up and rendered harmless. If the concentration camps became crowded it was an easy matter to set up additional ones.

The prohibition against the owning of radio receiving sets had been extended to include the whole country. To the home front this meant the loss of one of its chief sources of encouragement. This, together with the fact that the duplicating equipment of most of the "illegal" newspapers had been seized or destroyed, temporarily retarded any large-scale underground work.

But more important than all the foregoing was the fact that nothing came of the invasion which everyone had been expecting. This was a tremendous disappointment. During the early stages, when reports of German victories in Russia dominated the foreign news, faith in the Allied Powers' strength sank dangerously.

People had been so sure that an invasion was coming. They had reconciled themselves to the sufferings and misfortunes which a new war on Norwegian soil would surely introduce. All the destroyed towns and villages still lay as unpleasant reminders of what had happened in the spring of 1942.

But what good was a house if no one could feel safe inside its doors? What good was a town when no one could feel safe on its streets? The Norwegians stood ready to welcome their liberators and to lend them all possible aid, no matter what the cost.

The feeling of having been forgotten which gradually took hold of the people was far more dangerous than all German propaganda. Large as Norway is, with its widely scattered population, people generally had a feeling of carrying the whole burden alone. This feeling was accentuated when the radios and underground papers disappeared, when travel restrictions were extended, and when curfews became more and more frequent.

Every little home in the valleys and along the coast became a little world by itself, a world which hurtled along its own dizzying course through a dark and endless existence. Considerably weakened was the sense of solidarity which had up to then been the main source of everybody's strength. People had lost contact with one another. Their connection with the outside world—the news broadcasts from London—was cut off.

Beyond that little circle of light, the individual's private existence, was the dark, and out in the dark the Gestapo reigned supreme.

Never during the entire period of occupation had the pressure on the individual been so great as during the fall months of 1941. Another winter was at hand, long months of hunger and loss and black-outs. Spring seemed endlessly far away—spring, with its bright days and silvery gray nights. Hope was far, far off—the hope of liberation, peace, and happiness.

Hidden somewhere in the past was a pale memory of days when the Gestapo, concentration camps, and executions were things one read about in books, when war was exciting entertainment at the cinemas, and when hunger and privation were strange concepts.

It was like living in a tunnel. Far, far behind could be seen a bit of daylight where the entrance was. But around about and ahead were only darkness and cold. And one had to go on through the dark. Only one's thoughts could turn back.

Hopelessness held sway. But in all these little worlds hidden forces were seething and seeking escape, for no power in the world could shut in the hatred for the invaders. They were forces of nature which could not be kept in check.

In a thousand different ways these forces found the escape they sought. Censorship and oppression sharpened men's inventive genius. Germans found road signs turned around so that they pointed the wrong way. They found their automobile tires punctured. They found that someone had added water to their gasoline, that the fish they stole tasted of paraffin, that boats which they thought firmly tied broke loose and drifted away in the darkness of the night. On roadways, fences, and walls appeared huge Vs with extra inscriptions that told plainly what was on Norwegian minds.

They forced people to wash off the inscriptions, selecting prominent citizens to do the work. No sooner had night fallen than the patriots were at it again. By morning all the inscriptions had been restored.

A German soldier marches back and forth on a wharf in a small town in southern Norway. The iron heels clatter on the cobblestones. Back and forth, back and forth. A dark shadow steals forward along the wall of a shed. A stifled cry. Some scuffling in the dark. A splash in the sea. No more heels clattering on the cobblestones.

The roar of planes far out over the horizon. It comes nearer. Soon the engines are thundering directly overhead. Shouts and commotion from the German barracks. Cursing and turmoil and curt commands. But nothing happens until the bombs fall with deafening explosions on the airport. No searchlights. No firing from the anti-aircraft guns. Someone has cut the cables leading to the batteries. The planes swoop over the airport several times, then head out to sea again. Somewhere in the hills Morse code signals are transmitted by flashlight.

Ålesund is fined 100,000 kroner, Haugesund 50,000, Stavanger 2,000,000. The Germans call it a "war tax," demand it in reprisal for the "unruly conduct" of the people. And the fines are paid promptly.

The following night the cables are cut anew.

Trondheim is fined 60,000, Bergen 100,000.

The money is paid, but nothing changes.

At a west coast town the Germans decide to seize hostages. Local officials are asked to prepare a list of twenty-five persons. These shall with their lives be held responsible for the ending of sabotage.

The list is ready almost immediately. On it are the names of all the Quislings in the town.

The following night a German ship is set afire in the harbor, and before daybreak it is a sunken wreck.

The hostages are seized and taken away. The town breathes more easily. At least the Quislings have been put out of sight for a while.

When the orders to turn in all radio sets were received, there was little to do but obey. The Germans had lists of all who owned radio sets. If a set was not surrendered voluntarily, the Germans would come and get it.

But not all the radios were necessarily gone for good. In Bergen, for instance, a large building was being used for the storing of confiscated radios. One night the doors were forced open and a large number of radios disappeared—nobody knew where.

When people were ordered to turn in their woolen blankets, rucksacks, sweaters, ski pants, and tents, human ingenuity again came into play. Nobody had lists of people owning such articles. A father's ski pants or sweaters could be quickly remade into boys' clothes. Many people simply burned up their blankets and rucksacks rather than see them fall into German hands.

But the Germans meant one thing that they had said. The courts-martial operated overtime. The firing squads were busy: at Oslo, Bergen, Stavanger, Ålesund—Karl Engen, a construction worker; Tönnes Winther, a merchant; Johan Olsen, a miner; Rolf Lea, a business leader; Sigurd Johannesen, a telegrapher; Bjarne Langseth, a laborer; Ingvald Garbo, a teacher; Andreas Bertnes, a student . . .

Day by day the list of those executed grows.

Simultaneously the arrests continue.

A man spits as a German passes by. Three years in prison. Another hums the "King's Song" on the street. Five years in prison. A third is caught with an underground newspaper in his pocket. For him, a concentration camp in Germany.

The queues in front of the meat markets seemed endless. Housewives were abroad long before daylight, but their baskets were almost as empty when they returned late in the morning as they had been when they set out.

The children were growing pale and gaunt, and their parents were deeply distressed. They were ready to face any hardship themselves, but to see the children suffer . . .

On December 1 the authorities made plans to raid private homes for food. "The food is gone," they said. "It must be somewhere." The small stores found in homes here and there were confiscated and the owners were arrested.

But the seizures produced no change for the better in the food shortage. Everybody remained as hungry as before.

Industrial production decreased steadily. The Germans raged. Now and then workers were arrested for sabotage. With a shrug of the shoulders they allowed themselves to be led away. There was no need any more to loaf on the job in order to slow up production. The black, sticky bread and the substitute coffee could not satisfy the hunger of workingmen, who were no longer physically able to put the same energy into their jobs as of old, even if they had wanted to.

But appearances had to be kept up. The Nazi-controlled papers published reports and statistics to prove that unemployment had disappeared and that the living standard had been maintained. People were no longer reading the papers, however, at least not the "legal" ones. The time had passed when the brief, hidden-away items carried a kernel of truth. Newspapermen had been able to stave off the New Order, at least in part, for an unbelievably long time, but at last they, too, had to give up. One newspaper after the other had suspended publication, and those that remained had gradually lost many of their best men. It was not permitted for a newspaperman to quit his job, so there was no other choice. No other profession in Norway is as well represented in the concentration camps as that of the newspapermen.

Beneath the surface the work goes on. Little by little new leaders have risen to take the places of those arrested. The underground newspapers reappear, more lively and alert than ever before. And the news from the outside world is also better. The German advance into Russia is halted; even the "legal" papers admit this. The underground newspapers supply the details of Russian resistance.

Hope increases, and the wave swells.

Then America entered the war.

The effect was tremendous. Nearly everyone had almost given up hope that the United States would actively join forces with the fighting democracies. It had taken so long. The wait had been so endless. But now it had happened.

What if the path ahead was long and hard? What if many sufferings and humiliations still remained? Perhaps many countrymen would still have to give their lives, and it may be that more towns and cities would have to be reduced to ruins.

The war had been won—definitely.

Far, far ahead in the tunnel a faint light had appeared.

The state of civil emergency and the events preceding it had resulted in the destruction of the administrative machinery of the large organizations. All of them, from the National Labor Federation on down through the list, were in Nazi hands. The headquarters and local offices were occupied by people willing to run the Germans' errands.

But an organization without members, or whose members think only in terms of opposition and sabotage, is no longer an organization. It can accomplish nothing unless the members support it, for the organization *is* the members, and the members cannot be conquered. They can be killed, imprisoned, or otherwise rendered harmless, but as long as they live and breathe outside the walls of the concentration camps they are still, all together, an organization.

The Nazis had torn the many bonds that had held the members together, and it was a big and difficult job to tie the several bonds together again. This could not be done openly, as was the case before the state of civil emergency. Bitter experience had taught the people that much. But it could be done, and it was done.

Cautiously but systematically people within the same professions sought contact with one another. Committees were formed to replace the leaders who were under arrest. New representatives took the places of those in prison. Connections were made, and battle plans were formulated. Thus the foundation for a united action, like that which had earlier paralyzed the Nazi authorities' hands and feet, was established.

The Germans discovered that the organizations which they thought they had subdued were still alive and active. When, in December 1941, the Nazi authorities ruled that all the teachers in Norway must devote at least one hour a week to lessons on the New Order, and that they must all take a pledge of loyalty, they discovered that the wall was still standing. Not only did the teachers from top to bottom refuse to pledge their loyalty, but throughout the country they made their decisions known through identically worded statements. It was evident that the opposition was well organized and well directed. Everywhere the Nazis ran up against the same wall, the same well-organized defiance.

It was at this time that the first signs of panic began to appear within the thin ranks of the Quislings. The Nasjonal Samling's chief newspaper, *Fritt Folk,* proved a good barometer in this respect. Its tone became constantly more furious. And *Hirdmannen,* the official weekly newspaper of Quisling's *Hird,* did not hesitate to make some remarkable admissions. Towards the end of November this paper wrote as follows regarding a young man who had joined the *Hird:*

It did not take long before he was made to feel what he had done. He was met with cold glances, or, if necessary, frigid politeness. Acquaintances suddenly got busy peeking through windows at him whenever he approached, or they passed him on the street with set faces. He could not deny that all this aloofness hurt a little. A friend said to him: "You must realize that things cannot be as before. You have failed us. We had not expected this of you. We did not think you were so weak that you could not stick it out during this waiting period. It's a shame that you should be the one to break away now while Norwegians for the first time stand united—united against the barbarians."

The *Hird* man telephoned a girl friend and asked her to go out with him one evening. But she answered: "I could never do that after what you have done. You have betrayed all of us. I regard you as a traitor."

The *Hird* man received a letter from his mother, who wrote:

"To think that you could do this and betray your country and your people! Have you no pride or patriotism? No doubt you have done this for the sake of personal gain. No doubt you have been lured by the offer of a high position, and you have been too weak to refuse. I had never expected that you would bring such great disgrace upon the family. At my age such a sorrow is heavy to bear. I am glad your father lies in his grave. He could never have survived a sorrow such as this. I no longer have a son, but I will nevertheless pray day and night for your soul, and I will not abandon the hope that there is a salvation for you, too."

Early in December the local Nazi leader for Nordstrand and Bekkelaget sent the following letter to his "comrades in arms" within the district:

The attendance at the services conducted by Pastor Hagen at Bekkelaget Church has dropped to a point where only twenty-five persons were present the last time. Pastor Hagen is a prominent clergyman, and his sons belong to the Nasjonal Samling. We must attend the church when Hagen is conducting the services. It is doubtful if anyone suffers so much for their membership in the Nasjonal Samling as those pastors who have joined the movement, and it must be doubly bitter for them when even their comrades in arms fail them.

At the same time the Germans took steps to protect Nasjonal Samling members against various kinds of losses that they had sustained because of membership in the party. Merchants who had been boycotted after joining the Nasjonal Samling were assured of preferred treatment in the distribution of goods. Lawyers who had lost their clients because of Nasjonal Samling membership were given special assignments by the authorities.

The war of nerves against the party's members produced results more sensational than these. Even in the high ranks of the "constituted ministers," the war claimed its victims. In the fall the so-called Minister of Shipping, Kjeld Stub Irgens, suffered a nervous collapse and had to be placed in a clinic. The collapse came when Irgens was waiting in line at one of Oslo's banks, and it could not be kept secret since a large number of people had witnessed the event. Somewhat later two of the Nazi ministers, Ragnar Skancke and Birger Meidell, requested sick leave, and Gulbrand Lunde, the propaganda minister, was saved in the nick of time after he had taken poison; he was rushed to an Oslo hospital to have his stomach pumped.

Two thousand persons had gathered at the graveyard adjoining Bryn Church in Baerum one Sunday in November. No snow had fallen yet, but the air was crisp and clear, and people could see their breath when they talked.

A modest marker was to be unveiled. Its purpose was to commemorate the young men of the village who had fallen in the war against the Germans in 1940.

On this Sunday there was no ceremony to speak of—no band and no waving banners. It was only a couple of thousand people who had assembled to pay tribute to those who had given their lives for something in which they believed. There were two brief speeches, and the national anthem was sung.

The program was almost over when a young man stepped forward and asked permission to say a few words. Nobody knew him; nobody had ever seen him before.

His voice was firm:

I place these flowers on this stone with thanks for the contribution made and with a greeting from countrymen outside Norway who are today fighting for the same ideals that these men died for. I received the request to do this an hour ago, and I am glad that this duty of honor fell to me. These flowers I now place on the grave are wrapped in the flag for which we are all fighting.

He bent over to place on the grave a bouquet wrapped in the Norwegian flag. Then he stepped back into the crowd and a few moments later was seen riding away on a bicycle.

The home front's leadership had never lost contact with the Royal Government in London, not even during the state of civil emergency. The connections made during the summer of 1940 had been growing ever stronger, and the home front co-operated to a considerable degree in the Government's policies regarding conditions inside Norway. How this was done and is being done is still a secret and will continue to be so as long as the war lasts. But the co-operation is there, and it has been steadily improved.

At first it was apparent in the efficient news service as re-flected by the London radio broadcasts. Next, the home-front leadership began to make use of the London radio for issuing orders for nation-wide united action. As the connections improved, the home front began to play a part in the Government's legislative activity. One example of this was the law aimed at holding Quislings legally responsible for their acts on the day of reckoning. The amendments to this law, stipulating punishment and adopted by the Government on January 22, 1942, were in reality formulated by the home-front leadership and constituted another phase in the war of nerves being carried on against the little clique that calls itself the Nasjonal Samling.

These laws declared the Nasjonal Samling to be a traitorous party and membership in it a punishable crime. The provisions for punishment are so formed as to be applicable even though the person concerned has been only a passive member and has taken no part in the party's activity. According to law, penalties ranging from three years in prison to life imprisonment or execution may be imposed on anyone who aids the enemy by word or deed during a war in which Norway is a participant.

It provides further that Nasjonal Samling members shall be deprived of "public confidence." This means that they will lose their right to any position or privilege that calls for confidence in any form.

The home front's leadership understood the people's attitude, and it also wanted the Government to make its position clear. Since the Government was the people's Government, it acted according to the people's wishes.

By December 1941 the home front had become so well organized that it wanted its own representative in the Royal Government in London. When the request was made it was immediately approved by the Government, which replied that the seat was available and that it would leave it to the home front to select its own representative. Two days after the home front had made its choice, Paul Harmann, Oslo's mayor of finance, arrived in London and assumed his new position as a minister in the Royal Norwegian Government.

How all this was arranged and accomplished is a secret, though it is no secret that the Royal Norwegian Government has for a year or more been systematically getting much-needed individuals out of Norway. This has been true with respect to officers for the Army, Navy, and Air Force, and it has applied also to officials and experts needed by the Government. The co-operation continues without a hitch.

But the background for this co-operation is clear—clearer perhaps than in the case of any other occupied country. For if there ever had been any possibilities of discord or disunity on the home front, then the Germans themselves had destroyed those possibilities by their own encroachments and by their efforts to establish the New Order by means of Vidkun Quisling and the Nasjonal Samling.

In King Haakon and the Royal Government in London, Norwegians had long since found the "unifying symbol" that Quisling had hoped to become. The Government headed by

Prime Minister Johan Nygaardsvold has been in power since 1935, and it has long since ceased to be a partisan government although it was originally formed out of the Labor party. As early as April 9, 1940, when the Storting held its final meeting, representatives of the other leading parties had been added to the Government, and now the home front also has its representative at the King's council table. This was the outward expression of the national unity which had become evident on the home front during its hardest days.

The chief symbol of the unity and the determination to continue the fight was King Haakon, who, when he was elected King by an overwhelming majority in a plebiscite in 1905, had selected "All for Norway" as his royal slogan. He became the rallying point in the fight. In his name Norwegians found expression for their hopes and longings, for their determination to fight, and for their unshakable faith in the future. Through his courage and firmness of purpose, and principally through his unfaltering loyalty, King Haakon had become one with the people to whom he had come as a stranger in 1905.

With their profound democratic convictions, the Norwegians had never constituted a royalistic nation. As in England, the King had never been a ruling monarch in Norway. He wore the crown, but he did not govern. The power reposed with the nation's Storting and the administrative authority with the Government.

The war had not changed this condition. Quite the opposite, King Haakon had in every respect remained true to the policy which he had maintained throughout all his years as King: he continued to be constitutional monarch. He thus succeeded in emphasizing the constitutional aspect of the country's struggle and consequently in strengthening the resistance to the unconstitutional impositions of Vidkun Quisling and the New Order.

His purpose and the people's purpose were the same, and this program has perhaps been most clearly expressed in a New Year's review published in the underground newspaper *Free Trade-Unions* in January 1942:

In times of distress one learns who his true friends are. This is a truth which we have experienced ever more forcibly since April 1940.

What has happened has welded the Norwegian people together into a company of faithful friends. No one asks any more about one's political affiliations. Now the question is about one's national attitude. This can be summarized in three points:

1. Among all parties there shall be maintained a united front as of April 9, 1940.

2. All forces shall unite to blaze the trail for the country's legal Government. The Government has the Storting's vote of confidence, and it is composed of representatives of all the leading parties.

3. The King shall resume his legal position as given to him after the plebiscite of August 13, 1905.

More clearly than ever before shone the single purpose of the people's fight.

V. THE DAY WILL COME

1. THE CUP IS FILLED

TALL AND ERECT the towers of Akershus Fortress reach towards the heavy, gray winter sky. There is defiance in their bearing, but at the same time there is a certain gentle charm about the silhouettes, a charm that is in sharp contrast to the crooked, distorted swastika flags that flutter from the flagpoles of the fortress.

The winter day rests heavily over the Oslo valley. The chill, penetrating fog comes rolling down the hillside in giant waves. It blends with the frosty mist from the sea to form a coating of hoarfrost on the solid gray stone walls of the fortress. It forces itself into corners and crevices and makes the day raw and uncomfortable wherever it gains access. It is Nature weeping. The pearly dampness on the house walls is tears that shimmer faintly in the gray winter light.

It is Sunday, February 1, 1942.

Oslo, Norway's capital, is deserted. The houses seem neglected and dilapidated, after nearly two years of lack of attention, and they stare with blind eyes out into the empty streets where the slush lies ankle-deep. The silence that rests over the city is disturbed only now and then by the squish-

squish-squish of the worn-out shoes of some lonely person hurrying homeward.

It is Vidkun Quisling's day.

Twenty-one months had passed since that April day when a hoarse and excited voice sounded through the ether and called upon Norwegians to lay down their weapons and to greet the invader as a friend. Twenty-one months. Much had happened during this time. The coup of April 9, 1940, had not succeeded. For six brief days Quisling had been allowed to glory in his stolen title of Prime Minister. Then popular opinion had forced him out of sight. When he again appeared in the limelight on September 25 of that same year it was in a more humble position: as the Nasjonal Samling's *Führer*. Since that time Vidkun Quisling had again and again run his head against the wall of resistance which he found waiting for him wherever he and his comrades tried to push forward. There had been defeat after defeat and humiliation after humiliation. At first he had tried to win the people through flattery and fat promises. But as time passed and resistance increased, threats took the place of promises. The words grew constantly more sharp and the means of compulsion more hardhanded. But wherever the traitor sowed the wind, he reaped a storm. The New Order had long since passed the danger point. The Nasjonal Samling's membership, which never exceeded more than 20,000 or 30,000, diminished steadily. Chaos prevailed—chaos and corruption. Quisling's own acts reflected his desperation in increasing degree, and more and more frequently the Germans had to make use of their power in order to prevent open revolt.

Vidkun Quisling still possessed no direct power. He took his orders from Reichskommissar Terboven, who was the real leader of the civil administration. And the fact that the "constituted ministers" of September 1941 had been given permission to use the title of "ministers" made no real difference in the situation. They were still the errand boys of the Reichs-kommissar. They were responsible only to him.

During recent weeks the rumor that the Germans were about to give up their experiment with Quisling as a failure had recurred with increasing frequency. But Vidkun Quisling had not given up his plans of becoming the people's *Führer*. He had been affected by the resistance and was more nervous and upset than ever before; but his fanatical pride and ambition drove him relentlessly forward. And he had powerful connections within the German National Socialist party. First and foremost it appeared that Adolf Hitler was personally willing to give Quisling his full support.

Ever since the April days of 1940 there had existed a constant dispute between the German civilian occupation authorities and the military leadership over the problem of Quisling. General von Falkenhorst, who was at the head of the occupation troops, had early admitted the hopelessness of co-operation with the Nasjonal Samling and its *Führer*. He based his opinion entirely on military considerations. As an officer, he was not interested in unrest at the places of work. He had only one duty to perform. That was to wage war. Whatever the civil administration wanted to do with respect to the civil population was to him a matter of indifference, but he did not want anyone to be throwing monkey wrenches into the wheels that he was supposed to keep in motion. And he understood that no other monkey wrench was as big as Vidkun Quisling.

In the contest that went on behind the scenes, the party once more proved itself to be the stronger. Instead of being suppressed, Vidkun Quisling was promoted. That was why February 1, 1942, was Vidkun Quisling's day.

The Norwegian people had long known that something was to happen on that day. The espionage web spun by the home front reached far into the offices of the Nasjonal Samling and the occupation authorities, and it had snared the news.

The reports were published in the underground newspapers and forwarded to London. By the time the Nazis began setting up flagpoles along Oslo streets the last couple of days of January, everybody knew what was in the wind. At the same time everybody knew what to do. It was the same device as that used so often before during the occupation: boycott. The word was passed along from man to man. Empty streets were to show how the Norwegians felt about this turn of events.

There was activity in the courtyard of Akershus Fortress. Heavy soldiers' boots clattered on the cobblestones. Orders were barked. Weapons rattled as the troops saluted. A military band struck up a tune of quick, shrill blasts. To the top of a flagpole, which up to now had been standing bare, went the red-and-yellow colors of the Nasjonal Samling. Straight across the courtyard came Vidkun Quisling, marching. Goose-stepping German soldiers formed a guard of honor for him.

In the old, happy days, when peace was taken for granted and heavily laden ships came easing up the open Oslo Fiord, the towers of Akershus Fortress were the first visible signs of Oslo. They greeted the seafarer and bade him welcome. To stranger and countryman alike they seemed to say: "Come closer, friend!" Mysterious paths wound under the leafy trees and among the ancient moss-covered walls to the ramparts where young lovers sat and stared out over the harbor, hills, and ships as they laid their plans for the future.

At that time Akershus was peace.

Still longer ago, hundreds of years ago, Akershus was war. At that time the great, massive walls formed a rock which no foreign invader had been able to dislodge. Built in the 1300s, Akershus had stood off many a siege. But never had foreign soldiers set foot within its walls.

Not until April 9, 1940.

Akershus had always been freedom's protector. It was Oslo's

fort. It was Oslo's citizens whom it protected. The feudal system never gained a foothold in Norway, and lords of the manor never held sway there. It was free men who fought and died inside the walls of Akershus, free men who fought and died for freedom.

And in the consciousness of Norwegians, Akershus had remained the protector of freedom—even though nearly two years had passed since the Germans had raised their swastika over the ramparts. In that selfsame courtyard, where hundreds of years ago free Norwegians had given their lives in their fight for the things they believed in, other Norwegians during the past few months had shed their blood on the cobblestones for the same ideals. The Germans had made Akershus their execution ground. Here, in the course of the winter, many a Norwegian patriot had faced German firing squads, and the shots that had sounded through the courtyard had echoed and re-echoed throughout the land, and even beyond the country's borders.

It was through this courtyard that the traitor marched on that first day of February 1942, surrounded by the guardian soldiers of the occupying power. He walked on sacred ground. He had the blood of innocent men on his boots.

But no road led back for him, either.

The ceremony at Akershus was brief. Reichskommissar Terboven made a speech, announcing that he—with Adolf Hitler's approval and "according to the wishes of the Norwegian people"—had permitted Vidkun Quisling to form a government. Quisling's title was to be "Minister-President"—a title previously unknown in Norway. The Reichskommissar said that the day's events constituted a new forward step on the road to complete freedom and independence for the Norwegian people. Norway, he said, was facing a great and glorious future as a part of "the Greater Germanic International Fellowship" under the leadership of Adolf Hitler. After severely taking to task all those who had shunned Germany's "open hand of friendship," he congratulated Vidkun Quisling on his elevation.

The beggar lives on alms, and Vidkun Quisling was not the man to refuse this one. Fairly bursting with pride, he stood beside his master and accepted the tribute.

Then came Quisling's speech of acceptance—in German.

After the German national song and "Horst Wessel" had been sung, the Quislings present intoned the first stanza of the Norwegian national anthem. The program had to have at least one Norwegian aspect!

The following day a telegram from Berlin emphasized that what had happened in no way affected the position of the Reichskommissar.

At the head of the procession rode a couple of mounted policemen. Behind them came a band. Then a couple of thousand marching, uniformed Quislings. They marched two abreast with plenty of distance between so as to give the procession length and consequently the impression of vast numbers.

But despite the fact that the Nasjonal Samling had fetched members from all parts of Norway to Oslo for the occasion, the picture could not be changed. It was a picture of emptiness. Perhaps more clearly than ever before, the thin ranks of Quisling followers were displayed in all their desolation. The attempt to place a number of members in civilian garb along the line of march only accentuated the emptiness further.

Through the newspapers people had been ordered to display flags, but the flagpoles remained bare. And the people stayed away. Never had Oslo seemed so deserted as when the miserable procession stalked up Karl Johan in tribute to the country's first Minister-President. Even the flagpoles that the authorities had set up along the sidewalks pointed pale and lifeless towards the sky. Somehow they made one think of gallows waiting for their victims, and the ropes rustled ominously against the wood whenever gusts of wind swept through the streets.

As the procession moved up the slope to the Royal Palace, the faltering song and occasional cheers died away completely. The palace balcony was empty. But still it seemed as if the shadow of a man could be discerned up there—a tall, erect man with sharp features and a knowing face. The eyes were sad and yet severe as he gazed down on the wretched crowd slobbering along in the slush.

This was not the kind of people the King was accustomed to seeing from his balcony. He had known only the vast, rejoicing throngs that had paraded by on Independence Day—frank, smiling faces of young and old who had looked up to him as he stood by the balustrade sending his own cheery greetings out to one and all. There had been thousands and tens of thousands of them, pouring endlessly from all side streets and joining the masses that jammed Karl Johan and the park around the Palace. Happy, honest, industrious people.

For the motley mob that ruled the streets today, the eyes in the balcony showed only contempt—and a trace of sorrow.

The Quislings perhaps had seen the shadow in the balcony and inwardly knew that the shadow would one day again be the King himself. And they knew that when that day came, they themselves would no longer be marching in the streets.

Darkness settled over the city, where the ominous silence remained unbroken. But there were signs of activity on Karl Johan near the Grand Hotel. German soldiers and Quislings who had bolstered their courage by means of a few drinks were assembling in front of the hotel. They had been ordered to do so. The *Führer* was to be cheered.

Arrangements had been made for the "dramatic effects" which are always a part of the German pattern. As Quisling stepped out on the hotel balcony, a spotlight was turned on, and after a bit the groping beam found the little man who stood there with outstretched arm. For a few seconds he was visible against the black background. His face was glowing with fanatical pride while he listened to the hoarse cheers from the street below. He opened his mouth to speak.

At that very moment the spotlight went out. Someone had cut the electric wires; everything was dark, and confusion was complete.

In the midst of the confusion came sounds of explosions down near the water front. Shortly afterwards the howling sirens of fire trucks rent the winter evening, and a red glow appeared in the sky. Oslo's two railroad stations were ablaze. In the darkness of the night unknown men had added the home front's contributions to the day's entertainment.

And as the fires mounted and the skies grew redder, the silhouettes of the Akershus towers returned to view—defiantly and firmly confident.

When the Germans made Quisling Minister-President on February 1, 1942, they applied the finishing touch to a development that had been going on for nearly two years. On April 15, 1940, they had been forced to accede to pressure by removing Quisling. Later they had allowed him to edge forward again, but cautiously. He was to be sneaked in then through the back door.

But that experiment had failed. The Germans were faced with two alternatives: either to dispose of Quisling for good or else to go the whole way by putting him on top with the full support of the occupation troops.

They chose to do the latter.

But that left the situation exactly as it had been on April 9,

1940. Quisling's rise left the Norwegians with only one choice: to fight him.

That is what they did and are continuing to do.

A loud and emphatic "No!" has been the people's answer to every one of his appeals, plans, and orders.

2. THE FIGHT FOR THE YOUNG

A COUPLE OF DAYS after the affair at Akershus, Quisling had "completed" the formation of a government. With but one or two unimportant exceptions it was composed of the men who up to then had been serving as "constituted ministers."

The job of "New Orderizing" Norway could now be started in earnest. The Nasjonal Samling's plans for a corporate state on the fascist pattern were to be put into effect.

The program implied complete control by the State of all trades and professions in the land, of all business and cultural life, and of all political activity.

But the Nazis realized that they would run into considerable difficulty when it came to enforcing their program. Events of the last two years had taught them that they could not count on the support of the country's grownups. The young people, on the other hand, represented the nation's future, and it was therefore important to get the controlling influence over them as soon as possible.

Quisling's Government held its first meeting on February 5, and, of the laws proclaimed on this occasion, there were two of special significance. One stipulated that all Norwegian children between the ages of ten and eighteen years should serve in the Nasjonal Samling's *Ungdomsfylking*—the Norwegian counterpart of Germany's *Hitler Jugend*. The other required that all teachers, if they wished to continue in their positions, must be members of the newly created Nazi-controlled organization which had been given the name "Norges Lärersamband"— Norway's Teacher Association.

The two laws were closely linked to each other. They represented the first steps towards a systematic and compulsory nazification of the nation's young people.

The reaction was instantaneous. The announcement of the laws unloosed an avalanche of indignation and protest. Quisling had touched upon the most sacred thing in Norwegian life. He was trying to break into the home. And in doing so, he ran straight into a wall that knew no surrender. The months that followed became the most stirring ones of the entire occupation period, and gradually the struggle took on all the characteristics of a religious war. The conflict that had been going on between the Nazi authorities and the State Church was bound to result in an open break eventually; it was the Quislings' attempted encroachments on school and home that brought it about.

Time and events were to prove that the Nazis were unable to strike down the Norwegian resistance.

The first result of these two laws was a unanimous and well-organized protest by the parents, who flooded the Nazi Department of Church and Education with hundreds of thousands of letters. Every letter was signed with full name and address. When the flood of letters became so great that the Department was unable to handle them, let alone read them, orders were issued to the postal service to return to the senders all letters addressed to the Department. That order saved the Department's clerks from being buried in mail, but it helped not a whit to still the storm.

The teachers took action, and as the days passed the situation became intolerable for the authorities. From schools in all parts of the country teachers sent declarations to the effect that they would not agree to joining the Lärersamband. These statements were all identically worded, indicating that the teachers' front was thoroughly organized.

The authorities re-emphasized their demands by issuing a threat that all teachers refusing to accept membership in the Lärersamband would be put to "socially useful work in northern Norway, or elsewhere."

The threat had no effect. Of the country's 14,000 teachers—some of these were retired or in other employment and were thus unaffected by the demands—more than 12,000 joined in the protest against the Nazi scheme.

For such an attitude the Nazis knew but one answer: terror. They began to make arrests. Between 1500 and 2,000 teachers were in prison or concentration camps within a few weeks. The German police were busy all over the country, and there was scarcely a district that did not soon see one or more of its teachers taken into custody. No one was to be left in doubt as to whether the threats had been made in earnest. Those arrested were hostages representing the entire profession. What happened to them was to serve as a grim warning to all others.

But even this left the teachers' front undaunted, and, when the Norwegian Church late in February took its stand unconditionally on the side of the teachers, something akin to panic arose within the Nazis' own ranks. The situation had got completely out of hand. Partly for the purpose of concealment and partly for the sake of providing a breathing spell for themselves, the authorities decided suddenly to close all schools for one month. Officially they announced that the reason for this action was the "fuel shortage." The fact that many school boards objected and declared that they had sufficient fuel on hand made no difference to the Nazis. Late in February the schools had to close, and most of them did not reopen until May.

Simultaneously with the closing of the schools the Nazis halted all salary payments to teachers who had refused to belong to the Lärersamband—that is to say, 95 per cent of all the *active* teachers in the country. Next, on March 17, the Nazi Department of Church and Education ordered local school boards to discharge all teachers who had not joined the Lärersamband by March 28. The Nazis were trying their best to create the impression that the teachers had gone out on strike; the purpose behind this was to set the teachers at odds with the pupils' parents. The Nazi-controlled press began publishing "resolutions of protest," allegedly adopted by various groups of parents who "were concerned about the interruption of their children's education." All this humbug fooled nobody. The underground newspapers had long since made the truth known, and the teachers themselves saw to it that the Nazi propaganda was completely discredited—first and foremost by giving private lessons to pupils in their homes, and for no compensation whatever.

By the beginning of April 1942 conditions had reached a point where no retreat seemed possible for the Nazi authorities. The defeat could no longer be concealed, and the Germans decided to make use of their teacher hostages in a last desperate effort to turn the tide. Terror began in earnest. The entire Gestapo organization was brought into play.

Up to then most of the 1500 to 2,000 arrested teachers had been held in concentration camps in various parts of the country—particularly in the camps near Oslo, Bergen, and Trondheim. There they had been receiving the same sort of cruel and inconsiderate treatment that had been the lot of all political prisoners in Norway. But there are, nevertheless, degrees of "terror" as administered by the Germans, and for the arrested teachers the worst was yet to come.

The first days of April saw about 700 of them being taken to Jörstadmoen—an old military training ground near Lillehammer. They arrived there in open coal cars, most of them after having been en route for fourteen or fifteen hours. They had received no food during the journey, and when the train stopped at the Fåberg station in the middle of the night most of the teachers were on the verge of collapse from fatigue. But they were given no chance to rest. Once out of the cars, they were lined up, and then the ten-mile march through the night-enveloped countryside to Jörstadmoen began. It was hours before they got there.

Jörstadmoen had been made ready to receive these guests. It had been enclosed with high barbed-wire fences, and watch towers had been erected at all strategic points. From each of the towers gleamed a powerful searchlight, operated by Gestapo soldiers. All connections between the prisoners and the outside world were cut off.

The "treatment" of the teachers began at six o'clock in the morning after their arrival, and it was clear that the Germans were going to force them to submit by employing both physical and mental torture.

The day began with a meal that consisted of a slice of dry bread. Then followed four or five hours of gymnastics, according to the accepted pattern of concentration camps in Germany. Those who collapsed were given extra penal exercises to do afterwards. The Germans in charge seemed to derive particular delight out of ordering the schoolteachers to lie flat on their stomachs and then to wallow forward through snow, slush, or icy water while keeping their hands on their backs. One group of teachers was kept at this "exercise" for hours on the filthy ground immediately behind the camp latrine.

Following this long period of gymnastics came a work session under the supervision of German SS soldiers. The "work" consisted of such operations as carrying snow on broom handles, table forks, or in washcloths, or in moving woodpiles from one part of the camp to another and then back again.

After a scant and entirely inadequate midday meal came another period of gymnastics. And it happened often that the SS soldiers took rest periods for themselves while the teachers were ordered to remain in difficult positions.

Not even during the night were prisoners allowed any peace. Every now and then they were roused from their restless sleep to be told, for example, that they were to leave for the Russian front in two hours.

After a week of this the Gestapo could boast of some results. About forty or fifty of the teachers broke down. Most of them were ill, and in order to gain freedom and with it a chance to obtain medical attention they agreed to join the Lärersamband.

A few days later 150 more of the prisoners were sent back to the Grini concentration camp near Oslo. Most of these were elderly men, and all were in poor health. Not one of these, however, had agreed to join the hated organization.

By Sunday, April 12, the Germans had obviously given up hope of forcing the teachers to submit. It was then decided to send all those who were left—about 500 of them—to work camps in northern Norway.

For the day-long railway trip from Jörstadmoen to Trondheim the teachers were packed in cattle cars so tightly that there was not even room to sit down. Immediately upon their arrival at Trondheim they were marched aboard an old wooden ship named the *Skjerstad* and stowed away in the cargo holds. The *Skjerstad* was built in 1904, and it had been out of commission for many years. Because of the ship shortage the Germans had ordered the *Skjerstad* to sea again.

Conditions aboard were terrible. It was so crowded that the teachers could do little but stand upright. No bedding had been provided; there was, in fact, no place to lie. Cots or bunks were entirely out of the question. The food was wretched and insufficient. The hatches were closed, shutting out all light. Nor was there any fresh air.

People on the pier heard only the despairing groans of the prisoners. It was not allowed to do anything to aid or comfort them. Only a single doctor—a Nasjonal Samling member named Rian—was permitted to board the ship. What this Nazi saw terrified even him. He reported that at least a hundred of the teachers were seriously ill, and that at least ten doctors would be needed if any effective help were to be administered.

But no other doctors were allowed aboard. Instead, four of the teachers who were most critically ill were taken ashore and removed to hospitals. Two of these had lost their minds, one was suffering from a cerebral hemorrhage, and the other had developed pneumonia.

The following day five more of the teachers were removed to Trondheim hospitals, while townspeople worked desperately to prevent the voyage. Even the Nazi authorities in Trondheim joined in these efforts. They could see that a continuation of the terror would only serve to defeat its purpose. On April 14, Provincial Governor Prytz, nominally the highest ranking Nazi in Trondheim, sent Quisling the following telegram, which was promptly snatched up by representatives of the home front:

At least 500 teachers plus guards to depart from Trondheim on S.S. *Skjerstad.* Hygienic conditions on board are extraordinarily bad, according to Nasjonal Samling member Dr. Rian of Reitgjerdet Asylum. Many are not able to lie down at night but must stand since ship has room for only 250 passengers. Many of the teachers are very ill with pneumonia, stomach ulcers, asthma, bronchitis, cerebral hemorrhages, insanity. Two toilets for all. Kitchen capacity limited to 250 at most and cannot take care of all during trip. Water supply entirely insufficient. Several have expressed willingness to join Lärersamband. Suggest medical examination for all teachers.

On the same day Bishop Johan Stören and twenty-eight pastors of Tröndelag sent the following telegram to Ragnar Skancke, Nazi Minister of Church and Education:

In the name of Jesus Christ and humanity the undersigned pastors plead for mercy for the more than 500 teachers who are now being sent northwards. We cannot be silent in the face of the sufferings which we know they are going through. The echoes of these will soon resound throughout the entire country.

But the Germans had made up their minds, and it was too late to change them. They said that the teachers had been given their chance at Jörstadmoen. Despite the fact that the *Skjerstad's* captain tried to refuse to assume responsibility for the ship, the voyage from Trondheim started at three o'clock in the morning of April 15.

Besides the 500 teachers there were also fifty German guards aboard the overladen vessel. The guards reserved for their own use all cabins and other accommodations.

On April 28 the *Skjerstad* reached her destination, and the teachers were placed in a German work camp near the Finnish border far up on the Arctic coast. And there they are still, toiling as slaves of the occupying power. Even though some have died, and even though many are weary and ailing, not one has yet yielded to the Nazis.

At the close of the so-called "fuel shortage vacation" the teachers who were still free tried to reopen the schools. They did this purely out of consideration for the children and their education. The Nazi authorities sought to exploit the situation by publishing a notice to the effect that all teachers who returned to their work would automatically become members of the Lärersamband, but the teachers had anticipated this and were prepared. On April 9, 1942, thousands of teachers

throughout the country faced their classes for the first time
since February, and the first thing they did was to read the
following pledge to the attentive boys and girls:

On February 5, Norges Lärersamband was established. A few
days later I sent in my resignation because I found that membership in the organization might place upon me duties which I for
reasons of conscience could not assume. I am still of this opinion,
and I have recently sent the following statement to the school
board:

"I reiterate my protest against membership in Norges Lärersamband. At the same time I must in loyalty to my calling and
conscience declare that I, in consideration for my pupils and
their parents, wish to resume teaching. I request that this be
made known to the higher authorities. I have made this statement
because those two things—to be a member of Norges Lärersamband and to teach—are irreconcilable. For the same reason I cannot agree with the Department's opinion that those who teach
are automatically members of the Lärersamband."

One of our dearest national songs tells us that "every child's
soul we unfold is another province added to the country." Together with Church and home we teachers have the responsibility
to see to it that this unfolding occurs in Christian love and understanding, and in conformity with our national cultural traditions.
We have been charged with the task of giving you children the
knowledge and training for the thorough work which is necessary
if every single one of you is to receive complete development as a
human being, so that you can take your place in society to the
benefit of others and yourself. This is the duty with which we
have been entrusted by the Norwegian people, and the Norwegian
people can call us to account for it.

We know also that the sum of the knowledge and will to work
in a country is the greatest and most lasting of all that country's
assets. It is our duty to hold a protective hand over these resources. We should betray our calling if we did not put all our
strength into this task, especially during the trying times which

we are now experiencing. Every curtailment in the school's activity is an undermining of the foundation upon which our people's future is to be built.

However, the teacher's duty is not only to give the children knowledge. He must also teach the children to have faith in and earnestly to desire that which is true and right. Therefore he cannot, without betraying his calling, teach anything against his conscience. He who does so sins both against the pupils he is supposed to lead and against himself. This, I promise you, I shall not do.

I shall not call upon you to do anything which I regard as wrong. Nor shall I teach you anything which I regard as not conforming with the truth. I shall, as I have done heretofore, let my conscience be my guide, and I am confident that I shall then be in step with the great majority of the people who have entrusted to me the duties of an educator.

The immediate result of this action by the teachers was that the Quisling authorities again closed the schools, and a number of arrests were made. Nevertheless it was to prove a definite victory for the teachers. The entire nation was seething, and the Germans—fearing open violence—sought to quell the storm. On April 25, Quisling's Department of Church and Education was compelled to retreat. On orders from the Germans, the Department sent out a circular letter canceling the rule that all teachers who failed to declare their willingness to join the Lärersamband should be dismissed. The same letter served notice that all schools were to reopen on May 1.

During the first days of May teachers and pupils returned to schools throughout the country. To make sure that their position was clear, the teachers once more read their pledge of April 9 to their pupils. And the young folk, over whom the battle had been waged, knew that the spirit had registered still another victory over force and violence.

They knew also that hundreds of teachers were still enslaved in German concentration camps, and that the sacrifices of these teachers had not been made in vain.

The Nazis knew this, too.

On May 25 five or six cars turned in at the gates of the Stabekk School in Baerum, just outside Oslo. In the cars were enough policemen to arrest a whole town. They leaped out and cleared a path through the crowd of curious children, who were having a recess. Along this path and up to the doorway of the school marched Vidkun Quisling, followed closely by his Minister of Police, Jonas Lie, and his Minister of Church and Education, Ragnar Skancke. All three were decked out in Nasjonal Samling uniforms.

The teachers were hastily summoned to the gymnasium because the *Führer* was going to make a speech. While his bodyguard hovered close by, Vidkun Quisling stepped up on the platform. He was pale with anger and dismay, and his frenzied voice failed him again and again as he shouted his complaints at the listeners.

"It is the teachers' fault," he thundered, "that eighteen young boys were recently executed! It is the teachers' fault that Norway does not get her freedom back again!"

Sobs choked off his voice. Half weeping, he cried:

"You are spoiling the game for me! You are keeping me from making peace with Germany!"

He slouched forward over the table. The Minister of Police barked a few orders.

A few minutes later the automobiles disappeared through the gates, carrying with them as prisoners the teachers of the Stabekk School. The pupils, gathered about the gate, waved a tribute to their teachers as the cars sped away.

3. THE CROSS AND THE SWASTIKA

THOUSANDS OF PEOPLE are crowded about the entrances to Trondheim Cathedral, and others keep joining them. It is obvious that there will not be room for all in the church, but despite this there is no shoving, no mad rush for seats. Progress towards the doors is slow but orderly, and the people are silent, their faces somber.

It is nearing two o'clock in the afternoon of Sunday, February 1, 1942.

Suddenly the wail of sirens is heard and police cars storm into the square in front of the Cathedral. Armed policemen leap out; quickly they block the church entrances and form a line to hold the crowd back. Directing the police is the city's chief Nazi. For safety's sake German soldiers are stationed within beck and call.

The crowd is deathly still now; no one moves. Slowly an open space appears between the line of policemen and the front row of the crowd—a no man's land. Minutes pass, but no words are spoken. The atmosphere is tense, ominous.

Then, somewhere in the crowd, a lone voice is heard—singing. The song is Luther's famous hymn, "A Mighty Fortress Is Our God."

Other voices join in. Men bare their heads, and the hymn, now carried by the thousands of voices, rises with increasing volume towards the leaden winter sky.

The policemen, baffled, finger their weapons uncertainly and look towards their superiors for orders.

The hymn is ended, and a moment of silence ensues. Then someone starts Norway's national anthem, and again the thousands of voices join in:

"Yes, we love this land of ours!"

But now the police have their orders. Slowly but surely they force the crowd back towards the street. Here and there a policeman uses his club, but no one strikes back. Not for a moment does the singing falter; it only becomes more defiant in spirit.

Bishop Stören appears on the church steps and a lull settles over the square. Calmly the Bishop invokes a blessing on the congregation. Then he asks all to leave quietly.

Slowly, reluctantly the crowd disperses.

This Nazi encroachment against peaceable churchgoers at Trondheim on February 1, 1942, proved to be the turning point of the long, grim conflict that had been going on between the Norwegian Church and the Nazi authorities ever since the invasion. But it was not conclusive. It was only another step in a development which eventually must result in an open break. The course had long been clear.

The events leading up to the affair at Trondheim only confirmed this. On January 26 the Nazi Department of Church and Education telegraphed an order to the Bishop of Trondheim, Johan N. Stören, that the Cathedral should be "opened" to a Nazi pastor named Blessing-Dahle on February 1. The Bishop and all the pastors of Trondheim protested, but in vain. They were told that the Nasjonal Samling needed the Cathedral for a "festive service" in connection with the ceremony that was to take place in Oslo that Sunday—the elevation of Quisling to the office of Minister-President.

Dean Arne Fjellbu, who was to have conducted the eleven-o'clock service at the Cathedral on that Sunday, had to give way. Under the circumstances he postponed his regular service until two o'clock in the afternoon of the same day.

When Blessing-Dahle mounted the pulpit he faced a swastika-decked church that was all but empty. But even before he had finished his sermon thousands of persons were setting out from home to attend Dean Fjellbu's service. By the time the police interfered, hundreds had already entered the church and the service went on as announced.

The Nazis did not dare interfere with the service itself. By the time Dean Fjellbu began his sermon the police had driven a large part of his congregation away, and no doubt the Dean was aware of this. But his voice was strong and full of courage:

"If you build on lies and injustice, force and terror, you will reap misfortune for both yourself and others. If you build on truth and love, you will attain the blessing and the eternal values—yes, eternal life."

His words reached far beyond the church.

On February 3, the struggle between the Church and the State entered upon its decisive phase. On that day the seven bishops of the Church, meeting in Oslo, sent the Nazi Department of Church and Education a joint protest. The protest went unanswered.

The bishops convened again in Oslo on February 14. In the meantime Quisling had proclaimed the law requiring children to serve in the Nazi *Ungdomsfylking,* and the teacher conflict had grown acute. The bishops sent the Nazi Department of

Church and Education a letter in which they expressed their complete opposition of the *Ungdomsfylking* law which the teachers were also fighting. The bishops wrote:

At the baptism of a child the responsibility for the bringing up of the child is placed upon the parents. The children's school is a mutually arranged means of aid in this upbringing, and the first paragraph of the school laws states that the school's purpose is to assist in giving the children a Christian and moral education.

The homes and the Church have, therefore, also a right to share in determining the policies of the school. Every father and mother also holds full responsibility for how they have permitted others to take part in forming their children's character, faith, and conviction. This conscientious responsibility not only places a duty on the parents but also gives them an inviolable right. He who would attempt to force the children out of the parents' bonds of responsibility and to disrupt the divine right of the home would at the same time be forcing the parents to the utmost act of conscience.

As the overseers of the Church we recognize it as our duty to present this clearly and unmistakably upon the occasion of your having received orders to assist in the formation of a law aimed compulsorily to mobilize all children from the age of nine to ten years and upwards under an influence which countless parents must recognize as intolerable in relation to their conscientious obligations.

The bishops sent a copy of the letter to Axel Stang, chief of the so-called "Department of Labor Service and Athletics." It was to be Stang's duty to put the *Ungdomsfylking* law into effect.

No reply was forthcoming from Stang, but Ragnar Skancke, Nazi Minister of Church and Education, responded by declaring that the Government, as the supreme authority in the land, also had supreme authority over every individual citizen.

"This authority, responsibility, and right of the State," wrote Skancke, "means that the responsibility for the people's education also rests with the State, and it should be clear to the Church's bishops that this responsibility is particularly great with regard to our people, who have been neglected for many years."

During the days that immediately followed, the bishops were in constant contact with each other, and when they reassembled in Oslo on February 23 and 24 their minds were made up. They made their decision known to the Department of Church and Education through individual, identically worded letters. It was this: the bishops were resigning from their offices in protest against the Nazi administration.

The contents of the letter quickly became known throughout the country, thanks to the underground newspapers. The letter reviewed events leading up to the present crisis and concluded in the following unmistakable manner:

The Norwegian Church's bishops would be unfaithful to their calling if they continued to co-operate in an administration which in this manner, without trace of churchly reason, invades the rights of the congregation and even adds injustice to might. Therefore I submit that I hereby resign from the conduct of my office.

That is to say: I now divest myself of that which the State has deputed to me. The spiritual duty, assigned to me through ordination at the Lord's altar, is still mine with God and with right. To be a preacher of the Word, supervisor of the congregation, and spiritual adviser of the pastors is and will continue to be my calling. I will in the future look after this so far as it is possible for a non-official to do so.

But to continue the administrative co-operation which exercises might against the Church would be to betray the most sacred.

With Luther, we have tried in our service to be loyal to the authorities as far as word and commandment permitted. But as it came for Luther so also it comes for us, the moment when we must follow our conviction and assert the Church's rights against the State's injustice.

Forms of government may change, but with its church father the Church knows that against that which Luther called "the tyranny" stands God Himself in His Word and with His spirit's power.

Woe unto us if we did not here obey God more than man.

The bishops' decision to resign aroused a wave of sympathy, and the solidarity of the Norwegian people had never been greater. The bishops were speaking in behalf of the State Church, which includes about 98 per cent of the country's population. They won the immediate support not only of the state church membership, but also of all other religious groups and organizations, including the various "free," or non-state, congregations. The Catholic Bishop of Oslo was among the first to take a stand in support of the Lutheran bishops. It was a new popular revolt.

Within the ranks of the Nasjonal Samling the bishops' action created nothing short of a panic—a panic which, among other things, revealed itself in new outbursts of terror against the teachers. The Nazis set feverishly to work trying to force the bishops to retreat. One of the first steps taken was to summon the Bishop of Oslo, Eivind Berggrav, to the Royal Palace for a hearing.

Bishop Berggrav found Quisling himself waiting for him when he arrived at the Palace, and with Quisling were two of his chief lieutenants, Minister of Police Jonas Lie and Minister of Domestic Affairs William Hagelin. Present also were several police officers. The hearing lasted an hour and a quarter.

It ended with Bishop Berggrav's taking the offensive. He demanded to know why Quisling had falsified the bishops' letters of resignation by compelling the newspapers to print that the bishops had been dismissed.

"We in the Nasjonal Samling see it that way," answered Quisling.

"Then I have nothing to do here!" declared Berggrav.

"You triple traitor! You deserve to have your head chopped off!" bellowed Quisling.

"Well, here I am," replied Berggrav.

No one sought to stop him as he turned and left the room.

All seven bishops were still in Oslo. They had not been permitted to return to their homes. Instead, they had been ordered to report to police headquarters twice a day.

The bishops obeyed this order, but in a manner somewhat different from that anticipated by the Nazis. Twice daily a small procession marched with slow dignity through the streets to the prison. It was the bishops who, in full ecclesiastical attire and with their golden crosses displayed prominently on their breasts, were on their way to present themselves before the holders of worldly power.

This quiet form of demonstration quickly attracted tremendous crowds. People gathered in the market place opposite the prison and openly cheered and applauded the leaders of the Church.

The police soon found it necessary to order the bishops to report individually—and at outlying police stations.

But the Nazi authorities had not yet given up. A few days later the Nasjonal Samling appointed seven new bishops, selected from the forty or so pastors who had turned traitor and aligned themselves with the Nazis.

The Church's reply to this move was not slow in coming. The first Sunday in April the about 1,000 pastors of the Norwegian Church followed the example set by their bishops. Through individual, identically worded letters they notified the Nazi Department of Church and Education that they were resigning from their state offices.

As the bishops had done, the pastors stressed that they intended to continue to perform within their congregations all duties "which can be performed by non-officials according to the Holy Scriptures, the confession of faith, and the altar book."

The pastors justified their action by reading to their congregations a long document which bore the title: "The Foundations of the Church—a Confession and an Explanation." This occurred on Easter morning in all churches in the country with the exception of about forty where Nazi-minded pastors held forth. Long before the services were to start, the churches were filled to the doors, because the clergy had made no attempt to keep their actions secret.

The Nazi authorities knew what was going to happen, and Quisling's Department of Police had ordered its underlings to employ any and all means to prevent the pastors from reading the statement to their congregations. This order had been made known to the pastors, and the Nazis had thus turned the event into a test of strength between force and the spirit. The latter proved to be the stronger, and the occupying power realized this more quickly than did the Quislings. At the last moment the Germans countermanded the earlier orders to the police. The pastors were permitted to submit the message to their congregations.

This last-minute interference by the Germans was by no means an admission of defeat. Rather, it was an attempt to create somewhat peaceful conditions so that the next blow at the Church could be properly aimed.

And the blow fell. A few days later Bishop Eivind Berggrav was arrested and placed in the Grini concentration camp near Oslo. Simultaneously two prominent pastors, Ingvald B.

Carlsen and H. E. Wisloeff, were arrested and sent to Grini. The three were suspected of having prepared the statement that the pastors had read in the churches. Other arrests were expected, since the police had orders to apprehend all those who were implicated. During the following days a number of clergymen were arrested, and among these was Bishop Krohn-Hansen of Tromsö. At this time the Nazis also made a number of isolated thrusts at the Church, such as the confiscation of all property belonging to Bishop Hille of Hamar.

These measures, involving the use of force, served only to defeat their own purpose, and the Nazi authorities made their first retreat when, in response to orders issued by the Germans, Bishop Berggrav was released from Grini. It was a release in name only, however, since Berggrav was not permitted any freedom; he was taken immediately to a little cottage that he owned in Asker, just outside Oslo, and there he has remained ever since under the constant watch of a squad of police. As a prisoner in his own house, Berggrav has been denied all contact with the outside world.

The so-called release of Bishop Berggrav was intended to still the storm of resentment—a little, at least. But the Church had charted its course, and the clergy did not deviate from it. With painstaking care the pastors saw to it that no move was made that might be interpreted as submission.

The pastors continued to use the churches, holding divine services as usual. But they refused consistently to accept any salary from the State. Nor did they make any use of the official seal entrusted to them by the State. All letters to the pastors from Nazi authorities, and especially from the Department of Church and Education, were returned unopened. All official titles were dropped. Otherwise church activities continued pretty much as usual. The pastors conducted baptisms and confirmation, but they refused to officiate at marriages. They did, however, stand ready to bestow the blessing of the Church on civil marriages, if the couple concerned so desired.

The line between the Church and the State was sharply drawn, and it was never transgressed. The Church unyieldingly maintained that it should be above all political encroachments by the authorities.

For the Nazis the situation grew more and more intolerable, and the first peace feelers appeared as early as the closing days of April. These consisted of efforts by the Nazis to arrive at reconciliations with various pastors, one by one. All these attempts were brushed aside, however, with the comment that, if there were to be any negotiations, they would have to be conducted collectively and with Bishop Berggrav and the other bishops representing the Church.

Once more the Nazis tried to win through the use of might. More arrests were made, and a large number of pastors throughout the country were prohibited from speaking in public. Many were "dismissed," but notices to this effect made no particular impression, since the pastors had long before resigned from their offices.

The religious people were not willing to remain forever on the defensive. Letters of protest poured in to the Department of Church and Education from all parts of the country, from private persons and from congregational councils. Especially significant was a joint protest from the University Theological Faculty and the Congregational Faculty; these two bodies represent, respectively, the liberal and conservative schools of thought within the Norwegian Church. Employing plain and direct language that left no chance for misunderstanding, the two faculties declared:

We recognize it as our duty to present this *pro memoria,* which simultaneously is being sent to all pastors of the country. The

Evangelical Lutheran Church draws a sharp line between religion and politics. The Church is not the lord of the State, nor a state within a state, but the State's conscience. . . .

We cannot find that the statement, "The Foundations of the Church," has in any way a political character and much less that it is any anti-state or rebellious action. We must, on the other hand, declare that it is what it presents itself as being, a confession and a statement wherein the pastors take their stand with regard to the religious and moral aspect of events which have recently occurred in our society. . . . To act thus the pastors have not only a right but a duty. The pastors are duty-bound to obey God's Word without respect to persons and without taking into consideration extraneous factors of political or other character.

The faculties stated further that it was the bishops' duty to protest against the Nasjonal Samling's "youth service plan" as irreconcilable with the parents' and Church's right and responsibility with regard to the children's spiritual upbringing. Likewise the faculties declared that the "Church was duty-bound" to let its voice be heard in connection with the pressure and treatments to which the teachers were being subjected.

The letter from the faculties ended by declaring:

. . . The pastors' resignations are not an act of sabotage. This is revealed in the fact that the pastors are still performing their fundamental services as ministers and wish to continue doing so. The resignations are, on the other hand, a declaration of the Church's freedom and independence in spiritual matters. The Church has a right to demand that this freedom and independence is respected by the Government of the State.

In a joint communication to the Minister of Church and Education all the leading religious groups and organizations of the country expressed their complete agreement with the stand taken by the pastors in "The Foundations of the Church."

Faced with such a wall of resistance, the Nazis elected to retreat. Their first real effort to effect a reconciliation was made on June 13, when the Department sent to all pastors a long circular letter which opened the subject for general discussion. Carefully tucked away among all the theorizing and eloquence was a concrete peace proposal. It was introduced with an offer to the pastors to draw the salaries that they had coming to them, and it closed by offering them an opportunity to send a delegation to negotiate with the authorities. Quisling himself had signed the letter, along with Ragnar Skancke, Minister of Church and Education.

The letter was ignored.

On June 28 the Nazi authorities tried another approach. On that day Quisling presided at a meeting held at the Royal Palace to discuss ways and means of cracking the Church's resistance so that "peace and order" could be restored. The session produced the following compromise offer, which in due course was presented to the church leaders:

If the clergy would agree to resume co-operation with the State, Bishop Berggrav would be rewarded with a professorship in theology at the University of Oslo, Bishop Maroni would be retired in keeping with the old-age retirement law and would be assured a pension, and four of the bishops— Fleischer, Hille, Krohn-Hansen, and Skagestad—would be allowed to resume their former positions. No mention was made of the seventh bishop, Johan Stören of Trondheim.

But after so much struggle and strife the Church was not disposed to compromise. Long before, the fight had reached the stage where only a complete retreat by the Nazi authorities would be acceptable to the clergy as grounds for opening negotiations. It was obvious to one and all that the Church's fight was no isolated phenomenon, no mere dispute over words or shades of meaning. This struggle centered about ideals which were held sacred by the entire people. In concentrated form it was civilization's final reckoning with barbarism, and ideals were not to be bought or sold for a professorship in theology.

The Church's reply was curt. The compromise offer was flatly rejected.

On Sunday, July 26, 1942, the Norwegian clergy settled its account with the Nazi authorities for good. The lines for future action were clearly drawn for all to see. No attempts at compromise were involved. The Church spoke though its pastors from pulpits throughout the land, and it spoke so that both the people and the occupying power could hear and understand.

A recapitulation of the long struggle and of its purposes was read to the congregations. The document had been prepared at a secret meeting of church leaders held at Oslo late in June. It was sent to all Norwegian pastors, congregational councils, and congregations, and it was signed by "The Temporary Church Leadership"—a phrase which further emphasized the Church's conviction that existing conditions were only temporary and that victory, although still probably far away, was sure.

In its nature the statement was something far more than a lifeless ecclesiastical document. It was an attack, a quiet and yet flaming protest in behalf of all humanity against barbarism and terror, against untruth, falsification, and oppression. What its writers had produced was a clear and concise history of the occupation, a history stripped of all confusing details.

The document affirmed that the Church had been permitted to work in peace during the first few months following the invasion while the Administrative Council was looking after the civil administration in accordance with international law. But it also clearly stated that those conditions had changed with the Nasjonal Samling's so-called "assumption of power" in September 1940. Since that time, asserted the writers, the story had been a single, unbroken chain of increasingly brutal encroachments that led inevitably to the crisis of February 1942, when the occupying power turned terror loose and raised Vidkun Quisling to the office of Minister-President. What had happened since that time—the resignations of bishops and pastors and the creation of the Temporary Church Leadership—was declared to constitute a development that had been equally inevitable.

"It is not with joy that the Church has been forced to take the serious step of severing connections with the State," said the document. "But it had to do so. It was at the behest of conscience and after earnest consideration that it occurred. The Church would not have been true to its Master if it had calmly allowed all this to happen without taking action."

This, continued the statement, did not mean that the Church had suffered a defeat. Quite the opposite; because the Church, when the test came, had obeyed God more than man it had won a spiritual victory.

"During the very days of the Easter season, and immediately thereafter, when the men of the Church were being subjected to police hearings, dismissals, prohibition of speech, arrests, confiscation of property, threats of deportation, and even of the death penalty—precisely at that time it was established that the Church could not be frightened; it continued to preach openly God's Word and gospel, and as the conscience of the State it continued to protest against the encroachments which the authorities had made upon the Church, the schools, the parents and children—in short, on the country's established legal system."

The tone of the statement was calm and dignified but nevertheless firm and unwavering. The consciousness of having truth and justice on its side gave the Church strength and

courage to fix its gaze far beyond the dangers of the moment—
that is, the punishment and reprisals which the occupying
power might conceive. And there was no tremor therefore in
the voices of the pastors as they stood in their pulpits and
summed up the aims of the struggle:

"Briefly, we can say as follows: We fight this battle so that
we may work free and unrestrained. Unrestrained outwardly
by the State's illegal encroachments. And free inwardly with a
clear conscience before the Church's Master and His sacred
Word."

The document was something more than a statement of
distant goals. It was a declaration of war and a command to
all Christians in Norway. Under the flaming sign of the Cross,
the Church moved forth to battle with the armies of the
Swastika. The instructions were clear and unmistakable:

1. The congregational councils will continue their duties no
matter whether they are dismissed or not, seeing to it that all the
church work in the congregations proceeds on schedule. They will
be in contact with the rightful deans and bishops. Pastors who
are members of congregational councils will continue in the
councils even though they have resigned from office or have been
dismissed.

2. The pastors will continue their ministry in the congregations
even though they have resigned from office or have been dismissed. As long as the Church has not deprived them of that duty
which they accepted upon ordination, they have the right to wear
clerical robes and to perform those services in the church which
a non-official can perform. In all ministerial matters they are to
consult their superiors, the rightful deans and bishops.

3. The deans will continue their regular duties in connection
with their rightful bishops.

4. The bishops will direct the church work within their respective dioceses by continuing to hold their offices as bishops,
conducting visitations and ordinations, and, on the whole, by
continuing their customary duties. They have the full authority

of the Church to wear the robes of bishops and to use the title of bishop.

The Church had spoken, and its voice resounded mightily throughout the land. Once again it was the single purpose, clear and uncompromising. The Cross against the Swastika.

4. REFERENDUM FOR REVOLT

LIKE BOLTS OF LIGHTNING the planes shot down out of the blue September skies. No one knew where they came from, and no one knew where they were going until, with engines roaring, they swooped low over the rooftops and dropped their bombs.

The explosions were deafening. Crash followed crash. Bricks, broken glass, and roofing slate filled the air, and soon vast billows of black smoke were rolling upwards from the ruins of the Gestapo headquarters, the *Luftwaffe* brothels, and the apartment houses in which German officers resided.

It was all over within a few minutes. The planes soared skywards again. Beams from the descending sun caught the circles under the wings—emblems of the R.A.F. After a final circle over the city the Mosquito bombers set their course southwestwards, into the sunset. Not until then did the air-raid sirens begin to howl.

It was then a few minutes past five o'clock in the afternoon of September 25, 1942, and the place was Oslo.

On the speaker's rostrum in the University of Oslo auditorium stood Vidkun Quisling. The hall was decorated for a celebration. Swastikas and German eagles adorned the walls, and the audience was fairly glistening with monocles and medals. They were all there: Reichskommissar Josef Terboven; Wilhelm Rediess, Gestapo chief and General der Polizei; General Nicolaus von Falkenhorst, commander of the army of occupation; and their staffs.

It was the second anniversary of Quisling's "assumption of power" that was being celebrated. The gagged and standardized Norwegian press had heralded it as an event of historic importance.

The monotonous voice from the rostrum buzzed on and on. It was repeating once again the old, familiar phrases about the New Order, about honor and Europe's future. The listeners moved somewhat uneasily in their chairs. They had been listening to this for nine years. Here and there some of them yawned discreetly.

Just then the roar of airplane motors filled the hall. A few seconds later came the crash of the first explosion. The slender pillars supporting the roof of the auditorium swayed precariously.

The speaker stopped suddenly in the middle of a flowery sentence. For a brief, electric moment everything was deathly quiet; then began the wild rush for the doors, and leading the stampede for safety were Minister-President Quisling and Reichskommissar Terboven.

A few minutes later they were all crammed together in the comparative safety of the basement.

Out in the streets of the city a spirit of celebration held sway. Germans and Quislings were as if blown away, and for the first time in many, many months the citizens of Oslo were, for the moment, at least, masters in their own town. Thousands of them had rushed to the housetops, where they waved and shouted to the fliers. Their cheers soon changed to song, the national anthem and the hymn for the King. The voices were full of hope and courage.

Allied planes had not been over Oslo for more than a year, not since early September 1941. People had peered daily into the sky, waiting and hoping. All previous disappointments were now quickly forgotten, because the planes had arrived at precisely the right moment. The British bombs supplied the dot over the "i"—the finishing touch to a successful action that had reached its climax on that very day, September 25, 1942.

The Germans had fixed this day as one of celebration. And that is what it became, for the home front. For the Nazis it meant only a new defeat—greater, perhaps, than any other they had suffered.

The plan that Vidkun Quisling had embarked upon with the Germans' blessings in September 1940 had as its goal the complete nazification of the entire Norwegian social system. The *Führer* principle was to be introduced in the national administration, in all civil activity, and in all organizations and associations. All trades and professions were to be made to goose-step, and all control was to be assembled in the hands of a few trusted Nazis.

The decisive period in this New Ordering had been introduced by Quisling's elevation to the position of Minister-President on February 1, 1942; and September 25, 1942, had been selected as the day when these nazification plans should reach their successful culmination. On that day Vidkun Quisling was to proclaim the "Riksting"—Norwegian parallel to Nazi Germany's Reichstag.

Like all other efforts to establish a new order in occupied Norway, the plans for the Riksting were in the true Nazi pattern. It was designed as an advisory agency for the *Führer,* and it was to be composed of 150 sub-*Führers*. Further, it was to be divided into a "Näringsting" and a "Kulturting"—that is, into two councils, economic and cultural. Of course, the

150 members would have to represent somebody, and the plans called for the compulsory reorganization of all the trades and professions in the land with a Quisling-named *Führer* and Riksting member at the top of each. Thus the Riksting men would be representing "the people." It was as simple as that.

The first real attempt at such reorganization was made on the teaching profession. That choice was not accidental. In the first place, the Nazi authorities believed that the teachers comprised a comparatively small and tractable group which could easily be forced into submission. Secondly, and probably most important, they thought that by going after the teachers they might be able to kill two birds with one stone, for gaining control over the teachers would almost automatically result in control over the children.

The experiment was most unsuccessful. The teachers were ready for action; they knew what they wanted and what they did not want, and they received instant and valuable support from the parents of school children as well as from the powerful Norwegian State Church. The battle between the representatives of the schools and the Church on one side and the Nazi authorities on the other, which began in February 1942 and continued throughout the spring and summer and which is still unended, completely upset the Nazis' plans. The nazified teachers' organization, the Lärersambandet, as conceived by the Nazis, never became a reality. Nor did any other *samband* called for in Quisling's program.

The first visible result was that the authorities had to give up their plans for the formation of a so-called labor *samband*. This was designated as the second project on the list, and the date was set for May 1, 1942. The idea was to create a counterpart of what had already existed in Germany for many years, an *Arbeitsfront*.

But the Nazis took warning. When a small group such as the

teachers—about 12,000 people—had succeeded in creating an opposition wave of epic dimensions, what could one expect of 350,000 unionized and well-informed workers?

May 1 came and went and nothing happened. The idea of a Riksting was not abandoned, but it became necessary to revise the plans.

The Nazi officers worked feverishly throughout the summer. They tried to keep their preparations absolutely secret. But the home front knew what was happening. By the time the Nazis had completed their new plans, the home front also had its battle plans ready. And the unbelievable came to pass. Despite Gestapo, despite regulation and control and censorship on every side, the Norwegian home front arranged and carried out what was nothing less than a popular referendum on the question of Riksting or revolt—this in the heart of German-occupied territory!

To be sure, the referendum was not conducted according to the old, cherished, democratic principles of an open and above-board election campaign followed by use of the secret ballot. As it worked out, it had an even greater significance as an expression of opinion than the ordinary referendum, because every one of the voters gave expression to his opinion at the risk of his very life.

It began on September 12, 1942. On that date the underground newspaper *Free Trade-Unions* explained the Nazi plans. Simultaneously it staked out the course for the home front's counteraction. The paper addressed itself first and foremost to the workers. "Are we not made of as good stuff as the teachers and pastors?" it asked. "Shall we be the ones to tear down what the Church and schools in their battle have built up?"

The workers themselves supplied the answer in the days that followed. By the hundreds of thousands their letters poured in to the Nazi-named heads of the National Labor

Federation. Word for word, these letters were identical, but each carried the personal signature and address of the writer.

"Since I am now informed," said each of the letters, "that the Federation's present leadership intends to send representatives to the Nasjonal Samling's Riksting, and thereby to exploit my membership in promoting a political philosophy which it is against my innermost convictions to support, I hereby report that my membership in the organization is discontinued as of this date."

It was not for nothing that a unity between capital and labor, employer and employee, had been built up in Norway during the preceding two years, a unity fronting against the common enemy. Simultaneously with the workers, the employers also took action. The procedure was precisely the same: mass resignation from the nation-wide employers' organization through identically worded, signed letters.

There was no mistaking what had happened, and the Germans reluctantly had to take the consequences of such a clear expression of the people's will. It was publicly announced that the plans for establishing a Riksting had been postponed indefinitely. The festivities of September 25 were to take place as planned. But that was all.

It was the joy over this all-important victory that received its unbridled expression in the pandemonium that broke loose when the British bombers attacked Oslo that September afternoon. Pent-up feelings had to be aired, and the bombs that fell on the Gestapo headquarters came straight from heaven. Exactly at the psychological moment the home-front patriots received new proof that the world outside had not forgotten them, that mighty and growing forces were on the march, forces which someday would come to liberate them from the unequal battle that they had now been carrying on for two and a half years.

Even in the midst of their jubilation every single Norwegian patriot knew full well that the victory which had just been won was by no means final. He understood clearly that there was only one reason for the Riksting postponement: namely, that the occupying power wanted no further unrest among the workers. But the iron grip still rested heavily on people's necks, and the power behind it might at any moment decide to tighten the squeeze. Many evil days were still to be endured before the hour of liberation struck. Many Norwegians would still have to pay with their lives in front of German firing squads. Many tears were still to be shed.

In Norway two currents have been running parallel throughout the past two years: the home front's mounting hope for aid from the outside, and the Germans' correspondingly mounting fear that this hope will be realized.

Much water has poured into the sea since the summer of 1940, when the Germans conducted maneuvers along the entire western coast of Norway in preparation for the invasion of England. Today the situation is the reverse. Day and night the occupying power toils at the construction of fortifications designed to prevent an Allied landing in German-occupied Norway.

The developments on the war fronts of the world are also reflected in the activity of the home front. To an increasing degree the opposition has resorted to open sabotage against the German fortifications and the German-controlled industrial plants. For each act of sabotage the Germans strike back with increased force. It is a war of life and death.

At the beginning of October 1942 this sabotage activity reached a new high. Mysterious fires blazed up; inexplicable train wrecks occurred. When an explosion in the pumping plant of the German-operated Fosdalen mines put the mines out of commission, the hand of the "friends" was laid on. On October 7 Trondheim and the surrounding area was declared to be in a state of civil emergency. The Gestapo took over. In the course of three hectic days thirty-four Norwegian patriots were executed and hundreds of persons were arrested.

The Germans exploited the situation to the utmost for the purpose of spreading terror. They set up loud-speakers in the streets of Trondheim, at all railroad stations, and in all thickly populated sections of Tröndelag. As the executions took place, the names of the victims were shouted through the loud-speakers. Thus the Germans hoped to warn and intimidate the Norwegians. At the same time the occupying power let it be known that complete hostage lists had been prepared for all towns and localities throughout the country, lists of persons who would be instantly liquidated if an invasion of Norway should be attempted.

The Germans do not underestimate the importance of the Norwegian home front. They know that mighty forces are only biding their time, waiting until they can assert themselves; and the Germans know that that time will come the moment United Nations troops set foot on Norwegian soil.

The Germans fully understood the importance of the action taken against the Riksting in September 1942. They knew it could only be interpreted as a referendum for revolt.

5. FOR THE SKY IS RED

THE MAN who had built the house was an ill-starred speculator, and his name had long since been forgotten. Through
many years the mammoth mansion had stood amid the
neglected, overgrown grounds as a monument to explode
illusions of grandeur.

It had been built in the early 1920s with money harvested
during boom times, but misfortune had caught up with the
speculator, plunging him into disaster and disrepute before
his masterpiece was fully completed.

And because the mansion had in reality been built more for
show than for use as a home, it had remained unoccupied. In
the midst of a peaceful villa colony on Bygdöy, just outside
Oslo, it towered as a sinister and terrifying reminder of a
time when the world was out of kilter.

"The All Fools' Castle," it was called.

On an autumn day in 1942 a man walked restlessly back
and forth across one of the vast, high-ceilinged rooms. He was
alone, and he was dressed in a uniform that was a true copy
of German Nazis' uniforms—riding boots, riding breeches,

brown shirt, black tie, and bandoleer. On the left arm just above the elbow he had a white band with a circular emblem of red and yellow.

The man's face was dull and bloated, and his light, stringy hair hung lifelessly down over the low forehead. Only the eyes showed signs of life—light, watery-blue shifting eyes that reflected the mental derangement behind them.

The man was Vidkun Quisling.

Now and then he paused and looked about the room. It was luxuriously furnished now, and the walls were adorned with valuable paintings that once had hung in Norwegian art museums. A look of satisfaction passed over the man's countenance. Now they belonged to him.

Silence settled heavily over the room the moment the man ceased walking. But quiet as it was, the air was nevertheless filled with sounds—strange, unreal sounds that lived only in the man's own imagination, that plagued and tortured him all night long and would never leave him in peace.

He was alone, and yet he was not alone. There was someone behind him—always. Someone who wanted his life. Someone he feared.

Again he started pacing, an animal in a cage.

The thoughts took wing.

Two years had passed since that day in September 1940 when Reichskommissar Josef Terboven, acting in Adolf Hitler's behalf, had entrusted the New Ordering of Norway to Vidkun Quisling. Two long years.

And where was he today? What were the results? How near were the plans to fulfillment?

Quisling paused again, this time near the large window facing Oslo Fiord. He stood there, gazing out. His eyes followed the guards, heavily armed, as they trudged back and forth at their stations. He could hear the crunch of the iron heels in the gravel of the roadway.

It was as if the sight of the guards made him feel safe for a while. They were his bodyguard, and they had barbed-wire fences, anti-aircraft cannon, and machine guns to help them out if need should arise. And at last he had what seemed an adequate number of guards for a man of his position—about 200 of them. It had not been easy to get so many, because the rules had stated that in order to qualify for appointment the applicant had to be fully normal mentally and at the same time be a member of the *Hird*.

He could not escape from his own thoughts, however. They gnawed at him day and night, giving him no peace. And they were forever the same. What had he actually achieved?

Well, he had assured himself of this house. That was true. With the aid of the occupying power he had requisitioned it, and with the aid of the occupying power he had found workmen to complete and renovate it. Today the house was a fortress.

And he was well protected. In Norway were 300,000 German soldiers. They were to safeguard the country against an invasion from the west, but at the same time they were to safeguard his personal security. For the moment, at least, he was not running any risk of physical harm.

Besides, he had the *Hird*—or, at any rate, what was left of it. Regrettably, the occupying power had needed soldiers for the campaign against Russia, and, since no Norwegians felt the call to join the crusade against communism, the *Hird* had been forced to supply the men. As a matter of fact, this was no catastrophe for him personally, but there was no denying that it had caused a serious dent in the meager membership of the Nasjonal Samling.

Even at that it was worth the sacrifice.

But as for the New Order. What had it achieved?

Well, with the aid of the occupying power he had got rid of many personal enemies and dangerous opponents. There were at least sixteen concentration camps in the country, and German skill had not been wanting when it came to operating effectively. Between seven and eight thousand persons were tucked away in those camps, besides the many others who had been sent to Germany—some to concentration camps, and some to do slave labor. All of them had been taken out of the picture. And still others—many others—had been executed, wiped out.

But it was strange. Nothing had helped. The underground newspapers were still being published—and regularly, too. No sooner were illegal placards torn down than new ones appeared in their places. Trains were still being derailed. Mysterious fires kept on occurring. Stores of ammunition were being blown up. All work was being sabotaged.

The opposition could not be cleared away even though individual opponents were rendered harmless. Quisling tried to brush the thought aside, but it always reappeared: the memory of Russia, where the German propaganda department had won so many conclusive victories, yet where there always remained a Russian front that could not be crushed.

And take the Church, for example. Was not Bishop Berggrav locked up? Was not he, as Bishop of Oslo, the Church's leader? How could it be that a church without a leader still refused to submit? Christianity, after all, was only weakness, decadence. . . .

Or the schools. Could anyone explain how grown-up, educated people could bring themselves to submit to compulsory manual labor just for the sake of some cheap ideals?

Or the shipowners. Or the lawyers. Or the sports lovers. Or the doctors, the nurses, the architects, the engineers, the housewives.

For they had all acted in exactly the same way. Directly in conflict with their own materialistic interests.

Or the laborers.

Quisling began anew to pace the floor. His footfalls echoed hollowly in the big room.

Yes, those laborers.

Only a few days before, 500 men had been arrested and sent to Germany because they refused to have any part in converting their own country into a German prison.

How could one ever expect any co-operation from a people who persisted in being narrow-minded and negative, despite repeated threats and despite the examples set for them?

And plenty of examples had been set. The list of persons executed grew from day to day. New names were constantly being added—names of persons from all classes or strata of the population. Laboring men, students, lawyers, teachers, doctors, businessmen, newspapermen.

But nothing helped. Nothing seemed able to quell the people's spirit.

Quisling shrugged his shoulders. As if he were freezing.

Take those Commando raids, for example. There was no mistaking that people hoped and expected that every new raid was to be a real invasion. There was no other explanation for the way the civilian population cheered and carried on when the soldiers came ashore. There was no other explanation for the fact that the Commandos received all manner of help when it came to apprehending the Nasjonal Samling members whose job it was to spread the gospel of nazism in the coastal areas.

Again Quisling shrugged his shoulders. He was thinking of his own party comrades who had been taken to England by the Commandos and who now sat in prisons over there waiting to learn their fate. He knew that the punishment would be severe, because it was to be dictated by the Norwegian people themselves.

It was not the pangs of conscience that he felt when his thoughts wandered to the acts of terror which had been employed the last two years. It was fear—frantic, helpless fear.

He thought of Televaag, the little weather-beaten fishing village outside Bergen. At the end of April a couple of Norwegians had come ashore there. They were two Norwegian soldiers returning from England on a special mission. They had been discovered, and the Gestapo had sent a detachment of SS soldiers out to arrest them. But those two soldiers were soldiers, and they had not yielded without a fight. Before they fell they had shot two of the Germans to death. One of these was the Gestapo chief of Bergen.

Reichskommissar Terboven had personally gone to Televaag to supervise the reprisal measures. And, as a matter of fact, it was the Germans who bore the responsibility for what later happened at Televaag, in the same way that they bore the responsibility for all encroachments in Norway. But Quisling knew that he himself had not protested. Simply because he did not wish to protest. Because he knew that there was no road leading back.

Eighteen innocent hostages who had been in the Grini concentration camp for months, and who could not possibly have had anything to do with the Televaag affair, were marched out and executed.

All the men of the little village, about sixty of them, were arrested and sent to Germany to do slave labor there.

The women were arrested and placed in concentration camps. Their children were taken from them and turned over to the Nasjonal Samling for "proper education."

And after all the domestic animals had been brought to Bergen and slaughtered, the entire village of Televaag was burned to the ground—house by house.

It was a thorough piece of work. Quisling had to admit that much. But it was dangerous, too. People's eyes, which had long been burning with hate, took on new fire from the flames that laid Televaag waste.

It warned of a day of reckoning.

Quisling's thoughts wandered across the sea to the west. He knew that the thoughts of three million Norwegian people were making the same journey, day and night and week after week. Out there, beyond the sea, was the source of the hope of liberation. And it was unbelievable how well informed people were—despite the fact that their radios had been taken from them and despite the fact that the newspapers were prohibited from printing anything except reports of dazzling German victories.

They knew, for example, that England was stronger, far stronger, today than two years ago. They knew that the United States of America had laid its shoulder to the wheel and that the Americans meant business. They knew that the Russians— who, according to Hitler, had been wiped out again and again —were not only still fighting, but were fighting hard and effectively.

They knew the day was coming.

And they were proud of their own country's contribution to the combined Allied war effort, a contribution which even Quisling had to admit was one of considerable dimensions.

They were proud of their merchant marine, which was in the thick of the battle every hour of the day, and which had proved such a decisive factor in the United Nations' war program. They were proud of their seamen, who had consistently scorned all the fat promises made by the Germans if they would only sail their ships into German harbors.

They were proud of their Army, which was training in England and Iceland for the invasion of Norway.

They were proud of their Navy, which today was greater and more powerful than ever, despite the heavy losses suffered during the German invasion in April 1940. They knew it was the fourth largest navy serving with the Allies.

They were proud of their Air Force, which had been built

upon foreign soil and which had already proved itself a dangerous opponent to Hitler's touted *Luftwaffe*.

They were proud of the thousands of Norwegian young people who had defied all dangers in order to get out of the country and join the fighting forces.

And most of all they were proud of their King and the Royal Government, which in the midst of all the confusion and misfortune had pursued the single purpose so determinedly and uncompromisingly, and had thus made it possible for the occupied country to continue its existence as an unconquered nation side by side with its allies, and without becoming a burden on the others. For they knew that Norway, through the King and Government, was still paying its own way in the waging of the war, that all Norwegian war projects were financed by the nation itself, that all interest and amortization payments on foreign loans were being made promptly on the date they were due.

They were proud that their country was no burden on the other fighting nations, but was an active and valuable partner in the battle.

Quisling understood that all this helped to stimulate and strengthen the people of occupied Norway for further resistance. And there was nothing he could do about it.

He made a gesture of helplessness as he stood there before the window. He knew he would have to continue to travel the road he had once chosen. There was no road back. But in his innermost self he knew also that his whole scheme was hopeless, that no weapons—neither tanks, planes, nor cannon, neither firing squads, arrests, nor terror, neither promises nor flattery—would or could force the people to submit.

There were forces stronger than all the weapons in the world lined up against him. He could not see those forces, but he felt them. He knew that these forces, taken together, were called democracy. He uttered the word half aloud, as if tasting it.

A word? Yes, a word. But a word with meaning.

Nazi terror had been able to crush the tangible institutions of democracy. At least, it had tried to do so.

They might erase the word from all the dictionaries in the world, but they could never kill its meaning. It would live as long as man remained on earth. It could not be arrested or executed.

Quisling shook his fist in rage at the invisible enemy. Then he screamed. A lonely man in a big, empty room.

The guard who was just passing by shot a quick glance up towards the man at the window. Then he trudged on, somewhat uncertain of mind. The same thing had been happening so often of late. There was something eerie about it. But most likely the *Führer* was only practicing for a speech. For safety's sake, the guard made a "halt and front," and saluted with outstretched arm towards the window.

A man came sauntering down the path. He was poorly dressed, and his face showed the signs of undernourishment. But his eyes were clear and alert. Under his arm he carried a brief case.

Outside the forbidding iron fence he paused and peered towards the mansion that had at last found an occupant. He spat. Then he sauntered on. With a quick motion he dropped an underground newspaper into the mailboxes as he passed by the villas. He did not look back.

The sun had set, and the day was fast lapsing into night. Out to the west the heavens were glowing red. Still another night was to be endured, but a new day would soon be born. A new and happy day.